Acclaim for Mark and Delia Owens and SECRETS OF THE SAVANNA

"A fascinating look at the interplay of social and wildlife upheavals in Africa . . . a worthy follow-up to the authors' *Cry of the Kalahari*."
— *Publishers Weekly,* starred review

"The book is filled with some remarkable characters, including the local leaders, as well as the inspiring core of it all, the animals."
— *New York Times Book Review*

"A stirring account by two dedicated and courageous conservationists."
— *Kirkus Reviews*

"The Owenses have proven that the hard work of two people can improve the lives of thousands, if not millions, of people."
— *Contra Costa Times*

"Each of the Owenses' three books is a standalone page-turner that reads like a novel, with characters, both human and animal, that are so compelling you just can't wait to see what happens to them next. Both Mark and Delia have warm and accessible voices that invite the reader into a world that few will ever experience." — *Cape Codder*

"A wonderful story of a highly successful conservation initiative [that is] thrilling, heartwarming, and dramatic . . . This book will be one you cannot put down." — *Wildlife Activist*

"This story describes the complex interaction between people and wildlife in Africa." — *Science News*

"The authors had the pleasure and trials of exploring one of the last wild places on earth . . . Their story comes to life in *Secrets of the Savanna*."
— *Midwest Book Review*

"Full of adventure and a few hair-raising moments . . . One hopes there will be many more follow-ups to delight us." — *Library Journal*

BOOKS BY MARK AND DELIA OWENS

CRY OF THE KALAHARI

THE EYE OF THE ELEPHANT

SECRETS OF THE SAVANNA

SECRETS of the SAVANNA

TWENTY-THREE YEARS
IN THE AFRICAN WILDERNESS
UNRAVELING THE
MYSTERIES OF ELEPHANTS
AND PEOPLE

MARK AND DELIA OWENS

A MARINER BOOK
HOUGHTON MIFFLIN COMPANY
Boston · New York

TO BOB AND JILL

From guinea fowl pie in the Kalahari

to camping in the Luangwa bog,

thank you for everything.

Love always.

First Mariner Books edition 2007
Copyright © 2006 by Mark Owens and Delia Owens

For information about permission to reproduce selections
from this book, write to Permissions, Houghton Mifflin Company,
215 Park Avenue South, New York, New York 10003.

Visit our Web site: www.houghtonmifflinbooks.com.

Library of Congress Cataloging-in-Publication Data

Owens, Mark.
Secrets of the savanna : twenty-three years in the African wilderness
unraveling the mysteries of elephants and people / Mark and Delia Owens.
p.   cm.
Includes index.
ISBN-13: 978-0-395-89310-4
ISBN-10: 0-395-89310-0
1. African elephant — Conservation — Luangwa River Valley (Zambia
and Mozambique) 2. African elephant — Effect of hunting on — Luangwa
River Valley (Zambia and Mozambique) 3. Nature conservation —
Economic aspects — Luangwa River Valley (Zambia and Mozambique)
4. Owens, Delia. 5. Owens, Mark. I. Owens, Delia. II. Title.
QL737.P98095 2006
599.67'4 — dc22   2005023842

ISBN-13: 978-0-618-87250-3 (pbk.)
ISBN-10: 0-618-87250-7 (pbk.)

Printed in the United States of America

QUM 10 9 8 7 6 5 4 3 2 1

CONTENTS

FOREWORD

NOT SO FAR, relatively speaking, from where I spent the last years of my childhood in Zambia, there is a valley so rare and surprising in its beauty that once seen and heard and smelled, the sense of it stays with you always. Forever after, a tiny breath of it might come back to you in other places — say in a hint of dust in Italy or in the way the sun catches the land in Mexico — and you feel the tug of memory of that place. This valley is so rich with life that it seems entirely possible that Life itself started here, or at least that it congregated here in uncommon splendor and diversity. The landscape seems ideally suited to such majestic sights as herds of elephants casually fording a river or the philosophic stare of baboons at sunset. Perhaps that is why memory settles on the valley as a place of origin, as if we knew it in some other, wiser time.

But this valley — this template for what we might all have grown up with, or lived near, if we had not so carelessly eaten our way through our own wild lands long ago—was almost completely lost. When I was young, in the 1980s, North Luangwa National Park (for this is the valley of which I am speaking) was so rotten with heavily armed poachers and so corrupted with the blood money of elephants that anyone who ventured near it was considered foolhardy, if not downright stupid. Not only was the valley itself infested with armed gangs, but the villagers who lived in the land surrounding the park had been pressed into the service of the poachers — who were very often in the pay of powerful government officials and business people in the cities. Many thought that the valley was as good as gone.

But that was before Mark and Delia Owens happened upon the park and fell in love — illogically, incautiously — with a land so very nearly reaped of all its life that it had all but been left to die. This book is an account of the Owenses' years in that valley and with the people who live on its periphery. It is the story of how, together with the villagers and their chiefs, Mark and Delia gradually peeled away the dark years of elephant poaching and allowed both the valley and the settlements to flourish. In other words, the Owenses and the local people achieved what has been replicated in very few places in the world: a balance in which humans and wildlife have found strategies to coexist, not in some unsustainable primitive dream but in a viable, respectful way, with new ideas and resources building on the best of the old traditions. And in the process of saving the park, the Owenses found pieces of themselves in the sly, sometimes wickedly funny wisdom of the men and women with whom they worked. This book tells that story too.

However, as romantic as it sounds to hitch oneself to a dream and to attach oneself to an impossibly noble goal, the reality of years of gritty, flies-in-your-eyes, malarial loneliness in the name of love of land, humanitarianism, and science is not for anyone with less than a lion heart. I can't emphasize enough what courage and dedication — to say nothing of sheer stubborn passion — it must have taken for Mark and Delia Owens to rescue North Luangwa National Park while poachers and corrupt politicians and officials did everything they could to hurt them and derail their work and while even the land and the animals sometimes seemed ungrateful for their efforts. But with almost superhuman perseverance, the Owenses refused to give up until their goal of a valley without poachers had been achieved.

I recently returned to Zambia for a magazine assignment and spent time with Hammer Simwinga (the Owenses' protégé, a sort of

agriculture extension officer for the region, and every bit the hero described in these pages), and I met some of the traditional birth attendants, beekeepers, farmers, fish farmers, and shopkeepers described
here. The work that the Owenses instigated has outlived their time in
the valley, and there can be no greater tribute than that. In the words
of one villager, "You cannot separate the Owenses from this place.
What they have done has changed our lives for the better." It is true,
the Owenses cannot be separated from this place, which is ingrained
in them forever.

— ALEXANDRA FULLER

MARK

PROLOGUE

One touch of Nature
makes the whole world kin.

—William Shakespeare

A heavy fog, thick and white, settled lower over the hills of Masai-land in Kenya. I eased off the power and slowed down but pulled back on the cyclic stick, giving up altitude grudgingly. Our chopper's main rotor tore ragged chunks out of the cloud's underbelly and stirred great corkscrews of vapor that trailed behind us as we flew on. Fifty feet below us, malachite green hilltops dotted with flat-topped acacias and running giraffes — snapshots of Africa — flashed into view out of the white, then were lost to opacity. We flew on, while the fog squatted heavy on the hilltops, forcing us to skirt around and between them. But then the vapor began filling the valleys ahead; we were fast losing sight of the ground.

I keyed the intercom: "We've got to land while we still can; help me look for a place." Delia pressed her forehead to the cockpit window, scanning the terrain. Forested valleys and too steep hillsides all around: no place here.

To our right and slightly above us, a single rounded peak was still visible. But the clouds were already settling over it, like a goose on a nest. I banked hard right, pulled on some power, and climbed the slope. We popped onto the hilltop and planted our skids; even before the rotor wound to a stop, we could barely see beyond the blades.

Our camp in the remote northern Luangwa Valley of Zambia was still almost nine hundred miles and more than ten flying hours away. We would never make it before dark.

We unbuckled our safety harnesses, opened the doors, and stepped into the fragrant, misty air and into a surreal, palpable quiet. I have experienced such an utter absence of sound only among the old-growth Sitka spruce and hemlock forests of southeastern Alaska, where the wisps of moss clinging to tree trunks and branches and matting the forest floor absorb sound so completely that you can hear your pulse swishing in your ears with each heartbeat. Now, as Delia and I stood by the helicopter, we could see nothing beyond the ground immediately around us, could hear nothing but the occasional flinty *ping* of the chopper's cooling turbine.

Then, through particles of fog so thick they tickled our noses, came the merry, melodic, clear tinkle of little bells. At first they seemed far off, coming from everywhere at once. Then they grew louder, somewhere to our right, and we took several steps in that direction, yearning to discover the source of a melody that seemed to emanate from the heart of the hidden hills around us.

At first I thought I was imagining the faint crimson apparition, the red smudge that appeared in the fog. Then, like a distant memory gradually returning to consciousness, it gained form and definition, growing taller and still taller as it came toward us over the brow of the hill.

The Masai warrior, nearly seven feet tall, strode out of the swirling cloud, a red rubega cloth draped around his broad shoulders and large copper hoops dangling from his ears. His sharp, stern face was an ebony sculpture, and in his left hand he carried a long throwing spear with a broad blade.

"Jambo." He strode past us to our Bell Jet Ranger and began circling it, running his hands over its smooth, ivory-colored skin and Plexiglas windshield. "Tsk-ah!" He smiled and twiddled the ship's tail rotor back and forth as if it were one of his giant earrings, laughter rumbling deep in his chest.

Three women appeared carrying gourds and leading goats wearing necklaces of little bells. They stood back, gazing at the helicopter, chattering softly, their dark eyes wide with curiosity. Gradually a murmur of voices rose from all directions, and as the fog slowly thinned and began to lift, small groups of gaily dressed Masai streamed toward us across the green velvet hills. Soon they crowded around as I poured jerry cans of jet A-1 fuel into the chopper's tank, everyone trying to get at least a finger on the can so that they could help feed our strange bird.

After refueling, we stood waiting for the clouds to lift, surrounded by perhaps thirty or forty Masai. Delia begged a closer look at one of the beaded gourds — full of sour milk and ox blood — that a young girl carried around her neck on a strap of hide. Others showed us their bangles and bracelets, their spears and knives, apparently surprised that we should find these as interesting as they found our aircraft. Giggling shyly, one girl reached out and carefully lifted a lock of Delia's silky hair, massaging it gently between her fingertips. The cultural canyon that separated us was as wide as the Rift Valley, yet we felt a warm connection to these people, as though we had known them before, sometime in the distant past.

The fog lifted and the sun peeked through, bathing the green and golden hills with a buttery light. Reluctantly we bid goodbye to our new friends. Before starting the chopper's turbine, I led the warrior with the spear to the tail rotor, made spinning motions with my hands, and then drew my finger across my throat, to let him know what would happen should anyone get too close. He opened his long arms and, like a pelican gathering fish, stalked around the chopper, sweeping everyone back to the edges of the hilltop. We jumped in, lifted off, and then circled back to wave at the cheering crowd below, still standing around the space where the chopper had been. As I lowered its nose and we began speeding away, they closed in, still waving, and covered the spot — as if we had never been there.

Ten hours — and three countries — after the Masai, darkness fell, black and impenetrable under the solid layer of cloud that snuffed out sky light from above. Except for a stop to refuel in Dodoma, the capital city of Tanzania, and another on a remote plain in the southern part of that country, we had been flying continuously since leaving Nairobi, where our helicopter had passed its airworthiness inspection. Forty minutes earlier, the scattered lights of settlements west of Kasama, Zambia, had slipped away, leaving us alone with our worries about finding camp in this ink, our faces a Halloween green from the chopper's instrument lights. Somewhere, miles ahead beyond the mountains of the Muchinga Escarpment, in a five-thousand-square-mile tract of raw wilderness near the bottom of the Luangwa Valley, lay Marula-Puku, our bush camp, home, and conservation research base for the previous eight years.

With stars, with luck, and sometimes with the moon to light my way, I had often flown over wild Africa at night. It was always a beguiling experience, like swimming around in a womb with only faint flashes of nerve impulses and the lumps and bumps of a muscular landscape to lead me onward. But now I was extremely tired, and we were flying without navigational aids. My dead reckoning would have to be good.

Ahead, a jawbone of low mountains capped by clouds studded the rim of the Muchinga Escarpment, the western wall of the Great Rift, and I could not tell for sure whether the clouds were higher than the peaks. Before beginning our three-thousand-foot descent into the Luangwa Valley, we would have to fly east long enough to be certain we were beyond and clear of the Muchinga, while staying below the clouds. I dreaded the thought of blundering into the clouds in the dark; and if they were lying on the mountains, we would have no way to get through. My Global Positioning System (GPS) had burned out weeks before. Without it I had only the log of my time since leaving Kasama, my compass heading, our speed, and my altimeter to tell me whether we were safe. And I did not know if my message to light the milk-tin flares along the runway — sent by telephone from Nairobi to the United States, by fax back to Mpika, by radio to the main camp, and finally by truck to the airstrip — had been received and understood. If not, I would have to carefully descend until I could see the ground with the chopper's landing light, find the Lubonga River, then follow it north or south to camp. And finding the airstrip to land could be just as tricky.

Below and to our right I saw a scattering of yellow-orange lights, flickering, as though made by campfires.

"That should be Mano," I said to Delia, not absolutely sure it was. I had never seen the game scout camp from this high or from this direction in the dark. Something didn't feel quite right. But if I was correct, the mountains would be just beyond. The helicopter climbed higher, until wisps of cloud began breaking over her nose — and, I hoped, the jutting peaks were well below us. I imagined that I could feel them reaching up to gut the thin aluminum skin under our feet. "We must be high enough," I kept reassuring myself. But fatigue and darkness had planted a growing malignancy of doubt.

Leaving the cooking fires of Mano behind, we flew into the black void over the Luangwa Valley wilderness. The solid wall of darkness, and the lingering worry about flying into a mountain, so intimidated me that I suddenly and unconsciously reduced power and pulled up the nose, slowing us down to sixty knots instead of our usual cruising speed of one hundred. I picked up the lost air speed, tried to relax, and flew on.

"Where's camp? Shouldn't we see our lights by now?" Delia asked in a thin voice.

"Hang on; they'll be coming up anytime."

"So what are you going to do if there are no lights?"

In 1971, as young college students concerned about Africa's disappearing wildlife, we took temporary leave from our graduate programs and worked for two years at odd jobs to earn the money to field our own conservation research project on cheetahs. Early in 1974, one year after we married, we auctioned off all our belongings, bought one-way tickets, and flew to Johannesburg, South Africa. From there, over a period of several months, we found our way into the "Great

Thirst," Botswana's Central Kalahari Desert, and into Deception Valley, an ancient fossilized riverbed, where we set up a primitive camp in an island of thorn trees — and stayed for the next seven years.

Other than a few bands of roving Bushmen, we were the only two people in an area the size of Ireland; Maun, the nearest village, was more than a hundred miles away, so we often would not see other human beings for months. There was no rainfall for eight months each year, and droughts sometimes lasted for years. But the hardships of living in isolation, on a ration of little more than a gallon of water a day, every dry-season drop hauled to our camp in drums, were more than worth it. Most of the lions, leopards, brown hyenas, and other wildlife had never before encountered humans. They had never been chased by trucks, shot at, and in other ways abused by man, so they were naive and immediately curious about us — which often led to interesting close encounters.

Unable to afford a tent, we slept on the ground or in the back of our dilapidated Land Rover while observing the habits of black-backed jackals, brown hyenas, and lions. The latter two became our long-term research subjects because cheetahs were too rare and hard to find. At the beginning of our second year, a hunting company based in Maun gave us a faded, ripped cabin-style tent. Our first night in the tent we were sleeping on a thin piece of foam rubber when a *sssshhhhh*-ing sound and pressure on my feet awakened me. The night was moonless, but some light came through the mesh window near my head; I could see the silhouette of the wooded sand dune beyond our tree-island camp. A snake, no doubt a puff adder, seemed to be moving across my sleeping bag, its scales scraping along the nylon. I froze. The sound came again. The pressure began moving slowly up my leg. Carefully I reached behind my head for my flashlight. I would club the poisonous snake if it came near my face. But then came rumbles, squeaks, and heavy breathing — like something big digesting a heavy meal.

Resting on my back, I eased my head up and saw two black-maned Kalahari lions crouched at our feet, their noses roaming over our sleeping bags, their whiskers scratching the nylon like a scrub brush. I clamped my hand over Delia's mouth. Her eyes popped open as I whispered, "Lions — *in the tent!*"

We lay unmoving for a minute or two as the two male lions satisfied their curiosity. Then they withdrew and sauntered, one behind the other, along the footpath through our camp. We stood up, pulled on some clothes, and followed along behind as they strolled to our outdoor kitchen. They pulled down and tore open bags of cornmeal and onions we had hung in a tree for safekeeping and sniffed the spot where we had emptied some dishwater the night before. Then they sprayed urine on their favorite bush and lay down in the short grass just beyond our campfire. Delia and I sat quietly not ten feet from them and watched the sun rise over their shoulders.

During our seven years in the Kalahari, lions and brown hyenas sat at our campfire and smelled our hair, and the hyenas' cubs even nibbled our fingers as we took notes on their behavior; leopards hung out in the trees over our tent, and jackals stole meals off our table. Once while we were asleep on the savanna, a pride of lions lay down to rest in a circle around us, some of them an arm's length away.

We were with some two-year-old lions when, after a drought broke, they saw their first pool of standing water and took their first drink. We discovered that brown hyenas are very social rather than solitary, as had been thought, and that female clanmates, all relatives, faithfully adopt and rear the clan's orphans. We documented one of the largest antelope migrations in Africa — and learned that cattle fences built by the government with soft loans from the World Bank and trade subsidies from the European Union were blocking their migrations, killing hundreds of thousands of them, choking the life from one of the last great relatively intact ecosystems on the continent. When we wrote about this disaster in our first book, *Cry of the Kalahari,* the government of Botswana forced us to move on, though it rescinded the order a year later, after we had left.

In May 1986 I flew our Cessna 180 from Johannesburg to Lusaka,

Zambia, to begin looking for a new research site. But a week earlier the South African air force had bombed African National Council (ANC) bases around the city. Understandably, Zambian emotions were wound clock-spring tight with worries about a full-scale invasion. Government-issued posters and civil-defense radio and television announcements urged every citizen to be a "policeman" on the lookout for terrorists — all of whom were depicted as Caucasians because the country had been bombed by white-ruled South Africa. The U.S. State Department advised Americans not to enter Zambia, but we were anxious to find and settle in a new research site, so we had gone ahead with our plans anyway.

I landed in Lusaka, taxied to the terminal, and was locking up my plane when a squad of military police armed with AK-47s rushed up, grabbed my arms, and marched me to a small room in the terminal, where they began questioning me. At the time I didn't know that our newly purchased Cessna was the same model used by the South African air force for reconnaissance; it even had the same color scheme and bore a South African registration. The police held me for eight hours until they were sure I was not a spy, then released me.

I flew back to Johannesburg on a commercial flight, and Delia and I headed north with our trucks, towing a trailer and a shipping container loaded with gear needed to set up our new research project, at a site as yet unknown. A father-and-son film team from *National Geographic* followed us on our odyssey.

Shortly after we crossed the Zambezi River from Botswana into Zambia on the Kazangula ferry, we noticed two poles lying on opposite sides of the roadway. We had been warned about Zambia's notorious and often obscure roadblocks, so we stopped. But no one appeared, so we drove on. Twenty minutes later, I saw in my rearview mirror a large, battered East German army truck bristling with more than thirty soldiers and civilians, jeering and shaking their fists in the air as they drew up behind us. Lurching drunkenly from side to side, half on and half off the narrow road, the truck crowded beside me, its passengers shouting and waving AK-47s and bottles of beer from the back. One soldier aimed his rifle at me and forced me to stop. Then he jumped into the cab of my truck, jammed the muzzle of his weapon into my neck, and threatened to shoot me for running the "roadblock." His breath reeking of hops, he ordered me to turn around and drive back to the poles, where we were led to a small thatched hut hidden in the bushes. For more than an hour the soldiers questioned us, and all of our answers seemed to make them even more hostile. Then Delia remembered a photo we were carrying of our luncheon with President Kaunda, who had invited us to the state house while arranging our research permits earlier that year. I relaxed a little as she pulled it out of our file of papers.

Suddenly the men were very sober — and apologetic.

"Ah, you will — please — tell the president that we were only doing our job."

"Of course." And we were on our way again.

Numbed by the surreal roadblock incident, we drove on to Lusaka, which seemed as tense as a coiled snake. Even little children tugged at policemen to report our passing by. A lawless kind of martial law was in effect, and we couldn't get out of the city fast enough. On the long drive north on the Cape-to-Cairo Road from Lusaka to Mpika, we camped in darkness and hid our trucks in the bushes far off the road, sweeping away the tracks with tree branches so that bandits and military patrols would not find and follow them to our campsite. At more than a dozen roadblocks along the way, armed soldiers dressed in camouflage with helmets sprouting tree branches rifled through our belongings, demanded *nyama* (meat, usually from poached wild animals), and fingered their triggers, their eyes bloodshot, angry, and shifting. The air was gunpowder dry and seemed ready to explode.

A few years later, Zambians would begin yearning for a genuine democracy with a two-party system — and then demanding it, and in one of the most remarkable and benign political transformations in modern history, in 1992 they would hold their first free and fair presidential election since gaining independence from the colonial government three decades earlier. But the political atmosphere that greeted us in 1986, and in which we would work for the next decade, was much more ominous than it is today.

When we proposed working in North Luangwa National Park, officials told us that they had "written it off" because they lacked the resources to protect and manage it. Consequently, highly organized gangs of commercial poachers and ivory smugglers, sometimes in encampments of more than one hundred men, were slaughtering its wildlife with impunity.

We finally reached Mpika and found our way into the remote and ruggedly beautiful Luangwa Valley, near the northeast corner of Zambia. The North Luangwa National Park had been left undeveloped, its pristine wilderness a standard against which other parks in the country would be measured. It was largely undiscovered and little known to the outside world — except to poachers. We decided to continue our study of lions there.

As we packed mud on the walls of our first hut, gunfire broke out near our camp. We soon discovered that commercial poachers had wiped out all of the park's nearly two thousand black rhinoceros, that they had killed twelve thousand elephants for their tusks, and that they were still shooting one thousand elephants each year. Gangs numbering as many as 140 men were making regular forays into the national park and the wilderness around it. Two thirds of its area was largely depopulated of all animals larger than rabbits. Operating much like drug cartels, these poachers had virtually wiped out the wildlife in seventeen of Zambia's nineteen national parks.

It is difficult for Americans to fully comprehend the level of persistent instability in a country where people are always living on the edge because of political strife and shortages of even the most basic commodities, like firewood, water, and food. And that is why commercial poaching, which is motivated by greed, is such a crime, for it ultimately deprives people of the one renewable resource that can feed and clothe them and ensure their future when all else fails.

We drove to the local game scout camp for assistance but found only seven men there, who were supposed to protect the entire park. They lacked virtually everything they needed to patrol against poachers. At the time, in fact, many of the scouts in Zambia were poaching or taking payoffs from poachers just to survive.

Over the next ten years, with the help of generous sponsors from all over the world and a dedicated staff, we developed the North Luangwa Conservation Project (NLCP). The project brought to the area many more wildlife officers, who were equipped and supplied so they could do their jobs. And they did.

At the same time, we offered jobs to poachers, would-be poachers, and other villagers, provided loans and training for small business development and improved agriculture, trained village women in first aid and midwifery, provided basic medicines for clinics, offered conservation education programs and curricula for village schools, along with much more. In the beginning we focused this assistance on the fourteen villages in the area that were most involved with commercial poaching. At first we were met with suspicion and antipathy, but after four years of pilot projects, the fires of initiative and self-help began to flare among the people. Representatives from other villages began inviting NLCP to help them set up community development programs.

By the early 1990s, when this story begins, the United Nations had banned the international trade in ivory, devaluing it and making the alternatives to poaching offered by our project more attractive to villagers. Commercial poaching in North Luangwa was declining rapidly, but 93 percent of the elephants had been killed, and we did not know whether the population could ever recover. The ivory ban was to be reviewed every two years; if it was reversed, ivory poaching would intensify once again.

The success of the project brought its own ominous problems. Powerful people had made millions of dollars from poaching, and because we had helped put them out of business, they wanted to get rid of us. Their lackeys shot at our aircraft, sent assassins to our bush camp, and attempted to discredit us politically. The villagers, including many former poachers, had warned us that our adversaries had too much money at stake to give up, and it was only a matter of time before they would get us, one way or another.

On our long flight back from Nairobi this night in 1993, we could not know what lay ahead.

"Mark, there's a star!" Delia pointed through the windshield, and I studied the faint yellow light for a moment. It was directly ahead of us — but below where the horizon would be if we could see it. And it seemed to creep even lower as we flew onward.

"That's not a star — it's our beacon!" I exclaimed.

"But it's not flashing."

"We'll see the flash when we get closer." I tried to sound hopeful while resisting a strong urge to begin our long descent. I was still not absolutely certain that that single light, the only light for thousands of square miles, was coming from our airstrip.

As we flew nearer, we could see the solar-powered beacon winking like the light of a firefly, and I knew we had found our way home. A sun rose in my chest for all the people we had trusted to get that beacon lit. As we drew nearer, orange-red flares flickered to life on either side of the runway as Milfred, our assistant, ran along the airstrip lighting old powdered-milk cans filled with sand, rags, and diesel fuel.

I lowered the nose of the helicopter and began putting thousands of feet and miles of darkness behind us.

AUTHORS' NOTE

ZAMBIA'S CURRENT PRESIDENT, Levi Mwanawasa, has made unprecedented and commendable attempts to abolish corruption from the government of his country. He has made significant progress in this regard, and the people of Zambia and their wildlife have benefited. The corrupt officials named in this story were members of the previous two administrations. Acting with impunity, they were heavily involved with the poaching of elephants and the smuggling of ivory. They worked against us and others who tried to reduce poaching. In this narrative we have changed their names and their positions so that they cannot be identified. Many of them have been fired and/or jailed by the current government.

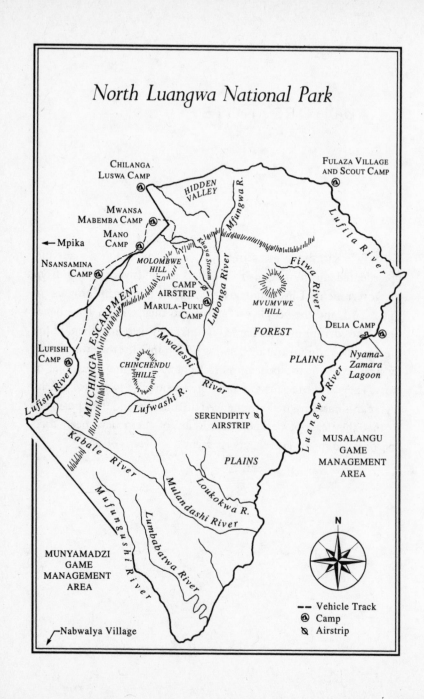

North Luangwa National Park

CHILANGA
LUSWA CAMP

HIDDEN
VALLEY

FULAZA VILLAGE
AND SCOUT CAMP

MWANSA
MABEMBA CAMP

MANO
CAMP

← Mpika

NSANSAMINA
CAMP

MOLOMBWE
HILL

CAMP
AIRSTRIP

MARULA-PUKU
CAMP

Khaya Stream

Mfungwa R.

Lubonga River

Lufila River

Fitwa River

MVUMVWE
HILL

FOREST

DELIA CAMP

MUCHINGA ESCARPMENT

Mwaleshi

River

Nyama
Zamara
Lagoon

LUFISHI
CAMP

CHINCHENDU
HILL

PLAINS

Lufishi River

Lufwashi R.

SERENDIPITY
AIRSTRIP

Luangwa River

MUSALANGU
GAME
MANAGEMENT
AREA

Kabale River

PLAINS

Loukokwa R.

N

Mufungushi River

Mulandashi River

Lumbabatwa River

MUNYAMADZI
GAME
MANAGEMENT
AREA

-- Vehicle Track
Ⓐ Camp
☒ Airstrip

→ Nabwalya Village

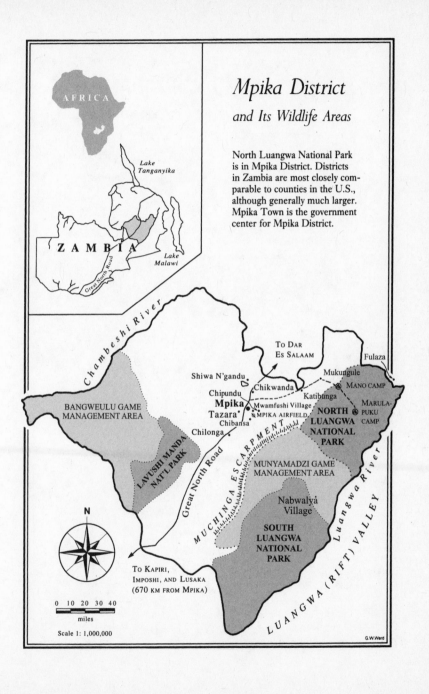

AFRICA

ZAMBIA

Lake Tanganyika

Lake Malawi

Great North Road

Mpika District
and Its Wildlife Areas

North Luangwa National Park is in Mpika District. Districts in Zambia are most closely comparable to counties in the U.S., although generally much larger. Mpika Town is the government center for Mpika District.

Chambeshi River

To Dar Es Salaam

Fulaza

Mukungule

MANO CAMP

Shiwa N'gandu

Chikwanda

Katibunga

BANGWEULU GAME MANAGEMENT AREA

Chipundu

Mpika

Tazara

Mwamfushi Village

MPIKA AIRFIELD

NORTH LUANGWA NATIONAL PARK

MARULA-PUKU CAMP

Chibansa

Chilonga

LAVUSHI MANDA NAT'L PARK

Great North Road

M U C H I N G A   E S C A R P M E N T

MUNYAMADZI GAME MANAGEMENT AREA

Luangwa River

N

Nabwalya Village

SOUTH LUANGWA NATIONAL PARK

L U A N G W A   (R I F T)   V A L L E Y

To Kapiri, Imposhi, and Lusaka
(670 km from Mpika)

0 10 20 30 40
miles

Scale 1: 1,000,000

G.W.Ward

1 DELIA

GIFT

A gift into the world for whoever will accept it.
— RICHARD BACH

... there are conflicts of interest between male and female
in courtship and mating.
— J. R. KREBS AND N. B. DAVIES

BETWEEN THE TREES of the forest, amid the thorny undergrowth, under tangles of twisted twigs is a space that is more color than place. It is a grayness painted by drooping limbs and distant branches that blur together and fade into nothingness. It is not a shadow but a pause in the landscape, rarely noticed because our eyes touch the trees, not the emptiness on either side of them. And elephants are the color of this space. As large as they are, elephants can disappear into these secret surroundings, dissolve into the background. When poachers slaughtered the elephants of North Luangwa, the few remaining survivors slipped into the understory. They were seldom seen and almost never heard because they rarely lifted their trunks to trumpet.

When we first came to the Luangwa Valley we could barely grab a glimpse through our binoculars of the elephants' broad, gray bottoms and thin tails before they tore into the thick brush and disappeared. As poaching decreased, a hushed peace settled over the valley, like the silence of fog folded among hills at the end of a rain. In 1991 fewer than ten elephants were shot in North Luangwa, down from a thousand killed illegally every year for a decade. It was an unexpected

1

yet natural quiet, as if a waterfall had frozen in midsong in an ice storm, leaving the land humming with the soft sounds of life. And then, once again, the elephants began to trumpet.

Slowly, beginning with Survivor, then Long Tail, Cheers, Stumpie, and Turbo — the Camp Group — a few of the male elephants learned that they were safe near our camp, Marula-Puku, which we had built in a large grove of marula trees on a small river, the Lubonga, halfway between the massive mountains of the escarpment and the Luangwa River. The elephants came at all times of the year, not just when the marula fruits were ripe. Sometimes they turned their giant rumps to our thatched roof and scratched their thick hides on the rough grass, closing their eyes in what appeared to be the most blissful glee. Elephants can make a lot of noise while feeding, tearing down branches or pushing over medium-size trees, or they can feed as silently as kittens, munching on fruits for long moments.

One night, as Cheers fed on one side of our cottage and Long Tail on the other, both only a few yards from our bed made of reeds, they let forth with full vocalizations. Mark and I, shrouded in our mosquito net, sat up as the sounds shook us. A lion's roar pounds the chest like deep sounds reverberating in a barrel; an elephant's trumpet, especially after decades of being stifled, stills the heart.

In the years before they learned to trust us, they must have watched from the hillsides, remembering the fruits of the marula grove yet afraid to come near. But once they made up their minds that we were harmless, nothing we did seemed to bother them. No matter whether Mark flew the helicopter low over the treetops, or our trucks rumbled in and out, or we cooked popcorn on the open fire, the elephants came to camp. When we stepped out of our cottages, we had to remember to look carefully both ways, or we might walk into an elephant's knee.

That nearly happened one dark evening when Mark walked quickly out of our open, thatched dining *n'saka,* or gazebo, where we were eating a dinner of spicy beans by candlelight. He was headed toward our bedroom cottage to retrieve the mosquito repellent and, having his mind on other things, played his flashlight beam along the ground looking for snakes. He heard a loud *wooosh* and felt a rush of wind. Looking up, he saw an elephant's chin and trunk swishing wildly about against the stars. Cheers stumbled out of Mark's path, twisting and turning to avoid the small primate. Both man and elephant backpedaled twenty yards and stood gazing at each other. Cheers finally settled down. He lifted his trunk one last time, flicking dust in the flashlight beam, and ambled to the office cottage, where he fed on marula fruits, making loud slurping sounds.

The elephants were not always so amiable. On a soft afternoon when the sun was shining through a mist of rain, I was reading in the n'saka by the river. Cheers marched briskly and silently into camp and fed on fallen marula fruits next to the bedroom cottage some thirty yards away. For a while he and I, alone in camp, went about our work, only glancing at the other now and then. The occasional heavy drop of rain fell from the trees as the mist cleared, and a faint wisp of steam rose from Cheers's broad, warm back. The picture was too beautiful to keep only as a memory, so I decided to photograph him. To get a better view, I tiptoed out and stood under a fruit tree — not, as it turned out, a good place to stand in marula season. Suddenly Cheers turned and walked directly toward my tree. Within seconds he was only fifteen yards away. Surely he had seen me, but he came on purposefully, his massive body swaying, as though I weren't there. I was unsure whether to stand or run, but Cheers was not the least bit indecisive; this was his tree, his fruit. Flapping his ears wildly, he mock-charged me. I ran backward about ten yards, turned, and jumped off the steep bank into the river, where Ripples the crocodile lived.

Even as the poaching decreased, the small female groups — the remnants of those once large family units — were shyer than the males. Finally, after several years, one or two females with their young calves would feed on the tall grass across the river, not far from Long Tail or Survivor. But they never ventured into camp, just wandered nearby and stared at us from the bluff above our cottages. Their backs glistening with mud, the youngsters would splash in and out of the river and romp on the beach across from the n'saka.

To KEEP OUT the African sun, we built our camp cottages with stone walls fourteen inches thick and roofed them with thatch about two feet deep. The huts stayed cave-cool even when the dry-season heat exceeded one hundred degrees. One afternoon, as I sat in the dim office cottage analyzing elephant footprint data on the solar-powered computer, a soft knock sounded on the door, and I looked up to see Patrick Mwamba, one of the first four Bemba tribesmen we had hired, years before, at the door. When he first came to us asking for work, the only tool he knew was his faithful ax; now he was our head mechanic and grader operator. Patrick is shy and gentle, with a fawnlike face.

"Dr. Delia, come see," he said. "There is a baby elephant. She is coming to us by the river."

I switched off the computer to save solar power and rushed to the doorway, where Patrick pointed to a small elephant trotting along the river's edge toward camp. Her tiny trunk jiggled about as she rambled along the sand. Suddenly she changed directions, galloped into the long grass, and reappeared upstream jogging in yet another direction, looking wildly around. Finally she halted and lifted her trunk, turning the end around like a periscope.

"Patrick, have you seen her mother — any other elephants?"

"No, madame, she is very much alone in this place."

An orphan. The park was sprinkled with these tiny survivors, youngsters who had watched every adult in their family mowed down by poachers. From the air we had seen infants standing by their fallen mothers or wandering around in aimless search for their families. Some died right there, waiting for their mothers to rise again. Some never found the herd. By the time we arrived at the site, the young elephants were usually gone or dead. Now one youngster had stumbled onto the shore opposite our camp and stood still, trunk hanging low, looking away as if we did not exist.

I could see Harrison Simbeye and Jackson Kasokola, our other assistants, and Mark watching the small elephant from behind the marula trees at the workshop. She wandered around the beach again for a few more minutes, then disappeared into the thick acacia brush. Without speaking and alert for crocodiles, the men and I forded the shallow river. We stood in a long line staring at the lonely prints in the sand.

Elephants grow throughout their lives, so their age can be determined by measuring the length of their hind footprints. The size of the prints suggested that this elephant was five years old. We named her Gift, after the recently deceased daughter of Tom Kotela, one of the Zambian game scout leaders. But we doubted if we would ever see her again.

There are two species of elephants in Africa. One, *Loxodonta cyclotis,* is the forest elephant found in Congo. Most of the others, including those of the Luangwa Valley, are *Loxodonta africana,* the savanna elephant.

Normally, when there is little or no poaching, female elephants live in family units whose matriarchal gene lines persist for generations. As is the case with many other social mammals, a female remains in her birth group all her life, so the group is made up of grandmothers, mothers, aunts, and sisters who feed, play, and raise their young together until they die. Males born into the group remain with the family only until their hormones send them off in search of unrelated females with whom to mate. Then they wander on their own or with a loose alliance of cronies, taking risks, fighting, or showing off to attract as many females as possible. So there are no adult males permanently attached to the family unit.

Female elephants touch often, rub backs and shoulders, gently tangling trunks. From their mothers and older relatives, the young-sters learn which plants to eat, where the waterholes are, and how to avoid predators. When an infant squeals, any of the female group members will run to the rescue. An elephant family is a fortress of fe-males.

But little Gift was alone. She was old enough to be weaned, yet how could she survive without her family unit? Elephants rarely adopt orphans, and never nonrelatives.

The next day we spotted Long Tail and Cheers across the river, tearing up long grass and shoving it into their mouths with their trunks. Gift was forty yards away, feeding on shorter, tenderer grasses. From then on, whenever Long Tail, Cheers, or the other males wan-dered into camp, little Gift bounced along behind them. She looked minute next to them, a windup toy circling on her own in the back-ground. In the absence of her family unit, and abandoning all normal elephant behavior, Gift had taken up residency near the Camp Group males.

For the most part, the males ignored her. At five, she was much too young to breed and, as is true of most male mammals, they had no other use for her. Before poaching was rampant in the Luangwa Valley, female elephants usually ovulated for the first time at fourteen years of age and delivered their first calf at sixteen. So, as the males roamed around in their habitual feeding patterns, first on the hill-sides, then across the river in the long grass, the diminutive Gift stayed within sight of them but fed on her own. Sometimes she stepped gingerly up to one of the towering males and reached out her tiny trunk in greeting. Her mother, sisters, and aunts would have snaked their trunks out to hers and twisted them together. Her female family would have circled her, bumped heads, rubbed backs like af-fectionate tanks. Gift would have observed older mothers suckling their young and played with other infants, all the while learning the elephant alphabet. But the Camp Group males turned away from her, their huge backsides blocking her only chance at companionship. A cold shoulder from an elephant is a big rejection.

It would be an exaggeration to call any female elephant dainty. With their tree-trunk legs, thick ankles, and heavy shoulders — not to mention their less than elegant profiles — it's difficult to describe them as at all feminine. However, Gift came close to being ladylike, at least for an elephant. Perhaps it was just that compared to the males, she seemed so much more delicate in her feeding and lighter of foot. She had other little habits that reminded me of a young girl who had somehow found herself in a male world. One afternoon while feeding on a small tree, she broke off a branch covered with fresh, green leaves. Instead of eating the forage, she wandered around rather aimlessly for over thirty minutes carrying the branch in her trunk, as a girl might carry wildflowers in a spring meadow.

With no group, Gift had no playmates. More than a pastime, play with peers and elders is essential for forming lifelong bonds, perfecting trunk-eye coordination, and testing dominance. Gift had to play alone. Once she stepped into the flooded river and submerged herself completely. Rolling over and over, she splashed about, with a leg poking up here, her trunk there. Now and then she would burst out of the water like a breaching whale and dive underneath again.

Gift's special trademark was her jig. We often blundered into her when we rushed around camp. In a hurry to get to the plane for an elephant survey or to the office for binoculars or notebook, we would stride around a tree and come face to face with her. But she never charged us. If we got too close for her liking, she would trot away about five steps, stop, lift her tail slowly to the side, throw her head around dramatically, make a one-eighty turn, and trot back toward us. She would repeat this several times, as if dancing a jig. She also performed her dance for the massive buffaloes who fed in our camp and sometimes got in her way.

Gift was never a pet; we never fed her and certainly did not touch her. But she must have felt safe around us, because she lived nearby as though she had set up her own camp near ours. She sometimes stood near our cottages watching the small female families across the river, as the youngsters frolicked and the adults greeted one another with tangled trunks. We hoped that she would join them, that against all elephant tradition they would adopt her. But she never ventured near them. As she grew older, Gift wandered farther from camp during her feeding forays, and sometimes we would not see her for weeks, and then even for months. We always worried that she had been shot, and then she would show up at our camp again.

Whenever we flew over the valley, observing the elephant families from the air, taking notes on every detail of the groups, counting to see if their numbers were increasing, I always searched for Gift. I longed to see a little elephant among the others, one who would perhaps look up at us and dance her jig.

2 MARK

POACHER CUM MILLER

That old law about "an eye for an eye" leaves everybody blind.
— MARTIN LUTHER KING, JR.

NOT LONG AFTER Gift began coming to camp, I was flying the Cessna along the Lufila River, surveying elephant movements in the northern regions of the park. Whenever I flew I made a special effort to patrol the areas where Gift had last been seen, hoping to keep her safe from poachers.

The clipped voice of Tom Kotela, the unit leader of Mano, one of the five game scout camps responsible for securing North Luangwa, came through on my headset. He was relaying a message from "Spider," one of his informants: Mabu Kabutongo, one of the most determined and ruthless poachers still active in the area, had headed into the park along the Shatangalala poachers' route to kill elephants on the Mulandashi River. I rolled my eyes and groaned. I had hoped that those hard-core poachers who had refused the jobs and business opportunities spun off from our project had moved on to softer targets elsewhere. But apparently Kabutongo and a few others were still around, waiting for our project to fold and for the United Nations ivory ban to be lifted. Then they could get back to killing elephants full-time, with lots of big-league support.

For years some police, military, and other government civil servants in towns like Mpika had provided the poachers with guns, ammunition, and transport and had helped them smuggle ivory, skins, and even trophy heads south on trains and trucks to Lusaka and

9

South Africa; north to the port of Dar Es Salaam in Tanzania; and across Lake Tanganyika aboard the SS *Liemba* to Burundi and thence to Belgium. Our own network of informants and our contacts in Zambia's Anti-Corruption Commission told us that officials in virtually every branch of the government charged with protecting wildlife had been involved in profiting from the animals' demise, from game scouts to police, magistrates, military personnel, customs officials, departmental directors, government ministers, and others even higher up in the government. According to Paul Russell, then director of the Anti-Corruption Commission, the black market in wildlife parts was second only to the illicit drug trade as a secret source of revenue for the country. For a cut of the action, officials had laundered much of the contraband, providing documents to make the ivory and animal parts appear legal before passing them on to ships and aircraft, most bound for central Europe, Asia, and the Middle East.

Romance Musangu, a civil servant equivalent to the head of the U.S. Secret Service, was one of these officials. Later we would come face to face with him, but for now we knew him only as one of our informants described him — reluctantly, nervously, in secret meeting places, usually at night. Musangu was one of the "Big Boys from Lusaka," a man with the face and personality of an angry pit bull, who sat near the top of a tower of corruption. That tower was built with the body parts of wild animals and the wasted lives of people hooked on Mandrax and other drugs.

The local wildlife ranger Banda Famwila was one of Musangu's minions. A handsome, graying man with the refined, retiring air of a deacon, Famwila had for years been ordering his scouts to poach and to smuggle tusks, skins, and meat to his bosses in Lusaka. Tom Kotela told me that twice each week during the early 1980s two wildlife department trucks loaded with contraband from North Luangwa had traveled to Lusaka under cover of darkness. First the trucks stopped to offload some of the cargo at the ministry in Lusaka, then drove on to deliver meat to the Mundawanga Zoo, directly across the road from the Parks Department headquarters. Despite these regular deliveries of meat, the lions and other carnivores at the zoo had always looked more than half starved — because most of the meat was actually being delivered to Parks officials.

With cover from Banda Famwila, who kept the poachers informed of the game scout patrols' movements, Mabu Kabutongo had eluded Kotela and his scouts for years, once even hiding out for months in an abandoned termite mound. He had shot at my aircraft several times and had killed elephants very near our camp. On a circuit board with a tiny speaker, two wires, and a battery, Kabutongo had recently learned from a BBC radio report that the United Nations was considering relaxing its moratorium on the international trade in ivory. He and other poachers knew that the ban was voted on every two years and that it could be partially or wholly reversed at any time, allowing the legal sale of ivory, which could be used as a cover for an intensified illegal trade. If the ban was reversed or even weakened, the market price of elephant tusks would skyrocket. He and other ivory poachers would be back in business again. In the meantime they remained hopeful, and some, like Kabutongo, continued shooting elephants on speculation. Now that the scouts had blocked off most of the poachers' routes into the park from the west, he planned to mount operations from the villages of Nabwalya, to the south, and Fulaza, on the park's northern boundary.

✍ "The elephants have been coming back nicely along the Mulandashi, sir," Tom said over the radio. "We must capture Kabutongo before he kills them. But it would take my scouts at least three days to get there on foot, and by then it would be too late. Maybe you can chopper them into position."

I sat back in my seat, exhausted. Just two nights earlier I had flown the scouts to intercept three corrupt policemen who for years had been supplying big-league poachers with weapons and ammunition from the police armory in Tazara, a railway settlement near

Mpika. The NLCP's support for wildlife law enforcement, along with our village outreach programs, had virtually put these police out of business. Armed with AK-47s and dressed like poachers, they had headed for our camp to "kill Owens and any scouts who get in the way." I had tried to intercept them by landing the scouts at night near their campfires in a deep ravine along the escarpment. The passage was so narrow that the chopper's main rotor had clipped tree limbs along the steep slopes. I had very nearly crashed. Badly shaken, I gave up and flew the scouts back to camp. The game warden told me later that before the corrupt police could get to our camp the next morning, they ran into a group of poachers dressed as scouts. In a shootout between policemen impersonating poachers, and poachers impersonating game scouts, one of the poachers had been wounded, and the cops had turned back to Tazara. Those hours of low-level night flying had left me haggard and raw. And now this.

"Copied, Tom, have them on standby at four o'clock tomorrow morning."

After a short night's sleep, I drove to our airstrip, where Milfred and I set out milk-tin flares along the runway. At 1:30 A.M. I took off in the Cessna to find Kabutongo and his bearers. The new moon hid behind a high layer of clouds; I could see only a hint of the sandbars along the rivers as I flew over. After I had been airborne for about twenty minutes, I put on my night-vision goggles and immediately picked up a hot spot of light from the poachers' campfires along the Mulandashi River northeast of Soma Hill. I climbed to eight thousand feet to avoid detection, and as I passed over the camp, I stored their latitude and longitude on the plane's global positioning instrument. The men did not snuff out their campfires, so I was pretty sure they had not heard the plane. I flew back to camp, preflight-checked the chopper, transferred the lat-long position of the poachers' camp to its GPS, catnapped for fifteen minutes, then took off for Mano to pick up the scouts.

Seven minutes after I landed at the Mano airstrip, Tom Kotela and Isaac Daka, Tom's stocky camp-in-charge and one of his most trusted officers, appeared out of the darkness leading two other scouts. They carried full packs so they could spend several days in the bush if needed, and they were armed with two rifles and two shotguns. We stuffed their gear in the cargo hold and took off. I slipped on my night-vision goggles again and began scanning the landscape — the image a grainy pea green in the starlight intensifier. Flying low-level along the forested foothills and ridges of the Muchinga Escarpment, I headed for the spot where the headwaters of the Mulandashi crept through the hills below the scarp and began their journey to the Luangwa, nearly twenty miles farther east. We were high above the valley floor — and still thirty miles from Kabutongo's poaching camp.

Minutes later, with dawn breaking, I slipped off my goggles and glanced at Kotela, sitting beside me, and then back at Daka, in the open doorway of the aft cabin, the cold wind rippling his crisp new uniform. Seven years earlier, on our first visit to Mano, Delia and I had found seven scouts dressed in rags seated around a frothing clay pot of beer. Only one looked up when we said hello, and the camp-in-charge, the man Isaac would eventually replace, scoffed when we told them that we hoped to start a conservation project in North Luangwa. Those seven men — armed with one working rifle and one round of ammunition — were the entire staff at the Mano Unit headquarters. The outlying camps had been abandoned, leaving a park the size of Delaware open to poaching. The scouts had no boots, uniforms, patrol food, medicines, or transportation; their mud-and-thatch houses were crumbling and leaky, they had not been paid in almost eight months, and their children did not have a school. They had not gone out on patrol for a year, maybe two — so long they could not remember for sure.

We would learn later that some of the scouts were poaching themselves; others were bartering their ammunition to poachers for meat. And even when they caught poachers, the magistrate would quickly release them for a small bribe.

One morning early in our third year I discovered more than a hundred poachers camped beside elephant carcasses on the Mulan-dashi River. They had kidnapped three tourists from one of the first walking safaris in the area. I flew in scouts from posts well beyond North Luangwa and landed them on a short gravel bar little more than a mile from the camp. We agreed that I would take off, fly over the poachers, and circle them while the scouts, following the airplane, would rush in to make the arrests. They never showed up. I circled over the poachers and dead elephants for almost two hours until, low on avgas, I was forced to go back to Marula-Puku. Later, I found out that the scouts had feasted on barbecued baby elephant trunk with the poachers, who had released the tourists earlier that day, warning them to stay out of the park.

Thankfully, those days were mostly behind us. Now more than sixty well-equipped scouts regularly patrolled North Luangwa. With the help of the project, the Zambian government, and the United Nations ivory ban, they had almost completely stamped out the poaching of elephants and other wildlife, at least for the time being, not only in the park but also in the areas around it. Almost. We still had Kabutongo and a few others to reckon with. And recently "Talky," one of our most reliable informants, a man who had formerly worked for the office of the president, had given me even more alarming news: Ranger Banda Famwila was moving corrupt scouts into the area and transferring good ones out to undermine the project and promote his operations. The warden confirmed this, but even though Famwila was his subordinate, he could not get his department to fire him or at least move him to another part of the country. He asked me to inter-vene, but when I did, I was met with icy hostility. Famwila's connec-tions were too high up.

I was beginning to feel that permanently stemming the tide of poaching in North Luangwa was like trying to stamp out drug traf-ficking in an inner city. Talky had already warned me that certain of-ficials, frustrated because the NLCP stood between them and their il-licit interests, might move against us.

We joined the Mulandashi among the deep, fluted canyons of the scarp and began following it east, downslope toward the Luangwa. I watched the GPS count down the miles to the poachers' camp. Flying low and fast, we hugged the riverbank, hiding below its trees, stifling the slap of the rotor blade in brush and tall grass to cover our approach.

At three miles I warned the scouts to get ready.

At two-tenths of a mile I flew the chopper behind a hill at the river's edge, then snatched back its cyclic control and shot up out of the mist.

A column of smoke and vultures was rising into the air next to a waterhole where some poachers squatted around their morning campfires; others were still asleep in their bedrolls. I throttled up and we swept forward, flying fifty feet above the ground. Caught by surprise, men scattered from around meat racks and smoldering drying fires hidden under trees. One of them — Kabutongo — carried a rifle.

We dropped into a clearing beyond the camp, and as the skids kissed the ground the scouts jumped out. Seeing us land, the poachers broke and ran. I took off again and hovered in the sky a safe distance away while the scouts gave chase, rounding up one after another until they had captured three groups, each guarded by a single officer. The shooter was still out there somewhere — but so was Isaac, the scrappy five-foot-tall scout.

To my left, about two hundred yards away, I could see another clutch of poachers hiding in a thicket. Isaac was running toward them, his rifle pointed ahead of him, darting right, then left, going bush to bush, not sure where they were. Kabutongo raised his rifle as the "little-big scout" came nearer.

"Shooter at your two o'clock! Watch out!" I yelled into the mike. But Isaac had lowered his radio from his ear, and even at this distance the roar of the chopper had drowned out my transmission. He stalked closer, still uncertain which thicket held the poachers.

I lowered the chopper's nose, poured on full power, and rushed forward. In seconds I hauled the screaming aircraft to a hover with its skids not ten feet above the poachers' heads. The rotor's powerful downdraft sent a dust storm ripping through the thicket, thrashing its thorny branches. Kabutongo lowered his rifle and ducked down, covering his face with his forearm. Blinded, he staggered out of his cover just as Isaac arrived at a dead run. He hit the poacher with a right cross and chopped his arm with his rifle barrel, sending the shooter's weapon flying. In seconds Kabutongo was handcuffed.

Kabutongo had killed a waterbuck to black-market the meat, but the scouts captured him before he could poach any elephants. His failed expedition had cost him a firearm, money to pay the carriers, and a lot of credibility with men who might not be so eager to follow him into the bush again.

After the scouts had handcuffed the poachers for their march to the magistrate's court in Mpika, I landed nearby and switched off the chopper. Tom and Isaac questioned each man as to why he had joined Kabutongo's poaching expedition. Mulenga Mwengi, thirty years old and from Mwamfushi village, a former gateway into the park for poachers, was trying to support nine children. His three oldest had dropped out of school because he couldn't afford to pay for their education. Kabutongo and other commercial poachers, whom Mwengi referred to as "the big brothers from town," paid him little more than a lump of meat for his service as a carrier.

When we offered Mwengi honest work if he gave up poaching, he became the miller for his village, running the maize hammer mill installed by the project in Mwamfushi. We hired the other carriers to build a road into the national park.

After Tom and Isaac had finished interviewing Kabutongo's carriers, they turned to him. The rising sun was spilling its golden light onto the dusty hardpan and scrub brush near the waterhole where the handcuffed poacher sat watching us, shoulders back, head unbowed.

"You are a lucky man," Tom explained. "According to the laws of Zambia you would ordinarily go to jail. But if you like, the project will offer you a job as the maize miller at Mano Camp. So, what will it be?"

Kabutongo, his face covered with white dust, looked at me. The muscles of his square jaw softened, and his eyes seemed to brighten.

"I can be miller."

We immediately moved him and his family to Mano, built them a small home of bricks and thatch, and he began his new career. He nicknamed his wife Delia.

Later we received this note from Mulenga Mwengi:

I was offered the job, which I grandly [gladly] accepted. Life changed so much . . . I started buying agriculture inputs from my salary and the project helped with other inputs like seeds and out let market for my products. I would say my life would never been like this, I have managed to send my children to school, a thing that I terribly failed in my poaching career.

Mulenga Mwengi
Maize Miller
Mwamfushi Village

3 DELIA

UPSIDE-DOWN ELEPHANTS

Like a crowd of kids . . .

—WILLIAM GOLDING

One important variable affecting the development of aggres-
siveness is the type of mothering received by a young animal.

—JAMES F. WITTENBERGER

TWENTY YEARS EARLIER, more than seventeen thousand elephants roamed North Luangwa, but in the early 1990s only about
fifteen hundred remained. Now, instead of large aggregations of
families moving through the valley, little pockets of survivors were
tucked away in deep ravines and thick brush. We weren't sure
whether enough adults of breeding age had survived to allow the
herds to recover. To find out, we had to measure their feet; the age
structure of the population would reveal what percentage could
breed and whether or not the population was growing, stable, or
declining.

I had decided to make the trek along the Lubonga River to the
Mwaleshi River and on to the Luangwa, to measure elephant footprints in the sand. There were no roads or even primitive tracks near
the rivers, so I would go on foot, a walk that would take six or seven
days. Mark could not come along because he had to locate the elephant families every day by aircraft and support the village work.

I needed a tracker, someone who could distinguish one footprint from another, someone who knew where the elephants were
foraging, which ravines they frequented. It occurred to me that Mabu

Kabutongo, the ex-poacher who was now the miller at Mano, would be an excellent choice. Who could read elephant tracks better than a former poacher? I sent a radio message asking him to come to Marula-Puku with carriers, and he agreed.

Mark was not enthusiastic about my plan. He pointed out that Kabutongo had shot at our airplane and was probably waiting for another chance to shoot elephants. I insisted that he had reformed, and I would have a game scout and three carriers with me. Mark finally gave in, saying he would fly over our position every day to check on us.

I had meant to depart at sunrise the next morning, but an hour later I stood at the edge of camp with piles of gear — big white bags of mealie meal, a string of pots tied together with blue plastic rope, tents, and backpacks — spread out in a circle. Kabutongo grew impatient as the porters circled their packs, insisting that they needed another man to share the load. "Tien, tien. Let's go, let's go," he kept saying.

Finally everyone shouldered their loads, adjusted straps and buckles, and balanced bags on their heads. Mark, a steaming cup of coffee in his hand, reminded me that whenever I heard the plane or chopper, I should radio my position. We marched single file out of camp with Kabutongo, armed and dressed in old fatigues, in the lead. I followed him, and the carriers, clad in an assortment of mismatched missionary hand-me-downs, their tin cups clanking against their packs, were strung out behind me. Francis, a game scout, outfitted smartly in his official uniform, provided recently by Prince Bernhard of the Netherlands, brought up the rear, his rifle slung over his shoulder with a piece of old rope. Grasshoppers flew up from the grass in front of us, spreading their wings and exposing their stunning red underwear.

Low, dirty clouds scudded just over our heads, masking the normally bright African sky. We passed the cook's camp, a squat mud hut under a huge marula tree, and I called goodbye to Mumanga

Kasokola, Jackson's brother. He stood next to the fire, waving a white dishcloth in farewell until we reached the first river bend, four hundred yards from camp. All I could see before I rounded the turn was his cloth flitting above the grass like a large butterfly.

The Lubonga River is born in lush miombo woodlands, a two-story forest with a wispy open canopy, high in the mountains of the Muchinga Escarpment. Its birth waters seep out of rocky, moss-covered crevasses and silent springs. As an infant, it meanders slowly through forgotten forests and small marshy plains, inviting other springs to join it along the way, growing in size and speed. The terrain becomes more broken as it approaches the three-thousand-foot drop of the escarpment, and there the small river picks up speed, tumbling over rocky outcroppings as startled, unnamed waterfalls and gushing through deep gorges smothered in ancient forests.

After running the mountains, the river takes a rest, slowing its pace through the foothills. Here the canyons are fewer and wider, and the Lubonga meanders gently through wooded foothills and small grassy glades of the valley. It wanders by our camp at this point — where we began to follow it — and continues to twist and turn through the riverine forests, finally losing its identity altogether as it flows into the wide, sweeping waters of the Mwaleshi. We headed downstream, following the Lubonga toward its confluence with the Mwaleshi.

Standing on the opposite shore, his rifle pointed toward the water, Kabutongo shouted to me, "Keep up, keep up," as I waded into a rocky shoal. The river is clear and shallow, giving one a false sense of security. But last year, as Charles Phiri, one of the workers, waded into a clear pool in the river near our camp, an enormous crocodile exploded from the calm water and grabbed his leg with jagged jaws. The twelve-foot reptile shook him violently, ripping his leg. Bornface Zulu, our airplane guard, grabbed Charles by the belt and pulled him free. As Charles heaved and struggled for breath on the beach, the crocodile lunged from the pool and grasped his torn and bloody leg again. Bornface ran for his rifle, which was leaning against a tree, stepped into the water, and shot the croc in the head. Although we flew Charles to Lusaka for the best medical care in Zambia, he later died from his injuries.

I never stepped into the river without thinking of Charles. Kabutongo shouted for us to bunch together while wading across, so I moved closer to the others, scanning back and forth for reptilian scales hiding in the current that lapped at our knees. Finally we reached the far shore and trundled onto the beach. Every half mile or so we had to cross the meandering river again, and each time Kabutongo urged us to stay together and walk quickly: "Tien! Tien!"

"More footy-prints." Kabutongo pointed to a line of prints criss-crossing the beach. I expected to find the tracks of only ten or fifteen elephants along the Lubonga, but by midmorning we had measured twenty sets.

I pulled the calipers, notebook, and pen from my pockets and squatted down to measure. By now we had a bit of a system going: the men would spread out across the beach and determine how many elephants were in the group, and I would follow along measuring one print of each. It was essential not to measure the same elephant twice, but because the elephants often milled around while drinking, bathing, and playing, it was difficult to tell their tracks apart. It looked as if a circus had been to the beach.

"No. You have already measured that one," Kabutongo said over my shoulder, as I knelt next to a print.

"How can you tell?"

"It is my work."

"I know, but please show me how." He pointed to the faint, squiggly lines in the sand created by the spongy bottom of the elephant's foot and, tracing them with his fingers, showed me how each was different, like a fingerprint. I had to study them for long minutes to see any difference, but it was obvious to Kabutongo.

At noon we dropped our packs to the ground under a *Trichilia emetica* tree at the confluence of the Mwaleshi and Lubonga rivers, a spot where Mark and I had lunched on our first day in North Luangwa six years before. We could see the rushing waters where the two rivers merged. The purple mountains of the scarp lay as a backdrop to the west. A campfire seemed to leap from Kabutongo's hands as he knelt in the clearing under the tree, and soon the men began cooking their lunch of *nshima* (cornmeal mush) and *kapenta* (small dried fish). I nibbled on crackers and peanut butter, and boiled water for tea in a pot on the edge of their fire. We chatted and laughed about the morning's work, very pleased with ourselves. Kabutongo seemed to relax, now that he had whipped us into an efficient unit.

At half past one we started off again, crossed the Lubonga for the last time, and followed the Mwaleshi, which is blessed with hundreds of wide sandy beaches and grassy floodplains. Many of the beaches were laced with long lines of elephant tracks, and we went about the backbreaking work of stooping to measure them. Taking our packs off and putting them on again at each set of tracks was tiresome, so we worked awkwardly with the packs on our backs. The clouds were gone now, and the heat seemed dense, like a curtain we had to push through to take a step.

As I knelt to measure a spoor, a large wasp hovered close to my wrist. Her brilliant blue, transparent wings were lined with black veins and reflected the stark light like colored foil. She landed and walked up and down my arm with dainty feet, then hovered just above my skin. She had powerful venom; we had watched others of her kind tranquilize mice and drag their immobilized prey into burrows for their young. I knew she wouldn't harm me; she was after my salty sweat, which to her must have been as refreshing as Gatorade. And I considered it an even trade, for the ambient air was so still and hot that the tiny breeze from her wings felt cool against my arm. I remained still, encouraging her to fan me. Finally she lifted off and flew toward the river, taking away the wind on her blue-black wings.

I stood and wiped my brow with my bandanna, thinking how nice it would be to actually *see* live elephants instead of just their "footy-prints."

Other species of wildlife were splashed everywhere across the wondrous, unscarred Mwaleshi floodplains. Waterbuck males strutted their stuff on sandbars, groups of cinnamon-colored puku grazed the short grasses, zebras pranced in lines along the beaches. Once, on the opposite shore, a herd of fifteen hundred buffalo jogged across the plain, stirring a plume of dust that blocked the sun. They plunged into the shallow river, splashing sprays of water, and as they emerged, they veered slightly and ran directly toward us. Kabutongo opened his arms like a mother hen herding her chicks and quickly moved us onto a bluff, where we could watch in safety.

By 4:30 my legs ached. Hiking through the burning sand was like walking against a strong current. Judging by the slowing progress of the men, I guessed they felt the same, though I was quite sure Kabutongo could walk all night. I began searching for a place to camp, ideally one with a wide, shady tree, a lovely view of the wilderness we had just embraced, a clean, safe place to bathe in the river, and a handy source of firewood. Often the camping place is the most memorable part of a day in the wild, and it sometimes seems my life is defined by a long trail of abandoned campfires.

Kabutongo and the others clearly had different criteria from mine. They unshouldered their packs in a small, rough clearing surrounded by tall, itchy grass with no view whatsoever, no shade trees, no firewood, and only a stagnant oxbow from which to draw water. I took one look at this unworthy spot, hefted my pack again, and told them they could stay there, but I was going back to the last group of trees we had passed, about three hundred yards upstream. There thick fig trees stood in a clearing by the sparkling, not-in-a-hurry current of the Mwaleshi. In the distance the soft body of the forested escarpment lay on its side to the west, and a zebra-spotted plain stretched to the east toward the rest of Africa.

"Wait, Dr. Delia, you cannot camp so far from us. It will be very dangerous," Kabutongo called after me.

"I'll be okay over here, don't worry." But soon he had the others lugging their packs toward my site, and we set about making camp. Someone wandered off for firewood, someone else for water. Scuffing the ground with my boots, I cleared a spot for my tent, and they a spot for theirs. A large clump of *Combretum obovatum* bushes, more gray, gnarled thorns than leaves, separated our respective sites, affording just a bit of privacy.

After the men went to the river to bathe, it was my turn. Although the rains had ended for the most part, the Mwaleshi was still murky from the wet-season runoff, making it impossible to see if the tail of a croc was coiled under the ripples. We had a rule that if you walked along the river for a hundred yards and could not see crocs through the clear water, it was okay to swim or bathe. But searching for crocs in this café au lait was pointless. Out of sight of my campmates, I undressed next to the current and slipped into the tepid water. I wanted to linger to soak up the coolness, but I jumped out to lather up, then plunged in once more to rinse quickly. I dried on the bank, feeling very clean but cheated; however, this was not the time or place to break the river rules.

I shared the men's campfire; the world could have shared their campfire. As usual, they dragged huge logs from far and near and started an enormous bonfire. The undercanopy of the tree was lit up in the yellow and red fire glow, and thousands of sparks sprayed into the air and mingled with the first timid stars of dusk. To cook their mealie meal they raked hot coals from the pyre and balanced a huge pot on top of the glowing embers. I stuck my tiny billy next to the coals to boil water for dehydrated soup. As we watched our steaming pots, all dented and scratched from miles of trail, and as the blushing sunset paled beyond the mountains, Kabutongo entertained us with stories about his poaching. He told us of a buffalo he had wounded, "but it did not die and it ran with me to the tree. But I was too fast because I had fewer legs and I climbed the tree in front of the buffalo.

And from there I was very safe until I shot the buffalo and finished him off." The other men listened with awe. I encouraged them to join in. I especially wanted Francis, the game scout, to feel as important as Kabutongo, but he was a shy, quiet man and did not want to boast about his experiences capturing poachers. Kabutongo carried the sunset.

As we stirred our pots, our slow movements around the fire cast giant, wavering shadows against the glowing tree. We ate in silence, and then I wished the men good night and moved over to my tent. I was so fatigued I could have fallen asleep instantly, but it wasn't even seven o'clock. If I slept this early, midnight would wake me stiff and sore. I dragged a small log from their woodpile, placed it in front of the pup tent door as a stool, and sat reading by candlelight. The stars were so bright in the black sky I felt I could reach up and touch them — even move them around. But who would want to rearrange Scorpio or disturb Orion's belt?

The frogs were louder than the lions, who called from the distant plains. By 7:40 the Southern Cross was fully on her side, and the arch of the Milky Way was holding up my tent. Fruit bats with beautiful fox faces swooped around me so close I could feel the wind of their wings on my face. The flicker from the candle distracted me, so I blew it out and put away my book. I would read the night instead. A different lion roared, closer. I felt alive, tucked into the earth.

I awoke at four and peeped out through my little tent window. A tide of clouds was flowing in so fast the moon seemed to be drowning. Struggling for a foothold, the predawn sky was heavy gray, with only a few weak streaks of gold far away. I lay on my camp mattress listening slowly to the guys as they began to stir. Rousing myself, I rolled up my sleeping bag and stuffed yesterday's clothes in my pack, then crawled from my pup tent like a caterpillar casting off a cocoon. The men, still half wrapped in their blankets around the fire, began to move about like giant worms.

I felt a bit tired and sore from yesterday's long walk but was "quite okay," as the Bembas say. No blisters on toes or heels.

For three days we walked along the Mwaleshi aging elephants, Mark now and then checking our position from the sky. We saw no elephants, only footy-prints. Once at night we heard their shrill trumpeting, and one afternoon they were so close in the thick bush we could feel and smell their huge bodies moving near us. Otherwise they kept their distance, and we studied them only by the stories they left in the sand. Our backs and knees ached from the constant stooping and kneeling with heavy packs, so on the third day we set up a base camp on a high bank overlooking the river and began doing day hikes from there.

One afternoon we saw a startling green lagoon blinking at us like an enormous eye from under the shadows of some ebony trees. The surface was so covered in life you could watch it breathe. On long, stiltlike legs, lily-trotters darted across water lily pads as large as elephant ears. Hadada ibis and spur-winged geese waddled along the shore eating tidbits. Five fat crocodiles as wide as kitchen tables lolled about in bright sun spots. We left the river beach and walked toward the lagoon to watch twelve hippos, their broad faces and tiny eyes peering at us from the water. One large male glided toward us, ducking his head now and then through the tangle of water plants floating on the surface. When he was thirty yards away he stood and threatened us with huge squared-off teeth and head rolls. I suppose he was trying to look fierce, but unbeknownst to him his head was draped with brilliant tendrils of green Nile lettuce and lovely water lilies, making him look more like a bridesmaid than a mad bull.

After five days we had aged almost two hundred elephants. In the heat of the day, when it was too hot to walk on the blazing sand, I sat in front of my tent and studied the data we had collected so far. In the 1970s, before heavy poaching, 50 percent of the female elephants had been of breeding age, that is, more than fifteen years old. Now only 8 percent were old enough to breed. Later on, after we had aged more than 60 percent of the population annually for six years, those preliminary figures were confirmed. Normally female elephants between the ages of twenty-five and forty are the most reproductively active, but very few of the old matriarchs were left. Besides being the most important players in elephant reproduction, the mature elephants are the storehouses for the collective knowledge of the herd. Such survival secrets had been shot and smuggled away with the ivory.

And, as with humans, adult elephants keep some sense of order and peace within their strongly bonded families. In elephant populations that have not been devastated by poachers, three quarters of the family units are led by a matriarch older than thirty years — a real grownup. Group members are seldom aggressive toward each other; even battles between gigantic males over courtship rights rarely end in serious injuries. In all social species, families designed by nature buffer youngsters against trauma and stresses that would otherwise lead to enhanced violence and poor maternal behavior in the next generation.

However, in North Luangwa a third of the family groups had no adult females older than fifteen years, because they had been shot. Nearly 10 percent of the groups were made up entirely of unsupervised, inexperienced, and unruly teenagers — some all females, some all males — roaming around on their own in an elephant version of *Lord of the Flies*. The social structure was scrambled. These disrupted families and unchaperoned gangs seemed vaguely familiar, not unlike some aspects of our own stressed species.

As a result of this change, the family units of North Luangwa were less cohesive and the adolescents were more aggressive than in populations that had not suffered from poaching. From the air we had seen young males chasing and harassing females far too young to breed. Enhanced aggression was seen elsewhere as well. In the absence of adult males, a small group of orphaned male elephants in Pilanesberg Game Reserve in South Africa went on a rampage and killed forty white rhinoceros. The killing spree stopped when mature bulls were introduced. The fractured groups of North Luangwa engaged in much less reaching out and twining of trunks; we seldom witnessed gentle touching. When families are dismantled, agonistic behavior increases; there is much less quality time at the beach. Based on what has been seen in other species, including our own, calves who had experienced the trauma of seeing their families killed were probably more likely to grow up to be aggressive. Children raised in wartorn neighborhoods are more likely to be violent than those raised in peaceful settings. Like the elephants, people do manage to survive in fragmented families, but society must endure the consequences of increased aggression and unruly gangs. We weren't sure whether man had more to learn from elephants or they from us.

The question was whether these abnormal groups of adolescent elephants would have the know-how to survive until they were old enough to reproduce. If not, the population would never recover. Amassing numbers is not the most important factor, as we, more than any other species on Earth, should know. Could these rogue teenage elephants put their social system back together? Could they ever return to a time and place where the most precious of accords — the basic family unit with its fundamental softness and security — was restored? When you lose the knack of hugging each other or twisting trunks together, how do you get it back again? Can society ever find peace once the family has fallen apart?

The columns of footprint measurements also presented a mystery. Most groups included more infants than adult females. How could this be? Even though a third of the families had no adult females, small infants still toddled next to the adolescents. Ivory poachers had left many orphans like Gift, but most of them had not been weaned from their mother's milk and thus had died. Elephants seldom adopt unweaned orphans. As inexplicable as the numbers seemed, it was certainly good news that twice as many infants had been born into the population in the past year as in the previous two years combined. Perhaps a recovery was beginning.

As the river swallowed the sun, I wandered to the sandy shore to bathe, as I did every night. Perhaps the coolness would wash away the muddle of numbers in my mind.

Just as I was testing the water with my toes, I heard the haunting shriek of an elephant trumpet. Another answered, and within seconds a chorus of elephant songs broke the silence. I grabbed my towel and soap and ran toward Kabutongo's camp. He had heard them too, and rushed toward me.

"They are just around the bend, madame. Let us go; we can see them." The other men followed as we walked quickly through the tall grass toward the river's wide bend downstream. We climbed a small bluff that overlooked the water and, peering from the thick bush, we could see twelve elephants milling about on the beach only forty yards below us. Two calves frolicked in the shallow current, while two adolescent females sprayed water over their own enormous backs. Subadult males pushed and shoved one another. A family of elephants just being elephants in an African river. Except that there were no old adults, and all the elephants were tuskless.

Every population of elephants has a small percentage, 2 to 5 percent, that never develop tusks. But in North Luangwa, since so many of the elephants with tusks had been shot, and those without tusks had lived to reproduce, the genes for tusklessness were spreading in the population. Thirty-eight percent were now tuskless. Having no tusks was definitely a disadvantage when it came to fighting and feeding, but it did help save the elephants from poachers.

We watched from our hiding place for twenty minutes. Kabutongo pointed out that one of the females had no tail. The men laughed at two young bulls fighting. Finally, Francis whispered that it was nearly dark and that we must get back to our camps. Reluctantly, I began to walk away, but Kabutongo grabbed my arm and pointed to a large bull foraging on the distant shore; he also had no tusks and, like one of the females, he was tailless. It was clear that Kabutongo did not want to leave the elephants and followed us only after Francis motioned urgently for him to come.

Around the campfire, Kabutongo helped me describe the elephant family in my notebook so that we could recognize them again.

He remembered characteristics about each one — a tear in the right ear, a medium-length tail, a jagged scar. I had definitely found a good elephant tracker.

After three days in our base camp, we packed up once more and walked downstream toward the confluence of the Mwaleshi and Luangwa rivers. As we neared the Luangwa, we approached the boundary of North Luangwa National Park. Although we could not see them from here, on the opposite shore were scattered villages, hunting and fishing camps, poachers. We encountered fewer and fewer elephant tracks as we neared the boundary. Wilderness on earth is now so confined that you can venture only so far into its heart before every step starts taking you away again. I could feel the shift, swinging like a compass in my chest.

In late afternoon we stood on a high bank overlooking the confluence of the two rivers, still somewhat swollen from the rains. At the height of the dry season, when some stretches of the Luangwa shrink to a mere channel, we had seen more than four hundred hippos packed nose to tail in this spot, but now, with the high waters, they were spread out in small groups of ten to twelve. As if luxuriating in the clean, rushing current, they were fully submerged except for their broad faces and tiny ears, which flicked continuously, sending sprays of droplets through the air. The men pitched their circle of pup tents farther inland in a small group of trees. I chose a camp very near the bank and, as darkness fell, I sat in front of my tent to watch the hippos waddle across the moonlit beaches. As they entered the water they made loud, hollow splashing sounds as if they were walking in big rubber boots.

Chief Mukungule, the oldest surviving chief in Zambia, had told us of the days when long, slow lines of several hundred elephants crossed the river. By sun or moon, they could be seen splashing through the wide, lazy Luangwa. The sounds of their giant feet against the current could be heard for a long distance, far around the river's bend.

Today elephants occasionally cross the river, but they know that poachers set up ambushes along the shore, so they usually cross under cover of darkness and, of course, in much smaller numbers. Even after spending years in Luangwa we had never seen this spectacle.

As I sat watching the glistening hippos emerge from the water, loud splashes broke the silence. I checked for lions with my flashlight, then crept through the silvery trees to the edge of the riverbank. Only fifty yards away a herd of fifteen elephants was slipping and sliding very clumsily down the steep, uneven bank. One youngster slid all the way down on his backside. Kicked free by huge feet, clods of mud rolled down the bank into the water. The elephants splashed into the river and in single file moved across it, their giant bodies swaying with an ancient rhythm. The night was lit brilliantly by the moon, and as they forded I saw their tails and trunks perfectly. They were all tuskless and two had no tails; it was the same herd we had watched bathe upstream. They reached the other side of the river and walked onto the flat beach.

The river was dancing with moonlight, yet the wet mud of the other side was black. When the deep gray elephants stepped onto the shore, they vanished into darkness. Even shielding my eyes against the bright moon, I could see nothing of them. But suddenly the perfect reflection of upside-down elephants, moving gracefully in a line, came into focus on the platinum river. Slowly and silently the inverted images floated on the sparkling current. The mirror river was so calm that every part of the elephants — the wiry tufts of their tails, the crooks of their trunks, their faces — was visible in detail. Stolen by the night, yet revealed by the moon's smile, these silent creatures drifted past my shore. Only the occasional ripple reminded me that they were mere reflections as they faded from magic into memory.

✐ SUCH WONDERS COULD keep me following elephant footprints for days, but we had reached our destination, the Luangwa, and other duties called. The key to conserving the elephants lay in helping the villagers near the park. Within the next few days I was to drive across the wild, remote northern plains of North Luangwa to the village of Fulaza to discuss job opportunities with the people. Mark and I had gone there several times over the years. However, I had never driven there by myself, and since the trip included crossing several rivers crazed with floodwaters, I was a bit apprehensive about the journey. But first the elephant trackers and I had to get back to Marula-Puku.

Late the next afternoon, as the sun pounded down and the white beach blinded us and I began to hope we never found another elephant track to measure, the *whop-whop-whop* of the chopper drifted softly downwind. As Mark swooped in low, we waved and danced around the beach like the troop of primates we were — now to be airlifted home, avoiding the long trek back. To ferry us all, Mark would have to make two trips. He landed on a grassy knoll and handed out cold Cokes and chocolate bars — treats as rare as rain — as we talked furiously about our adventures and the success of the elephant tracking. Within minutes we had half of our gear stuffed into the aft compartment and were gliding over the beaches we had hiked. Along the Mwaleshi, not far from the orange-red bluff, the tuskless elephant family foraged in a thicket of riverine forest. They must have recrossed the river into the national park sometime during the night. I nodded a silent farewell and wished them well in their upside-down world.

4 DELIA

THE SONG OF
THE WINTERTHORN

. . . passions will rock thee
As the storms rock the ravens on high.

— PERCY BYSSHE SHELLEY

LOW, DARK CLOUDS with wispy bottoms skirted the treetops across the river from Marula-Puku, parting briefly to reveal the stars. One last flash of lightning mixed its eerie blue light with the golden moonlight, and the crack of thunder tumbled head over heels across the valley. Then, unbelievably, the sparrow weavers began to sing. These small birds, outfitted with startling patterns of black, white, and brown, had nested in the acacia trees of our Kalahari camp in Botswana years ago, and now this same species lived in our Luangwa camp. For more than fifteen years we had been awakened before dawn by their joyous chortles and throaty whistles. But now they were singing furiously at midnight. Perhaps they were bragging that they had survived the storm. Or maybe their nests had been blown out of the winterthorn tree, leaving them homeless in the night with nothing left to do but sing — that's the way a sparrow weaver would see it.

Earlier, during the rainy season, there had been other storms, hot and heavy like this one, leaving behind the signs of their passion — broken trees and flooded rivers. All that anger, all that energy spent, but not wasted. For they left behind wonders as well.

Every year at the end of the long dry season, every bit of scrub,

33

every tree, bursts forth with pure, bright green. Even before the first storm, when the heat is still stifling, miles upon unbroken miles of shrubs unfold their tiny, curled shoots at once. The rivers may still be parched and choked with dry sand, but the huge trees spilling over their banks sprout new leaves seemingly overnight. With the first drops of rain, a flush of new grasses spreads across the savannas in a tide of fresh life. The only time of year when Africa is free of dust or mud, she swishes around in her new green dress for all to see. Every bush, every tree joins the parade except for one, the winterthorn.

In the midst of this celebration of new life and color, the winterthorn stands barren and leafless. A stranger to Africa will say, "Look at that huge tree; too bad it's dead." But the winterthorn, impervious to such insults, stretches its dry, delicate branches in a mighty arc across the sky, as if it knows its moment will come.

For all this green will pass too, of course. The last drop of rain is not the beginning of the dry season; the signs of the seasons are much more subtle. But you awake one morning in March or April — maybe even May — and find the dawn less soft, the air less gentle. You know, as the geese do, that the dry season is just around the river's bend. Clouds still form, and it may even rain again, a time or two, but the thunderheads have shrunk to puffy pillows floating over distant mountains.

When the plains and rivers dry up, the green trees wither and fade. At that moment, when it has the stage all to itself and life seems too hard to bear, the winterthorn begins to sing. At first only a whisper of green touches the tips of the thorny branches, but soon a rich, deep color spreads across the towering limbs. And then the stranger will ask, "What is that magnificent tree?"

Like Africa itself, the winterthorn dances in its own season.

SINCE THIS WAS early in the dry season, the time of the winterthorn, the midnight squall had been all wind and no rain. I awoke again at dawn. After an early breakfast of hot sorghum porridge and campfire toast, I set off in the truck for Fulaza village, whose mud-and-thatch huts hug the bank of the winding, clear waters of the Lufila River, the northern boundary of North Luangwa National Park. No roads went to Fulaza. Only a few worn trails snaked out of the village into the bush beyond; one of the main footpaths led into the park.

Riding beside me in the truck was Sugar, a Bemba man we had hired a year earlier to oversee our village programs. Sugar, like many of the tribesmen, had attended only a few grades of school in his small village. Then, holding tight to his brother's hand, he had traveled on an overcrowded bus to southern Zambia, which had more opportunities than the quiet and wild north. The pulsing capital of Lusaka was surrounded by vast farms, and there Sugar had learned the agricultural skills he was putting to use in his homeland by setting up projects in the tiny outposts scattered across Bembaland.

Fulaza was one of the fourteen villages where we had set up programs to help people find alternatives to poaching. The other villages had fish farms, sunflower-seed presses, soybean crops, grinding mills, and beekeepers. Men who were once notorious poachers now sold honey from beehives, raised rabbits and ducks, and reaped peanuts for protein. However, poachers coming into the park from the north were still shooting some of the few remaining elephants every year. Soon these small herds would be wiped out, and then what would the people who depended on poaching do? We wanted to give them options, at least. Villages like Fulaza were so isolated that the villagers could not go to visit the carpentry shops or fish farms in Chobela. They had no cash economy but shot elephants and traded the ivory and meat for mealie meal or cooking oil.

Sugar was short and stout, with round cheeks and smiling eyes. His real name was Musakanya Chatukwa; we nicknamed him Sugar because he put at least five or six teaspoons of it in every cup of tea.

"That was a strange storm last night, hey, Sugar?" I said.

"Yes, Delia, this weather is lost."

I drove through a stand of tall, prickly buffalo grass, and shifted the Land Cruiser into low gear to ford the Lubonga. The truck rocked gently over the rounded stones lining the stream bottom as the clear water flowed beneath us. I drove upstream several yards to avoid a waterfall that cascaded about three feet into a pool, where Ripples the crocodile sometimes hunted. As I drove onto the far bank, Sugar opened his leather briefcase — polished to a copper luster by his constant rubbing — and rummaged through his papers until he found his notes about Fulaza and studied the names of the villagers.

It would take five or six hours to drive the twenty-three miles on the dusty track across the park to the village. Mark and I had cut the track a few years earlier, a job that took days because we had to devise river crossings. Once we had four flat tires in less than an hour in a mean thicket of thorny brush. On the last night of track-making we worked long into dusk, and the full moon rose ahead of us. I stood in the bed of the truck and peered ahead into the thick bush, searching for the best course around fallen logs or holes. "Stay to the left of the moon," I called to Mark. Then, "Now drive straight toward the moon. Back left of the moon." Finally we reached the river, which seemed to flow into the mouth of night.

I hoped that Sugar could not tell that I was somewhat nervous about driving to Fulaza for the first time. When we reached the second crossing, I stopped the truck on a steep bank that descended about fifteen yards toward the water. The freak storm had apparently brought rain somewhere upstream, for the normally small river was in a mad and muddy mood. It was only about thirty feet wide and probably less than five feet deep, but it was in flood and flowing swiftly through the narrow ravine. I eased the truck down the pitch in low gear and drove slowly into the current. Within seconds the water seeped under the doors and around our feet. The front end of the truck went under the water, which reached halfway up the cab doors. The raised, snorkel-like air intake kept the truck from sucking water and stalling, but the engine hissed and moaned as the truck crept forward over the uneven bottom. As long as I did not get stuck and kept moving, we would be all right. I had watched Mark do this scores of times, but my heart thumped against my ribs as water sloshed around my ankles. Sugar stared ahead and did not say a word. He held his briefcase high against his chest.

In midstream the water flowed over the hood in a brown swirl. It seemed surreal to push the gas pedal, which was now under water, but the truck churned ahead, rocking and rolling. Finally, the front tires found purchase on the far shore and pulled us up the steep bank. Water poured from the cab and the bed of the truck. I looked at Sugar and grinned.

"This truck is a very powerful machine. It can even be a boat," he said.

𝒟 ON ONE OF our previous visits, Isaiah, the one-eyed headman, standing outside of his grass hut, had told us that poaching was the only way the villagers could make a living. They wanted other jobs or opportunities but nothing else was available to them. So we had recruited a young Englishman, Edward North, to live in Fulaza and talk to the villagers about possibilities. Fresh from Reading University, Edward had set off one morning in a truck with a compass, a radio, and a few supplies to set up camp near the village. A few days later he radioed us to say he had built some grass huts under an enormous shade tree. He had no idea what kind of tree it was, but it offered deep, lush shade for more than thirty yards.

Edward moved quietly and shyly around the village, talking through an interpreter with one man or woman at a time about ways we could help them make a living. Sugar and I were on our way to a meeting he had set up with the villagers. We drove east across the park, cutting through several more steep river gorges, then turned north toward the Lufila River on an old colonial-era survey line. Dust swirling behind our truck, we crossed the Chimana plains, passing herds of zebra, impala, and Cookson wildebeest, which are blonder than the common blue wildebeest and are found only in the Luangwa Valley.

All wildebeests are curious and playful, and the ones on this lonely plain, perhaps because they rarely saw vehicles, seemed unable to contain their inquisitiveness. Each time they saw us driving across the dusty flats they trotted after us, tossing their heads. I played a game with them, as we often did. I stopped the truck when they were eighty or so yards away. Immediately, they applied their brakes, milling about and swinging their heads. I drove forward slowly, and again they cantered after us. I stopped, they stopped. Eventually, they were forty-five feet away, jogging after us like a string of circus ponies. When we had gone several miles in this strange parade, the wildebeests dropped out of formation. They galloped about in a small circle, shaking their heads, as if in farewell. We would see them in a few days on our return, when they would again escort us across their plain.

After a few more miles we saw no more wildlife; neither wart hog nor impala graced the savanna. There was lush grass, clear water, and nutritious forage, but no animals. Eden plundered. Although we were still deep inside the national park, these were the hunting grounds of Fulaza village. Wildebeest games behind us, Sugar and I drove on in silence.

"I worry that these people will never know this idea," Sugar said as we approached the waters of the Lufila, flowing gently through the tall papyrus.

"Panono, panono," I said. Kasokola, our camp cook, had taught me the expression, which means "little by little." He was always reminding me not to fret when a truck bringing supplies was three weeks late or when essential spare parts for the Cessna arrived eight months late and were the wrong specs. "Panono, panono," he would say.

I drove down a gentle grassy slope into the river. The bank on the other side was too steep and muddy to climb, so we slogged upstream through the clear current for about fifty yards to an old log. There I turned sharply and drove up the bank.

I followed Edward's directions along the small bush track and could soon see his enormous camp tree, the largest winterthorn I had ever seen. Edward strolled out, grinning broadly. He was obviously proud of his new camp. At the center was a tiny grass sleeping shack no more than twelve feet square. An even smaller hut held his supplies. Near the river he had made a reed n'saka with a mat floor. After a quick cup of tea in the n'saka, Edward, Sugar, and I drove to the village center for the meeting.

More than fifty villagers — mothers with infants wrapped tightly to their backs with bright *chitenje* cloths, strong young men toting axes, and bent old men and women in tattered clothes — waited on straw mats under a large fig tree. As we stepped down from the truck, four elders led by Isaiah greeted us. Isaiah, his blind eye staring into the bushes beyond me, shook my hand for a long moment and held on to it gently as he introduced the others. For three hours, with Sugar translating, we talked with the villagers about how they could support themselves in this remote and lovely spot. The farmers, who grew mostly corn and sorghum in small dry patches, said they could grow sunflowers if they had seeds, and if they had a press they could make cooking oil — a priceless commodity they referred to as *saladee* — which they had to travel at least five days by foot to obtain. The village needed a grinding mill, because crushing the maize by hand took hours of hard labor. A mill would provide an industry for at least one family. Several women wanted to be beekeepers.

Standing under the fig tree, the mud huts behind us, Sugar and I explained that the project would train them and lend them money for equipment. We explained that they would be required to pay back the loans. Free handouts have been a plague in Africa. The continent is littered with failed development projects that were too large in scope, too high-tech by design, and required no accountability. The result was broken-down tractors in dusty fields, dried rice paddies in ruined oases, sophisticated hospital equipment no one could repair in abandoned, wornout clinics. We assured them that no one had to participate; we were simply offering assistance to those who wanted it.

Sugar translated, going into long explanations complete with stories and parables. Sitting on the straw mats, faces fixed on Sugar, the villagers nodded their heads. They understood why they should pay back any loans.

After three hours the sun dipped below the branches of the fig tree. The rough drive from camp and the long discussions in the heat had made me weary. Just as we were about to close the meeting, an old woman with anxious dark eyes unfolded her bony frame in slow motion from the grass mats and spoke. Isaiah translated, "There is no school in this village for the children of us." Everyone nodded in agreement. One man said, "Our village will never find the world until we educate our children."

We did not have enough money in our budget to build a school, but as they leaned toward us waiting for our answer, I felt we couldn't disappoint them. Edward, Sugar, and I huddled together, and after a few minutes Sugar came up with a suggestion: the project would supply the materials and hire six villagers to make bricks, paying them with soap, cooking oil, and mealie meal. We would ask ADMADE, a government program that returned fees paid by trophy hunters to the villages, to pay for door and window frames. Later, when all the materials were assembled, we would hire a builder to supervise construction by the villagers. The people clapped, and several women swayed into a string dance that wound among the straw mats and blankets, leading us across the bush and sorghum patches to a small grove of trees not far from the main footpath. The village elders agreed that this was the right spot for the school.

"Madame, when do you think it will be finished?" Isaiah asked. Instinctively I looked at the sky and searched for clouds. When the rains came in three or four months, we would be unable to ferry supplies across the river.

"We must finish before the rains or a whole school year will be lost," I said, and he nodded.

We got busy right away. Edward and the elders chose six men — all of whom had been poachers — to make bricks from the local clay. When Sugar and I got back to Marula-Puku, I sent a truck to Fulaza with soap, cooking oil, and mealie meal for the brick makers. From his office in Mpika, Sugar arranged for a maize-grinding mill to be transported from Lusaka. Edward distributed sunflower seeds to the farmers and repaired the water pump for the small clinic staffed by a Zambian medical practitioner. The elders visited Edward at his camp and invited him to a wedding, then a funeral.

A FEW DAYS LATER Edward radioed to say that the brick makers had changed their minds about being paid in supplies. "They want to be paid in cash."

"Okay, Edward. I'll have to drive to Mpika for cash, then back to Fulaza. It may take a few days."

The next day I stood at the fuel station on the lonely stretch of the Great North Road, which transects the continent from the Cape of Good Hope to Cairo. To the east lay the Muchinga Mountains, whose lush forests spilled along the road and into the village.

"So, no diesel?" I asked.

"Yes, madame. The tanker trucks did not come from Lusaka, so there is no diesel. Maybe it will come tomorrow."

I had driven six hours over the mountains to the bank in Mpika village, but I could not drive back to camp or to Fulaza without more diesel. After staying the night with friends in Mpika, I went back to the station, where gumba music blared from the Dog Eat Dog Café.

"Sorry, madame. But we are sure tomorrow the tanker will come."

In the heart of the village the open market vibrated with colorful chitenje cloths that swayed on the hips of thin women toting baskets of golden mangos. Again loud music rang out from old ghetto blasters tended by young men. This time it was not tribal music but Western hits from the sixties like "I Want to Hold Your Hand." No matter what they were doing — selling cooking oil in Coke bottles or mending sandals — people tapped and clapped to the thumping beat, and I had a wild urge to break into a dance. Women squatted on straw mats, where carrots, cabbages, onions, and sweet potatoes were displayed in little piles. The odor of dried fish mixed with that of overcooked meat roasting over small pits. I bought two burlap bags of dried beans from a mother and daughter who had been up since dawn shelling them. The older woman grinned at me and insisted I take a small bundle of bananas for free.

Four days later the diesel tanker arrived. I filled the truck's tank plus several drums and drove back to Marula-Puku. The next morning I radioed Edward that I would drive to Fulaza that afternoon.

"Sorry, Delia, but the brick makers have deserted. Apparently they do not want to work now, even for wages. I'll let you know when I find replacements."

Edward found new brick makers, we paid them cash, and they began molding clay into blocks. Only a few bricks were fired before the rains started, and work on the school was delayed for another five months. Edward's time as a volunteer ended and he had to return to England. After the rains stopped, Mark and I drove to Fulaza to get construction going again. Progress was slow, and the school was not finished when the rains came once more.

Again I stood in Fulaza facing the headman. "When will we finish the school, madame? We must finish the school before the rains."

"This year, Isaiah. Surely this year before the rains."

Finally the bricks were finished, and one of our new volunteers, Alex Haynes, supervised construction. As promised, the villagers volunteered to do the labor as long as we donated soap, cooking oil, and food. The walls began to go up, but soon they ran out of cement and none was to be found in Mpika. It would have to come by train from Lusaka — maybe tomorrow, the shopkeeper said. Two months later it arrived, and we sent Moses Kunda off driving the tractor and trailer loaded with cement across the wildebeest plains to Fulaza. Moses had never forded the Lufila before, and he was supposed to wait at the river until villagers arrived to show him the crossing by the log. They would be able to hear the tractor coming for miles and would come to greet him. When Moses arrived at the river, he saw no villagers. The crossing looked easy to him, so he drove the tractor into the water and straight across to the other side instead of driving upstream to the log. Moses started up the far bank just as the villagers ran toward him through the papyrus waving their arms. The trailer stood nearly on its end as the tractor struggled up the muddy incline.

With a *whoosh*, one hundred bags of cement slid off the trailer and into the river. The brick makers knew about cement, but most of the villagers did not. They spread the contents of the soaked bags all over the ground in the sun to dry. And dry it did, making a huge, flat monument to the delayed school.

More cement was ordered, the rains came again, and then another dry season. A summer and a winter. Time and again the winterthorn where Edward had camped flushed green and turned barren. It became the tree of hope.

In the meantime the farmers planted sunflower seeds and sold their crop to the press operator, who sold cooking oil to the villagers or traded it for meat. Families raised chickens. The mill ground corn, so villagers no longer had to shoot wildlife in the park to barter for ground cornmeal. Farmers also grew soybeans and other protein-rich crops. The medical officer had a house, and the clinic was supplied.

One afternoon Mark and I flew the helicopter to Fulaza to return the mill engine, which had been repaired at camp. It was too large to fit inside the chopper, so Mark clipped it to the cargo line; it swung in gentle circles beneath us as we flew across the plains. Ahead we could see the mud huts, their thatched peaks sprouting among papyrus patches along the river. Herds of impala and puku grazed peacefully on the bank opposite the village. A family of wart hogs dug up roots on the riverbank, stirring up a plume of dust. The huts of Fulaza and the wild animals of North Luangwa stood within the same field of view, a sight I never thought I would see.

The villagers had been expecting the return of the engine for weeks. When they saw the chopper appear, the engine swinging below like prey in the clutches of a giant eagle, they swarmed from their huts and ran toward the millhouse. Scores of people dressed in bright yellow, red, and blue chitenje cloths streamed through the dusty green brush toward the village center. Mark hovered the chopper over the ground near the mill. Using the belly-mounted cargo mirror to see the load, he gently placed the engine on the ground. We landed beside the mill, and Mark helped the men restart the engine.

It took three and a half years, but finally the school in Fulaza village was complete. It stood near the river, its red mud bricks a rosy pink in the sun. Textbooks were sent from America, the Ministry of Education arranged for a teacher, and the children went to school.

After the opening celebration I said to Isaiah that we would be back next year, and he answered, "I know, madame. You will come with the winterthorn." Then he added, "How is it that you knew about our problems, that you did not come to arrest the poachers but to give them jobs?"

"There have been poachers in my family, too, Isaiah," I said. "In fact my grandpa was one."

5 DELIA
GRANDPA

Grandfather, . . .
Teach us love, compassion, and honor
That we may heal the earth
And heal each other.

— OJIBWAY PEOPLE OF CANADA

Destiny is made known silently.

— AGNES DE MILLE

ONE MORNING KASOKOLA was kneading bread dough under the thatched roof of the open kitchen *boma* (hut) while I picked weevils out of the mealie meal. He wanted to know where I had come from in America and why I had come to Africa. So I told him this story.

My grandfather, tall and handsome, with neatly combed white hair, sat behind the wheel of his Ford Fairlane in the summer of 1959. "Look here, HiDe, the gears are like an H. When you push the clutch plumb to the floor, you gotta ease the knob to the top here, up the left side of the H. Then let the clutch out thisaway, as you give 'er a little gas. Now give 'er a try. You can do it." I was ten years old, and as interested in pleasing Grandpa as driving, so I slid behind the steering wheel. Stalling and bucking, the Ford Fairlane lurched among the pecan trees as I honed my skills. Earth the color of dried blood stretched away toward crooked split-rail fences smothered in blackberry brambles as thick as fort walls and sweet-smelling honeysuckle. Hungry kudzu crawled across the nearby woods, consuming ancient oaks, lean-to shacks, even an abandoned barn. They say kudzu grows an inch an hour, so if you have nothing else to do — and some folks here can make that claim — you can watch it grow.

Gentle words and the occasional Baby Ruth candy bar encouraged me until I finally eased the Ford somewhat more smoothly over the red clay.

"Well, I declare, HiDe, you drive real good. Yessiree bobtail, you sure do." This was reward enough, but from his pocket he took a small white gold watch with rhinestones around its dainty oval face. My first timepiece, from the Kress five-and-dime, and now I could drive! I had surely grown up in a hurry.

My grandpa, Roy C. Johnson, had bought a small brick house on "plumb and nelly" street — "plumb out of town and nearly in the country" — on the edge of Americus, a small south Georgia town, in 1926, and he lived there with my grandma, Mary Belle, until she passed away, two days before their sixtieth wedding anniversary. Grandpa delivered the mail on Route 1 for forty-two years.

Grandpa hadn't always been a mail carrier. His grandfather and father had owned one of the largest plantations in Sumter County. Called Huntington, it stretched across the flat, fertile ground toward the Flint River. It was not a frilly estate, all columns and rose gardens, but a working plantation with expansive cotton fields, pecan groves, cattle herds, a milk and butter dairy, a brickyard, and a syrup factory fed by fields of sugar cane that marched between the pines.

But the Depression hauled off and kicked the South in the belly. Commodity prices wilted like dried tobacco leaves, and my great-grandfather could no longer pay the army of laborers required to pick and pack such a large plantation. Rows of cotton bales were left strewn across the fields like brilliant white coffins tied up with burlap, the soul of the old South interred within them. They waited for a market that never returned, and my great-grandfather died in debt. Grandpa, Mr. Roy, didn't have to pay off his father's bank loans, but he did. Every hot afternoon after delivering the mail, he and his brothers farmed for the bank until they paid off the debt. Then they sold the land, and Grandpa and Grandma moved to plumb and nelly street.

Most of the people on Route 1 were African Americans. They lived in unpainted wooden houses perched on rickety stacks of brick. Kneeling down, you could see under the house right to the other side. The dwellings may not have been brushed with store-bought paint, but they were colorful just the same, because thunderstorms splashed red mud onto the raw pine siding, mixing it with the orange rust that dribbled down from the corroded tin roofs. As Grandpa used to tell me, when you deliver mail to the same people for forty-two years you get to know them "real good": births, weddings, deaths, all the good times, all the hard times. Especially during the Depression, he got to know the people, and they got to know him.

Many a time, Grandpa told me, folks on Route 1 didn't have the money for a two-cent stamp. Grandpa would find an unstamped letter in the mailbox, and inside or under it would be postage: a single egg, a bundle of fresh turnip greens, or a brown paper bag of black-eyed peas, already shelled. He would supply the postage himself and either deliver the greens to another family who needed them or take them home to Grandma to fix for dinner, which was pronounced *dunnah,* and served at noon.

One item Grandpa refused to deliver. A few men on Route 1 made a living distilling corn liquor in the woods. Grandpa knew where all the stills were, but he never told the federal agents. One morning Grandpa found a big glass jug of moonshine hidden in the tall grass under one of the mailboxes. A rubber band around its neck held a note asking him to take it to a farm up the road. Turnip greens were one thing, but Grandpa worried that if someone saw him delivering moonshine, it wouldn't look too good for the U.S. Postal Service. He honked the horn of his Fairlane. Mr. Henry, a large black man in baggy bib overalls that were always too short for his long legs, came out, and Grandpa told him that maybe it wasn't such a good idea to leave moonshine right next to the road. Mr. Henry thanked

Grandpa for the advice and tried to give him another jug — this one for himself. Grandpa failed to mention whether he accepted it or not.

I lived with my family — Mama, Daddy, sister Helen, twin brother Bobby, and younger brother Lee — one hundred miles south of Huntington among the magnolias, plantations, cotton fields, and cattails of Thomasville, one of Georgia's southernmost towns. Ancient oaks adorned with wispy Spanish moss spread their limbs across wide avenues lined with antebellum mansions and flowering white dogwoods. The Big Oak, said to be four hundred years old, covered nearly an entire yard and was shored up with twisted steel cables, iron rods, and the unfailing love of the entire town.

My friend Libby Wine and I rode her quarter horses on the county's seemingly endless miles of winding back roads. We packed peanut butter and banana sandwiches in brown paper bags, which we tied to our saddles, and rode all day in the balmy breezes. One of her horses, a roan gelding named Strawberry, I considered my own. He never really belonged to me, but no one else rode him. He was the color of honey and had a thick mane and tail as blond as sunlight.

While riding along a creek in dense oak forest one morning, we discovered a nation of albino frogs, looking like delicate porcelain figurines in a fairy-tale forest. We thought the natural soggy debris of the creek — dead leaves, pine needles, and moss — was clogging the current and threatening these wondrous creatures. Day after day we rode the horses to the creek and, in a misguided conservation project, cleared the stream until it gurgled slightly faster over the rocks. (In fact, slower, meandering creeks provide richer habitats for wildlife. But Libby and I were in good company. Over the next twenty years the U.S. government would channelize streams, cement riverbanks, and drain wetlands, thereby destroying thousands of acres of prime habitat.) We told no one about the frogs for fear that men in white lab coats would come with nets and capture them in large jars for the Smithsonian Institution. Instead we kept their creek clean and watched until they dispersed throughout the clear water.

We were free to wander wherever the woods went. We found a

hawk's nest and shinnied up a nearby tree to watch the fluffy chicks. When the mother did not return, we crept quietly away, fearing that we had interfered with her brood-rearing chores. We never took anything, never collected bugs in bottles, and all we left behind were our footprints along with those of the deer in the soggy creek bottom.

One day a gunshot cracked through the bird songs and the pine-scented breeze. Like a posse, we galloped around a bend in the road and found a man standing next to a beat-up pickup, a shotgun bent over his arm. At his feet was a large bird, its blood-smeared wings spread across the red clay. When we asked why he had shot it, he said, "Because it was a buzzard." He then kicked it over and over in the dust until it flopped like an oil-soaked rag into the ditch. After he drove away, we buried the bird and marked the leaf-covered grave with a cross made of twisted twigs. We held a two-girl funeral, each saying a few words and a prayer "because it was a buzzard."

Maybe I didn't know it then, but the joy-sorrow of nature would never leave my heart again.

꧁ We heard grownups talking about the Cuban missile crisis, and civil-defense-test horns blared periodically on the radio between Elvis songs. Yellow signs with black triangles popped up around town, each marking a fallout shelter. Mama stored cans of chili and beanie-weenies and jugs of water under the stairs, where Tammy always had her kittens. I asked her to please also stash cans of Puss 'n Boots for Tammy, and of course she did. For my parents, who had been through World War II — my dad as a navy pilot in the South Pacific, my mother on the home front making bandages — the threat of a nuclear bomb attack was dire.

One day long lines of camouflaged jeeps and trucks filled with soldiers began passing by the intersection of Monticello Road and the unpaved lane where we lived. Bobby and I stood at attention under the stop sign and saluted the soldiers going south to protect us, and they saluted back.

To me the biggest worry of the Cuban missile crisis was that our beanie-weenie supply might give out and we'd have to eat Tammy's Puss 'n Boots. But the war never came. When the soldiers motored back through town headed north, we took up our posts, but the saluting on both sides was less enthusiastic this time around. Sitting in the dirt, teasing doodlebugs with pine needles, we chatted with the neighborhood kids. It was then and there that Hank Pepin told me how babies are really made, which to me was a much more alarming prospect than any missile crisis.

✒ GRANDMA SOMETIMES BAKED a plump caramel cake, wrapped it in foil, and sent it to us on the Trailways bus, where it rode on the floor next to the driver. But she and Grandpa visited us as often as they could, the Fairlane filled with sugar cookies, meringue pies, and corn on the cob. Knowing my love of horses, Grandpa often brought me toy ones made of plastic or wood. One autumn day he brought me a beautiful china horse, a golden brown palomino with rippling muscles and a waving blond mane. I named it Strawberry, though the resemblance to the real horse was a bit vague, and kept it close to my bed.

As far as Grandpa was concerned, one of the best things about being a rural mail carrier was finishing work about 1:30 every afternoon. He would sit down to Mary Belle's dinner of fried chicken, biscuits, gravy, butter beans, sliced tomatoes, corn off the cob, fried okra, and pecan pie or backbone stew, cornbread, turnip greens, sweet potatoes, black-eyed peas, and peach cobbler. "Pass me a hot 'un, HiDe," he would say, and I would pass the basket of hot biscuits that were as tall and light as clouds. Grandpa called me HiDe because when Bobby and I were babies, my mother would walk into our room and say, "Hi Bo. Hi De." So Bobby thought my name was HiDe, and called me that as soon as he could talk. Grandpa called me HiDe until the day he died.

After dinner Grandpa would take a nap in his reclining chair, since he had been up since four A.M. delivering the mail. The rest of the afternoon he was free: free to watch baseball in the spring, to make furniture in his garage during the winter, to go hunting and fishing all summer and autumn long.

Mr. Roy was the best man who ever lived on this earth, and I will argue that point with anybody, but he was not perfect. In fact, my grandfather was a poacher. He and Charles Jones, who was a banker and thus kept good hours, went hunting or fishing every day of every summer and fall and didn't pay too much mind to the limit of trout, quail, doves, or whatever their quarry. But catching fish and shooting birds were secondary to the thrill of outsmarting the game warden.

The warden didn't like to walk very far, so he could always be spotted driving his Ford pickup across the fields. This usually gave Grandpa and Mr. Jones plenty of time to run, hide, or dispose of the extra birds or fish. Once they climbed high in a big oak tree and sat watching as the warden ranted and raved below them when he found their cache of doves but couldn't find them. One day they illegally baited a whole field with corn and caught the game warden, who sat there all day waiting for them. Meanwhile they shot hundreds of doves that flew over an unbaited field a few miles down the road. Grandma cooked as many doves as she could in stews or pies and gave the rest away to the neighbors.

But the warden finally nailed Grandpa, and Ol' Dan was to blame. Grandpa swore that Ol' Dan was the best bird dog in the South; he would point quail and fetch ducks without a miss. Plenty of Georgia bird dogs can do that, but Ol' Dan was the only one who knew to bark at the game warden's truck, and *only* the game warden's truck.

One afternoon Grandpa and Mr. Jones shot about a hundred doves next to a small stream that runs down to the Flint River along the edge of a large, open field. They were just about to bag their birds and go home for the day when Ol' Dan gave a soft, short bark, warning that the game warden was coming. They looked up and saw the game warden's pickup rocking and rolling over the rough furrowed ground on the other side of the field. They were in the open, with no trees to climb and nowhere to run, so they started slinging the birds as fast as they could into thick blackberry bushes on the other side of the stream. They kept a few — a very few — over the limit, knowing the warden would be suspicious if he found them with the lawful quota. When the warden was close enough to see them clearly, Grandpa decided he still had too many, so he kicked a few into the stream.

The warden pulled up and strode over. Grandpa and Mr. Jones hailed him politely. He checked their licenses and shook his head as he counted the doves. "Looks like ya'll are a bit over the limit. But not too bad," he said.

As Grandpa pointed out some mallard ducks flying toward the Flint River, Ol' Dan pulled himself out of the stream with a dove in his mouth. He dropped it at Grandpa's feet, shook himself vigorously, ran across the stream, and retrieved another dove from the blackberry bushes.

"Well, well, what do we have here?" the game warden asked, as Ol' Dan retrieved bird after bird from across the stream. The old dog's enthusiasm cost Grandpa five dollars in fines, but it did give him another story to tell his grandchildren.

⬧ IT'S HARD TO KNOW which little things in life affect your decision to follow one course rather than another. There are probably hundreds of words and deeds — things you don't remember, or didn't think much about at the time — that make you turn one corner but not the next. I used to sit and listen to Grandpa's stories for hours. In later years, when he could no longer go hunting, he would shake his head and say, "There ain't as many birds as there used to be, HiDe." He would almost whisper, "There used to be so many doves they'd darken the sky when they flew over a cornfield. At dusk you could hear the ducks landin' on the river from half a mile away. You never heard so much squawkin' and carryin' on in your life. We didn't

figure our shootin' would make a dent in 'em. But I reckon we did."
He stopped short of saying the game warden was right all those years,
but that's what he was admitting, and he felt bad, real bad. He told his
tales to us and the "route folks" on their faded, weather-checked
porches until the day he died. Almost every family in town, black and
white, came to his funeral, and he was buried wearing his red vest.

Grandpa gave me a lot of things: my first wristwatch, a china
horse with a glorious golden mane, and an apple tree from Sears Roe-
buck, because a fruit seed I had planted in the spring turned out to be
a weed. But I think the best thing he gave me were his words, which
started out as only stories, then became something more, one of the
little things that changed my life and set me on a certain course.

6 DELIA

ANY TIME FROM NOW

> Females generally put most of their reproductive effort
> into "parental effort" while males put most of theirs into
> "mating effort."
>
> — J. R. KREBS AND N. B. DAVIES

AS THE DRY SEASON deepened, the elephants began to leave the valley for the lush browse of the mountains. Lines of the small families could be seen twisting through the ravines and gorges as they fed in the ancient forests. Mark airlifted six of the Mano Unit scouts, including Isaac Daka, into the rugged terrain to guard the elephants from any poachers who still trekked into the park to shoot them. The scouts hunkered in the bush along an old trail that was worn wide and bare from the days, only a few years earlier, when bands of more than one hundred men would march boldly into the park to kill for ivory.

Suddenly Daka pointed ahead. A pack of poachers, rifles slung over their shoulders, bundles on their backs, walked down the path single file toward the hidden scouts. Three of the carriers were balancing large white bags of mealie meal on their heads. Oddly, one of the poachers was outfitted with a sleeping bag, ground mat, and tent identical to those we had supplied to the scouts. With the poachers at thirty yards, the patrol leader squeezed the arm of his number-two man and pointed.

"Ah-way! But it is Mabu!" His bandy legs striding out, walking at a quick pace as always, Mabu Kabutongo, ivory poacher/miller/research assistant/tracker, who had helped me age elephants, a poacher once again, was leading the band of outlaws.

Stunned, the scouts half stood from behind the boulders and brush. Perhaps if Mabu had thought quickly enough, he could have waved warmly to the scouts and pretended to be bringing them a message from us. Instead he stopped suddenly, then slowly backed away, confirming that he was up to no good. Immediately the scouts felt betrayed. They had accepted Mabu into their camp, and he had repaid their trust, and ours, by pretending to go to the village for supplies, then organizing a poaching expedition from Mpika. He had even stolen their camping equipment.

The scouts shouted, "*Eway* — Y O U! Just wait for us there!" At that the poachers scattered, running through the bushes like rabbits, each pursued by a scout. Mabu escaped, but his carrier and three others did not. Daka radioed Mark, and within thirty minutes he had helicoptered the scouts back to Mano with their prisoners. From there a squad of scouts drove to Mpika to turn in the poachers and to stake out Mabu's old grass hovel — the one he used before taking up residence in Mano — which was forty miles over the Muchinga Mountains from where he had been spotted. Mabu walked back out of the park all night, feeling his way along the rocky, darkened trails over the mountains. The next morning he crept through the outskirts of the village and entered his hut. Seconds later, on a signal, the scouts, shouting and firing rounds into the air, ran from the nearby bushes and surrounded the dwelling. Mabu surrendered — even he could not put up much of a defense from inside a grass hut.

Acting as his own counsel, Mabu tried to convince the magistrate that he had received a tip that poachers were headed into the park, borrowed a rifle from his grandfather — his own had been confiscated — gathered some of his friends as a posse, and headed into the park to apprehend the criminals. The old magistrate might have believed this story or accepted a bribe, but the new one did not. Knowing that these men were repeat offenders, he sentenced Mabu and the others to six months in jail for carrying illegal guns in North Luangwa.

Another ex-poacher gladly accepted the job as miller at Mano;

he and his family occupied the house we had constructed for Mabu. His accompanying me on my elephant walk had not helped his poaching; Mabu had known for years where the elephants lived. He must have been laughing at me as I scribbled the measurements in my notebook. We had helped many ex-poachers find jobs, and most of them were now fish farmers or carpenters. But Mabu had a reason for returning to poaching.

Field Commander Banda Famwila, who was based in Mpika, was still encouraging poachers to shoot wildlife illegally for large-scale commercial operations that smuggled illegal meat and ivory to high-level officials in Lusaka. Because of Famwila's lofty connections with Romance Musangu, he operated with impunity right under the nose of the game warden, the magistrate, and the other scouts. They could do nothing to stop him.

To make matters worse, it was still rumored that the Convention on International Trade in Endangered Species (CITES) ban on the international trade in ivory would be reversed or relaxed, allowing tusks to be sold once again. Before the ban, 90 percent of the ivory sold legally on the world market was from illegally shot elephants. No signatory nation to the CITES ban could sell or buy ivory unless the restrictions were lifted, but there was constant pressure on nations like Zambia, which supported the ban, to change their position.

The ivory ban had been one of the most successful environmental policies ever adopted. As a direct result of it, elephant poaching had decreased by 70 to 90 percent in most areas where illegal hunting had thrived. The ban also protected other wildlife, because when poachers ventured out on extended expeditions for elephants, they also killed buffaloes, wildebeests, impalas, and zebras for their meat and skins.

Less has been written about the human suffering resulting from the ivory trade. Since the 1800s, when long caravans of men from the north snaked their way into Africa's belly and enslaved men to carry ivory, the trade in "white gold" has led to the mistreatment and abuse of tribal people. More than a hundred years later, in the 1890s and 1990s, villages were still taken over by the "big men," powerful poachers and smugglers who abused women, forced children out of school to be porters, and paid men less than a dollar per expedition to shoot elephants. Because there were few other opportunities in these remote mud-and-thatch outposts, the poachers could tempt or force people to join this dirty, dangerous, illegal work. In the process, they stifled chances for legitimate development, keeping the villagers in stagnant backwaters of poverty and isolation.

The ivory ban changed all that. When nations could no longer sell or buy ivory, the price dropped dramatically. When it was no longer profitable for poachers to shoot for ivory, they left the villagers, as well as the elephants, alone.

But CITES was soon to vote again on the ban, and some nations were lobbying to sell ivory. Men like Musangu, Famwila, and Mabu were patient. Whispers of a new trade in ivory were incentive enough for these men to shoot elephants and stockpile the tusks. After all the progress that had been made against poaching, we worried that the situation would backslide.

NOW THAT MABU KABUTONGO had been caught poaching again, I had to find another elephant tracker. Bornface Zulu, the man who had rescued Charles after the crocodile attacked him, was an ex–game scout whom Mark had hired as a guard for the helicopter. Tall and thin, Bornface has a kind face and a nonstop willingness to please. He knew as much about elephants as Kabutongo and maybe more.

I asked him to assemble a tracking team, and the six men and I walked the wild and stirring rivers of Luangwa — the Lubonga, Lufila, Mwaleshi, and Mulandashi — aging elephants. As poetic and mysterious as their names, these rivers cascaded through secret forests in the mountains, then snaked across the wide, sprawling valley. Not once did we come across another human being as we explored them. Poaching had been reduced for several years in these remote areas, so the elephants were calmer, and we watched them forage in the trees or frolic in the rivers more frequently. Using natural markings, lengths of tails, and scars, I identified and number-coded as many elephants as possible before we measured the footprints.

Bornface always waited for me when I lagged behind instead of yelling for me to catch up, as Kabutongo had done, and he always walked by my side, rifle cocked, when we crossed the croc-laden rivers. The men were more at ease under his leadership, and we all consulted on campsites and river crossings. Bornface would walk all the way across a hot beach to identify a bird's nest or investigate an abandoned lion kill. He knew most of the trees by name and could describe in detail which plants an elephant family had been browsing in the forests.

One morning as we hiked a remote, narrow canyon of the upper Lubonga River, we came around a bend and suddenly found ourselves too close to a small female elephant. Alone in a grassy meadow between us and the rocky walls of the canyon, she was cornered, with nowhere to run. Even the gentlest creature can become aggressive when trapped. Instinctively, we halted. The elephant whirled around to face us and threw her trunk into the air. But then she turned away, pranced toward the wall for a few feet, lifted her tail to the side, and jogged slowly toward us, dancing a little jig.

"Ah, it is Gifty," Bornface said. We were miles from camp, but she seemed to recognize us. After shaking her head in our direction a few times, she calmed down and completely ignored us as she pulled grass from the riverbank. Standing quietly, we watched her for some time. It was nearly two years since we had first seen her, and we had often observed her either near camp or miles away. She was still completely alone. It unraveled my heart. When we finally left her, we gave her a wide berth by climbing up the canyon wall on the opposite side. As we continued north, I turned to look until her gray back disappeared in the long grass.

We followed the Lubonga toward Hidden Valley, a small, tear-drop-shaped basin of spongy green meadows and meandering streams carved into the great scarp mountains. It is protected from the world by a fort of tall, rugged hills covered in thick forests of ancient trees and giant ferns. Steep, rocky ravines lace the hills like moats, warding off intruders. The only gate into this sanctuary is a steep canyon sliced through the rim of the lower escarpment by the river. We followed the river up through the dark gorge, climbing over huge boulders that blocked the way and wading through deep pools that reflected the towering walls around us. On a previous walk we had gotten to the very last pool of the canyon to find it guarded by a very large crocodile. Sheer rock walls, smothered with mosses and ferns, rose from the water on either side, so there was no way around the pool. Guardian of the valley, the croc lay on the surface, his eyes staring at us. We had had no choice but to turn around, hike back through the canyon, and spend an extra day climbing over the hills into the valley.

So on this trek, when we reached the last pool we leaned carefully over the edge to check for crocs. Our reflections were the only creatures staring back at us, so we waded through the pool and climbed the rocks on the other side. Before us lay the sun-splashed valley.

An enormous fig tree graced the entrance to the valley, and a smaller one stood about a hundred yards away. I said I would camp under the smaller tree; the men could pitch their tents under the larger one. I always wanted my own camp because the men liked to chat and laugh at night, whereas I wished to hear the owls and the hyenas. Besides, we all liked our privacy. The Bembas were extremely shy around women, and they would not come near my camp if they thought I was getting dressed. Even in our main camp I had to be careful about hanging my laundry; certain items were just not appropriate to fly in the wind.

Later, after dark, my pup tent set up, my forgettable meal cooked and eaten, I leaned against a big log, cocking my book at an odd angle so I could read by firelight. It was a great little camp. I had hung a kettle, a towel, and my clothes in the lower branches of the tree. My pack and boots fit in the fork of the trunk, just out of reach of the hyenas. The light from the men's huge campfire danced in the fig, the brilliant stars capping the scene. I was content reading one of my favorite books in one of my favorite places.

I heard a rustle in the grass to my right, maybe ten yards away. I lowered my book to my lap and peered in that direction. But the long grass stood like a wall on three sides of me, so I could not see very far. I began reading again.

I heard the sound once more — like a stick falling on duff — and jerked my head up. A lioness, her blond body shimmering in the light of my campfire, walked into the clearing just beyond my tent. Looking straight ahead, not in my direction, she sashayed through the shorter grass only twenty yards away, her tail forming a crook behind her. Clutching the pepper spray — my only weapon — I froze. She would probably satisfy her curiosity and then move on. I heard nothing for five minutes.

I went back to my book. The promotional spiel on its jacket stated that most readers were so touched by the story that they would always remember exactly where they were when they read it. I was sure that would be true for me.

Suddenly the grass crackled behind me — close. I stood up, shouted, and waved my arms. The lioness sprang away from me and trotted from the grass into the clearing. She stood, her head low, tail twitching, staring at me with a whole lot of attitude.

"Bornface!!! There's a lion over here!" I shouted.

Immediately, five flashlights swirled around in all directions as the men, silhouetted against the bonfire, rushed toward me. The lioness trotted into the tall grass as they approached, their flashlights illuminating her pale back.

But as soon as the men stood by my side, the lioness stepped boldly back into the clearing toward us, posture erect, tail lashing like a whip.

"Madame, this lioness may leave, but she will return any time from now."

"You're right, I can't stay here. Let's move my camp under your tree." The scouts moved toward the lioness, waving their arms, while the rest of us gathered up my gear. Two of the carriers toted the fully erect tent, billowing out like a sail, over to their fire. Bornface and I followed with armloads of pots, binoculars, clothes, and sleeping gear. Guarded by the scouts, the rest of the men went back for a last load and doused my fire with water, sending a plume of ash and steam into the night air. Within ten minutes my little camp was set up under the security of their huge fig tree. Without hesitation the lioness sauntered to my abandoned spot and sniffed around the extinguished campfire. Now and then she looked our way, ears back in annoyance that we had spoiled her game. But the six of us must have been a formidable sight against the large fire, for she finally disappeared into the tall grass.

I thanked the guys and wished them good night.

Five "good nights" echoed mine, and I slipped into my tent. I thought of reading by flashlight but instead lay very still. The men's soft laughter may have been at my expense, but I have never heard a more comforting sound in my life. Snuggled in my sleeping bag, the firelight glowing through the wall of my tent, I forgot about the calls of owls and hyenas for one night and drifted off to sleep to the music of their singsong voices.

The next morning, when I crawled out of my tent, Bornface was making tea by a small cook fire. The others milled about, folding bedding or stirring porridge. None of them looked directly at me or in the direction of my abandoned camp. Perhaps they were simply giving me my own space. I stretched and wished them good morning, which they all answered rather quietly. As I looked over the valley, whose muted colors waited impatiently for sunrise to give them life,

I noticed something flapping in the tree of my former camp. During our hasty retreat, we had obviously missed something. Dangling from a branch was my white, lacy bra, which, although very small indeed, somehow looked enormous in this setting. I sidled over, tore down the bright feminine banner, and discreetly stuffed it in my pocket.

BORNFACE AND I LEFT the others in camp that morning and hiked along the maze of streams that crisscrossed the marshy plains of Hidden Valley to look for elephant tracks. The day promised to be hot, so I wore shorts instead of long khaki pants. As we ventured northwest into the narrow part of the teardrop shape, the grass became very tall and razor sharp. In a half hour of breaking trail through the prickly weeds, my bare legs were cut to shreds, little beads of blood running down my calves. Then, as if they had been waiting for our arrival, the tsetse flies swarmed around our faces, and we had to apply fresh repellent every twenty minutes. Bornface cut branches for us to swat the tsetses. Nature so often turns out to be heat, flies, and saw grass.

Blue waxbills covered the ground like a pastel blanket, and paradise flycatchers flitted about the tall reeds, their long tail feathers flowing behind them like kite tails. Suddenly, breaking the silence, a hyena called with a voice as clear and sharp as a bell cut from crystal. We could not see him because of the papyrus, but from the direction of his yelp we knew he stood at the base of a canyon wall. A fraction of a second later his call echoed from the cliff and flowed through the meadow. It did not stop there. It bounced from canyon to cliff to rocky shoal all around us, over and over, filling the entire valley. It was unusual for a hyena to vocalize that late in the morning, but he called again and again as Bornface and I listened, entranced. Before one plaintive cry died away, the next one began, so there was a continuous rolling chorus of hyena song. In the end it seemed that he was as enchanted by his own voice drifting endlessly through the hills as we were. Or perhaps, being a social animal in a solitary state, the echoes made him feel, at least for a while, as if his clan surrounded him.

Just like that, nature can turn from heat, flies, and saw grass to paradise flycatchers and hyena sonatas.

Several days later, after aging the elephants of Hidden Valley — I always wore long pants now — we hiked higher into the mountains to find others. Like clues in a mystery novel, the footprint data had already revealed that the harassed female elephants of Luangwa had been reduced to groups of fewer than four elephants on average. The groups were odd assemblages, mostly adolescents and with too many infants.

And now we were learning more about the males. A male calf is snuggled, fed, and protected by his mother and the other females of his natal family unit until he is about fourteen; then his powerful instinct to reproduce sends him away in search of unrelated females. However, the young male usually has to wait a long time before he gains the right to copulate, because he must compete with the older males. In a normal population the males of thirty to sixty years — those mountainous "tuskers" with huge ivory — are the ones who usually mate with the females. The mere presence of a tusker decreases the aggressive and sexual behavior of a rogue teenage male and sends the upstart slinking into the bushes, his testosterone levels temporarily dropping to his socks. For a time the young male will lose all the physical characteristics advertising musth, or sexual readiness.

The females *choose* the mature tuskers for mating because their very survival demonstrates their genetic superiority. Genetically, young males may have what it takes to endure, the right stuff to thrive, but they have not had time to prove it yet. Why would a female risk so much of her time and energy — two years of gestation plus four years of maternal care — by allowing one of her few eggs to be fertilized with sperm from an untested male? The genes from such a male might be substandard, and she would pass this downmarket DNA to her offspring. Like almost all other female mammals on earth, female elephants look for successful males with whom to breed. There are always external signs to go by: large tusks, long antlers, deep croaks, rich territories — or big houses, expensive cars, higher degrees.

In a normal population estrous females will avoid young bulls, actually run away from them, and instead choose the mature males. But almost no large tuskers were left in North Luangwa. We had seen only one in ten years. The Camp Group males were barely twenty years old. In most populations of wild animals the sex ratio is even, with as many females as males. However, after the poaching in North Luangwa, the population of adult elephants was made up of 81 percent females and only 19 percent males. Since there were few older males to dampen the aggressive sexual advances of adolescent males, unruly gangs of inexperienced, untested males chased the estrous females and copulated with them. With so much social chaos on the surface, there was no telling how much genetic chaos — untested, possibly inferior DNA — was being introduced.

Of course, it isn't just young male elephants who try to prove themselves.

7 MARK

GULLYWHUMPER

For I have learned
To look on Nature, not as in the hour
of thoughtless youth;
but hearing oftentimes
the still, sad music of humanity.

— WILLIAM WORDSWORTH

ONE SUNDAY WHEN I was seven, Cousin Kent jumped from my uncle's car, the pockets of his bib overalls bulging with silver Blockbuster firecrackers, their green waxy fuses peeking out. Kent, my brother Mike, and I headed straight for the Gullywhumper — a small, spring-fed marsh in the creek bottom below our house. Choked with reeds and cattails, always too wet to plow, it was thought to be good for nothing — as all wetlands were in that day. But to the three of us it was a secret netherland of frogs, snakes, salamanders, skunks, minks, and other creatures hiding in its deep black, smelly mud, which regularly belched odoriferous natural gas. My fascination with nature began here, especially on spring and fall mornings when a dense fog stole silently among the cedar, poplar, and hickory trees guarding its mossy perimeter, their thick dark limbs outstretched in the mist, only their tops showing through.

No matter the season, whenever we weren't busy with chores or school, the Gullywhumper lured us, our eyes shining with excitement. In addition to our interest in the swamp's wildlife, we were captivated by the mystery of an eight-inch-diameter gas well casing drilled deep into its bowels. Whenever we put our ears to the pipe's opening we could hear mysterious hollow popping sounds as methane gas bubbled up through the water far, far below. The old well was a relic left from the bygone era when my great-grandparents had cooked and lighted their farmhouse with methane.

Mother forbade us to play in the Gullywhumper, worried that we might contract polio from its malodorous waters or sink in its quicksand. But whenever we could sneak away, my brother and I stalked barefoot through its depths, catching snakes, frogs, and salamanders and dropping pebbles down the gurgling pipe.

The Gullywhumper was our refuge from everything disagreeable about childhood: hoeing weeds, shucking corn, and picking strawberries. The tedium of these tasks not infrequently led to pitched battles between my brother and me on one side and Barbara and Anne, my two older sisters, on the other. We often peppered each other with overripe strawberries or other organic missiles before Mike and I went AWOL from the garden to our hideout in the Gullywhumper.

In 1831 DANIEL SAEGER, my great-grandfather, built our rambling white clapboard farmhouse, with its white and gray porches of turned posts and lattice, on a knoll above Swan Creek in Fulton County, Ohio. In summer its foundation and clapboard sides stood deep in spicebush, honeysuckle, and ivy. Fluffy pillows of snow buttressed its flanks every winter. My parents moved into the old homestead in 1941, shortly before the Japanese bombed Pearl Harbor and after my grandparents had settled into the new home they had built a stone's throw away.

When the crops were in the ground, summer Sunday afternoons after church were for family get-togethers. Pontiacs, Plymouths, Fords, and Chevys carried my uncles, aunts, and cousins, each family with its own baskets of food, to my grandparents' driveway. Everyone piled out and spent the day eating, lolling on the front porch, and chewing over the weather, the state of our crops, the fall prospects for Fulton School's basketball team, President Truman's handling of the

Korean War, and other weighty subjects. We kids played kick-the-can and hide-and-seek, climbed the apple trees, and jumped off high beams into the granary's wheat bins, playing until dark. Then we caught night crawlers and salamanders in Maxwell House coffee tins or fireflies in Mason jars stuffed with grass to give the bugs some habitat. I can still smell the sweet, dank perfume of pollinating grasses, corn, and honeysuckle, hear the soft, easy laughter, the croaking of frogs, and the rhythmic creak of the porch swing's chains wearing, back and forth, back and forth, on its ceiling hooks, setting my life's rhythm as a coxswain sets the pace for his oarsmen.

✐ AT THE BOG that fateful Sunday, our pockets stuffed with Blockbusters, Mike, Kent, and I rolled up our trousers and slogged barefoot through the black marsh mud to the standpipe of natural gas. We stood around it for a moment, convinced that the daring experiment we were about to conduct would blast us to the cutting edge of science.

I dug a firecracker and an Ohio Blue Tip sulfur match from my pocket, held the match at arm's length, scratched it on the side of the pipe, lit the fuse, and pitched the firecracker into the hole. Kent, Mike, and I bumped heads as we strained to follow the trail of orange sparks as it tumbled into the pipe's black depths.

BAA — WAAANG — WAANG — WAAANG! The Gullywhumper roared to life, a blue-orange flame shooting four feet straight up from the pipe. My eyelashes, eyebrows, and the hair above my forehead instantly burned to a crisp of black ash, and my lips were roasted like frankfurters on a grill. We staggered back and sat down in the mud, our heads rolling like bobble toys.

✐ IN THE SPRING of my fifth year, Dad had hoisted me to his shoulders, saying, "Let's climb the windmill, Mark." Though I dreamed of flying, scaling the windmill balanced on my father's shoulders was not exactly what I had in mind.

"Dad — no! I don't want to go up." I wrapped my arms tightly around his head.

"Don't worry, you'll be all right, just hold on tight." He began climbing, and as we rose higher than the roof of our house, the fields beyond it came into view.

The narrow platform at the top, forty feet above the ground, was a plank no more than eighteen inches wide and bolted to the windmill's four steel legs just below their union at its peak. No railings or handholds, just a board barely wide enough for a seat. There Dad peeled me off his head, carefully sat down, put his arm around me, and eased me down beside him. Our legs dangled in the air as we looked out on a neat tapestry of cultivated fields — corn, oats, wheat, and hay — spread out for miles, a sea of grasses undulating in the summer breeze, their sweet perfume thick on the warm air. It seemed a world in miniature, quieter and more peaceful, more harmonious and less threatening. In the distance all around were the tiny barns and houses of neighboring farms, including those of my aunts and uncles; a quarter of a mile away, at the end of the sandy lane that ran through our fields, stood the maple-oak-hickory woods that was our family's small but beloved private nature preserve. The essence of everything I loved lay at my feet. *So this is what it's like to fly,* I thought.

"Take a good look, son," Dad said, almost to himself. "It won't stay this way for long." We sat up there for perhaps half an hour, and then we climbed down the way we had come up. But this time my arms were relaxed and I held on around his neck.

LATER THAT YEAR, on a hot September afternoon, tall dark thunderheads began piling up in the sky above the field where we were working. Dad, driving our model-A John Deere tractor, pulled a grain drill around and around the field near our woods, planting wheat. On a wagon hitched to the smaller model-B John Deere, which was parked along the edge of the field, I dragged heavy bags of seed and fertilizer from a stack, hauled them across the wooden deck to the back of the wagon, slit them open with my pocket knife, and stood by, ready to help whenever he stopped to top up the drill. It was heavy work for a five-year-old, but I was helping my dad.

As he wrestled a bag from the wagon to the drill, ripped it open, and began pouring it into the hopper, he paused to glance up at me on the wagon above him, his Dr. Grabow pipe clamped in his teeth, a white cloud of fertilizer dust around his head, his glasses, face, and cap chalky with chemicals and loamy dust. He winked as though he and I alone shared some secret conspiracy. And then, the bins full, he slammed the covers closed, stoked his pipe, climbed back on the tractor, and began his rounds again.

Circling the field, Dad looked up at the darkening sky. It was late in the season and he badly needed to finish the planting before the rain came. From overhearing conversations between Dad and Uncle Harold about the cost of fertilizer and seed grain, I knew that our struggling little farm could not afford to lose the contents of my wagon or the crop that would come from that field.

A gust of cold wind swept in from the northwest, flattening the clover on the ridge above us and sweeping windrows of dust from the freshly tilled soil. It slapped the wagon, ripping loose the tarpaulin that covered the seed and fertilizer. The tarp sailed away across the field and fencerows. Dad quickly turned and drove straight to the wagon. By the time he reached me, fat drops of rain had begun to pock the valuable seed and fertilizer.

"Mark!" he shouted as he jumped down. "Get on that tractor and drive it to the house — right now!"

"I — I don't know how, Dad!" Until then my brother and I had only ridden with him occasionally, turned around on the seat behind him, our legs and feet dangling through a gap at the bottom of the seat's back as he tilled the fields. A few times he had let me steer.

"Yes, you do! Now get on and drive!" He grabbed me under my arms, lifted me onto the platform behind the steering wheel of the model-B tractor, and started its motor. I put my hands on the big wheel, trying to remember how I had seen him drive. I advanced its throttle, put it into gear, and pushed the hand clutch forward. The machine lurched ahead, and by the time I reached the gate to the field, I had learned to steer — at least well enough to clear the posts. I learned how to brake before smashing through the barnyard gate, and by the time I reached the barn I was confident enough to drive my precious cargo under its shelter.

Dad was so pleased that soon afterward he began letting me drive the larger tractor alone to till entire fields. I was so small that I could not steer from the John Deere's seat, but instead stood on the small steel platform ahead of it, looking through the steering wheel's spokes as I drove. And I did not have the strength to engage or disengage its hand-clutch lever, which was almost as tall as I was. My father would drive with me to the field, put me behind the steering wheel, set the throttle, engage the clutch, and then, with his lips near my ear, shout that he would be back at noon to get me for lunch. If he didn't come, I was to simply switch off the ignition and walk to the house. He then jumped off and left me to drive around and around the fields for hours as I prepared them for planting, haying, or harvesting. I was a farmer at five.

✒ WE HAD FINISHED the early morning milking, Dad and I, and we were walking in clover through the ridge field behind our big red barn, checking the young hay crop, a warm breeze in our faces. Bumblebees buzzed from one purple flower to another, their yellow and black bodies heavy with dew and pollen. Gradually, a deep-throated voice rose above the chorus of bees and blackbirds. It grew to a moan — and then a roar from the east. We turned to shield our eyes against the sun as a bright yellow airplane trimmed in black soared low above the barn, its wheels nearly clipping the lightning rods planted along the roof's peak. The craft dived at us, its propeller glinting in the sunlight, scattering flocks of blackbirds from around the field. Its wheels clipped through the clover, and I could see the pilot grinning as he headed straight for us. Dad and I dropped to our knees. At the last minute, the pilot pulled up and banked away, waving through his open side window.

"Well, I'll be damned, son. It's your uncle Kenneth."

Dad's younger brother circled the field again and landed. Before the plane's prop stopped turning he had run to Dad and hugged him, lifting his feet off the ground. Then, as we lay in the sun-warmed clover, he told us about the South Pacific island where he had hidden during the war, gathering intelligence on the movements of Japanese ships and planes; he talked about jungle rot and liberty and what he would do next with his life. Then he took off again and was gone for a long time from my memory. I don't remember if I knew then where he had come from, where he was going, or whose plane he was flying. But his brief visit, on his way home from the South Pacific, convinced me that someday I too would fly like the blackbirds from that field.

_✐_ MOWING HAY WAS one of the most dangerous jobs on the farm. When the cutter bar, with its guides and sickle, got plugged up with wads of stems, the operator had to get off to pull them free. If the tractor rolled forward or if the driver stumbled or in any way touched the chattering sickle knife as it sliced back and forth in its guides, he could lose a hand or a foot and maybe bleed to death.

Dad was reluctant to let me mow hay, even though by the time I was seven I was regularly driving our tractors while pulling hay rakes, wagons, tilling equipment, and other pieces of machinery. But to make ends meet, he had begun chopping hay silage for neighbors, and he had even less time to tend to our own crops. So one morning we drove the tractor and mower to one of our hay fields, where he rode with me for a round or two. Then, after sternly reminding me never to get off the tractor without locking the brakes and shutting down the mower, and never to stand in front of the cutter bar, he left me alone. Mowing a swath of plants almost as wide as a country road with a single pass, I would quickly finish the field. A day or two later I'd rake the cut hay into windrows that would be ready for chopping.

But then I began noticing the pheasants, cottontails, quail, blackbirds, and meadowlarks running, leaping, and flying to escape. A cottontail mother waited a split second too long before jumping, and when I looked back I saw her lying behind the cutter bar, the stumps of her hind legs hemorrhaging blood into the green grass, her squirming, squealing babies and the remains of her nest strewn across the ground. Horrified, I stopped and quickly shut down the mower. I jumped off, ran to her, picked her up, and held her shivering body in my hands, her black eyes staring at me. I wanted to put her back together, remake her nest, and put the babies back in it. But I could not, of course, so I turned her head too far around, to help her die quickly. I laid her back in the clover and then stomped on each of her young. What else could I do? Then I stood by the big back wheel of the tractor and cried for what I had done and what I would have to keep doing. I climbed back on the tractor, pushed the clutch in, and kept mowing, cutting off heads and legs, destroying more nests — because my father needed me, because there was no other choice. But I learned something about myself that morning: I learned that I cared more than I had realized about wild living things.

At noon Dad walked across the field and stood watching me mow. When I looked at him he pretended to be spooning in food, his signal that it was time for lunch. We walked side by side the quarter mile to the house. Dad talked about Barney, the red-tailed hawk who, with the help of red foxes, controlled the numbers of field mice; about earthworms that aerated and fertilized the soil; about the Maumee Indians buried on our farm. In the washroom, just off our kitchen, we pumped water from the cistern, scrubbed our hands in an enamel basin, and took our places at the table, where Mother had spread platters of chicken-fried steak, sweet corn, mashed potatoes and gravy, green beans, salad, and apple pie — all from the farm.

Dad loved the violent storms that most often came on hot August afternoons. The wind and hail flattened our crops, tore shingles from our barn, and in other ways made life more interesting. One afternoon we were baling hay in the field behind the barn when the sky turned purple-black and the wind sprang to gale force. We quickly drove our load of hay into the barn and ran for the house. We shed our dripping clothes in the washroom and joined Mother and my sisters and brother in the kitchen. A bluish white bolt of lightning shot down the trunk of a big maple tree in our front yard, showering our porch and driveway with bark. A large limb thudded to the ground in a blizzard of leaves.

"Jim! That was really close!" Mother's voice quavered.

"Don't worry, lightning never strikes twice in the same place," Dad said. *GZZZZZZZ-BOOM!* This time the kitchen light switch exploded from the wall. Bits of plaster showered the room, leaving a cloud of white dust and gray smoke hanging around the light fixture.

"Kids! Follow me!" Mother ran into the dining room and stood next to our potbelly coal stove. We left Dad in the kitchen and joined her there, watching the trees in the front yard reel wildly in the wind and rain, their leaves shredded by golf-ball-size hail. Above the din of the storm I could hear Dad laughing from the kitchen. "What's so darned funny?" Mother shouted. "I thought lightning never struck twice in the same place."

"It doesn't," Dad said, entering the room. "That was a fluke."

GZZZZZZZZ-BOOM! The telephone in the corner of the dining room jumped off the wall and hung from smoldering wires.

Mother huddled close to the stove, holding out her arms and shouting, "Kids! Come here, take my hands!" Dad stood in the archway to the kitchen, his smile crooked. His eyebrows seemed at war over whether to move up in surprise or downward in concern, and his pipe jutted at an odd angle from his clenched jaws.

"All together now — let's sing!" Mother commanded, her voice thin and wavering. "N-nearer my God to thee, n-nearer to, to thee!"

As the storm began to slacken, Dad peered from one window

and then another, his pipe chuffing smoke. "Okay, kids." He rolled his eyes impishly. "Who's going to run to the woods with me!" With that he headed for the washroom, stripping down to his shorts as he went. Mike, Anne, and I immediately broke ranks from Mother and took off after him.

"Jim Owens," she scolded, "if you get those kids killed I will never forgive you!"

Dad ran through the back door into the storm, his laughter trailing behind him. We followed him as he skipped across the yard, our bare feet splashing in the chocolate water of the mud puddles. The hail and lightning had ceased for the most part, but sheets of raindrops stung our shoulders and eyes as we headed for the barn-yard gate. Beyond it was the lane that led to our woods. Dad vaulted over the gate and, laughing and shouting, we sprinted after him down the lane into the dark, leafy sanctum of tall trees. As we ran along the paths Dad had cut through the undergrowth, rainwater poured through the canopy over our heads, coursing down the wagon tracks and across our toes.

We stopped to catch our breath in the heart of the woods, inhaling deeply of ozone, of the spirit of this tiny remnant of a vast deciduous forest and the Maumee Indians who had still lived there when my great-grandfather built our house. The Indians were gone soon after my grandfather Saeger was born, though we occasionally still unearthed their skeletons, bowls, and other artifacts from shallow graves when digging in our gravel pit. Most of these items were donated to a museum in Columbus. Dad spoke wistfully of the Indians and the great forest that had been their home. Even at an early age I had the sense that something profound had been lost, was still being lost, that there was not much left to lose and not much time to save what little remained.

⬡ ALL TOO SOON the seasons turned, the trees lost their leaves, and bitter winds blew in from the north and west, feeling their way through the cracks of our old farmhouse, its foundation buttressed with insulating bales of wheat straw to keep our water pipes from freezing. Without crops to plant or harvest, Mother and Dad had more time for us.

On dark and snowy winter evenings, in an age before TV, Mother read to us from *The Encyclopedia of Children's Stories* or opened the lid of our old grand piano and played "Bumble Boogie" or "The Mosquito Waltz." Sometimes she sent us into the yard to scoop fresh snow into a big bowl, and mixed it with eggs, vanilla, and sugar to make snow ice cream.

When we were a little older, Dad often lay on his belly, propped on his elbows before our coal stove, and read aloud to us from the works of Keats, Shelley, Frost, Byron, Poe, and other great poets. At the death of Annabel Lee, he cried unashamedly, wiping away his tears with a red bandanna. He recited from memory "The Cremation of Sam Magee," "The Rime of the Ancient Mariner," and Frost's "The Road Not Taken." When he read *Moby Dick,* his voice rose and fell as though with the sea's swells, until we could almost taste the salt air and hear the great whale spout. We sat rapt for hours, often until well past bedtime.

I shared one of the two upstairs bedrooms with my brother; my two older sisters shared the other. Before going to bed in our icy rooms, we dashed up the steps, grabbed our comforters and pillows, then took turns warming them on the potbelly stove, pulling them off, most of the time, just before they were scorched. After they had absorbed as much heat as they would hold, we wrapped our pillows in our comforters, bounded back upstairs to our frigid bedrooms, dived into bed, pulled our bedclothes over our heads, and then curled our bodies around our pillows, holding on to their warmth for as long as it lasted. Night storms often howled out of the west, rattling the windows and driving snow through cracks in the frames, leaving drifts inches deep on the floor and frost on the bedcovers. On many nights, long after I should have been asleep, I peered from beneath those covers to see, on our far bedroom wall, Sam Magee sitting on his funeral pyre, grinning at me in the darkness as the flames leaped and danced around him.

I often awoke in the middle of the night, stole from my bed, and tiptoed downstairs. As I opened the door to our dining room, the coal stove greeted me like some large friendly monster, its fiery eyes orange and flickering through their lenses of mica. I would sit for an hour or more, wrapped in my comforter, staring into those eyes, imagining the worlds in the books Mother and Dad read to us and wondering if I would ever see any of them. And then I quietly lowered the lid of our ebony grand piano, spread my comforter on its broad top, and slept there.

SNEAKING THROUGH the popcorn patch after getting singed by the Gullywhumper, Kent, Mike, and I couldn't see anyone sitting on the front porch of our grandparents' house, but the lights were on in our kitchen. Creeping closer, we could hear the murmur of voices and see the yellow light spilling through the doors and windows into the yard. Something didn't feel right. Why was everyone in *our* kitchen rather than on my grandparents' front porch? Their voices sounded tense, angry — with us? We hunched over, ran across the driveway, and hid in the clump of spicebush near the kitchen door. Through the window I could see Grandpa Saeger seated at one end of the table, his beefy fists in front of him, his thick, bushy eyebrows set in a scowl. Dad was in his place at the other end of the table, with Mother and our uncles and aunts shoulder to shoulder around it.

I heard Grandpa growl, "It's eminent domain. The lawyer says they can take our land for the highway and there's nothing we can do."

"It'll cut this farm in two!" Dad hammered his pipe on the ashtray, scattering flakes of charred tobacco on the table.

"I'm sorry, boys." Grandpa's voice was more tired than I had ever heard it. A heavy silence settled over the table; the fireflies in the yard seemed to dim, the crickets grew quiet. And then my aunts and uncles stood and filed out of our kitchen onto the porch and began calling for the kids. It was time to go home. I was already home, but for how much longer? I wondered.

*ᶜ*ᵍ ONE SUMMER DAY in my eighth year, my brother and I watched men with hardhats and yellow trucks tie orange ribbons in parallel lines through our cornfields. Not long after, our yards swarmed with neighbors and strangers, as all of our livestock and equipment were sold at auction. We still lived on the farm, but the right of way for the interstate had been staked through its heart. It left us with too few acres to make a living. The granaries where we kids had once jumped from the rafters into the wheat bins were now silent, hollow, and dusty.

Dad refused to apply for unemployment, although it would have paid more than his temporary job as a garage mechanic in a nearby town. At home he sat at the head of our table, quietly smoking his pipe and reading his paper. He played no more word games, read no more poetry. The rhyme and meter had been taken from our lives.

The next summer no corn grew in the field beyond the Gullywhumper, but the lines of orange survey ribbons were still there. Early on a morning in August, we awoke to a deep rumble from far across the fields. I ran to the windmill in our backyard, quickly scaled its forty feet, and stood on the platform at the top. With my hand shielding my eyes against the morning sun, I watched a phalanx of yellow bulldozers plow through our fields and our beloved woods, gutting our farm.

I heard a door slam below me and saw my father — a hardhat on his head and a lunch pail tucked under his arm — walking up the road toward the army of heavy equipment that was laying claim to our land. And to our way of life.

8 DELIA

NO SCHOOL FOR GIFT

Come forth into the light of things. Let nature be your teacher.
— WILLIAM WORDSWORTH

GIFT STEPPED UP TO a small mopane tree. Six inches in diameter and twelve feet tall, it was not much more than a shrub. Lifting her trunk straight up like a stick, she placed it flat along the bark and then lurched forward, pushing all of her weight against the tree. She had watched Long Tail and Cheers stretch their thick trunks against the massive sides of marula trees that were four or five feet in diameter and fifty feet tall. As their great knees bent, they shoved the tree until marula fruits rained down all around them.

The dry mopane leaves rattled as Gift slammed the tree. The small crown shuddered as she pushed. Lowering her trunk, she stepped back and looked around on the ground, her small eyes hooded under long, gray lashes. But of course there were no fruits to be found because this was not a marula tree. Gift tried again, throwing her trunk into the branches and ramming her head into the bark. She stepped back and swept the end of her trunk along the ground, back and forth, searching for the sweet fruits. After several more tries she finally gave up and walked to a dry streambed, where she pulled up wilted grass stems and poked them in her mouth.

The valley was drying up. The short, succulent grasses of the floodplains that fed everybody from geese to elephants during the rainy season had withered and turned to dust. The dirt had cracked into a jigsaw puzzle of gray hardpan. Many of the elephants were leaving the valley, following ancient trails — some fifty feet wide and five feet deep from years of wear — that traversed the escarpment. The air was twenty degrees cooler in the mountains and held more moisture than that of the valley. The forests were thick with small edible trees, ripe seeds, and tasty shrubs. As long as they knew where to go, the elephants could find plenty to eat throughout the dry season. But there was no one to show Gift where to go.

The Camp Group males had dispersed with the last of the marula fruits. We had not seen them for several weeks, which was not unusual. They kept an odd schedule, coming and going in every season. After all, some females remained in the valley in the dry season, inhabiting the scattered woodlands and shrub-covered hillsides. So the males had to be flexible, hedging their bets to be close to as many females as possible. They wandered in the mountains, then returned to the valley, usually stopping by camp on their way.

Gift had not followed them, and now she was left completely alone to find nutritious fare among the leaves and grasses, which were shriveling more by the day. The undergrowth crackled under her feet like broken glass. Our camp was about halfway between the verdant mountains and the parched valley floor, so there was surely enough nutrition tucked away in acacia seeds, bark, and leaves to allow one small elephant to survive. And this was not her first dry season alone, so she must have learned something about living with a dwindling pantry. Still, the coming months would be raw and lean for an unschooled orphan.

I stood at the edge of camp with Kasokola and Patrick Mwamba, who had first seen Gift. We watched her move from one mopane shrub to the next as she shook them and then looked on the ground for fruits.

The elephant population in North Luangwa had now bottomed out at thirteen hundred. The poaching had almost stopped, but even though many infants were being born, the population was not increasing. This probably meant that some of the infants were not surviving. Certainly many of the orphans were not.

"I wish this elephant would go live with the mothers and babies," Kasokola said.

"That cannot be," Patrick replied. "She is from a different tribe, and they are no longer in this place."

The next morning Gift was gone. We could not find her anywhere near camp. An unlikely dry-season shawl of clouds wrapped itself around the cool shoulders of the mountains. I hoped that Gift was walking in that direction, into the food-filled forests, following an ancient trail once used by her fallen tribe.

9 DELIA
THE WOMEN OF KATIBUNGA

Perhaps the healing of the world rests on just this sort of shift
in our way of seeing, a coming to know that in our suffering
and in our joy we are connected to one another with unbreak-
able and compelling human bonds.

— RACHEL NAOMI REMEN

ONE MORNING NOT LONG AFTER Gift disappeared from camp,
I headed up the back of the escarpment toward the village of Katibunga, where Dr. Philip Watt, known as PW, was teaching midwifery
to the women. The Muchinga Mountains appear to have marched
long ago to the rim of the Rift Valley. Some, it seems, halted at the
precipice, leaning their giant shoulders over the edge, while others
tumbled head over hills down the three-thousand-foot escarpment.
Set off by tectonic forces, avalanches of entire mountains came to rest
above the sinuous valley and along its deep gorges. Folded gently in
the arms of the higher mountains, not far from the elephants' dry-
season sanctuary, is a most unlikely forest of grand spruce and fir
trees planted many years ago by a European priest. The deep green
shadows of the exotic forest intermingle with the wispy, flat-topped
woodlands of the rolling hills. These contrasting jungles embrace the
tiny village of Katibunga, decked out in its own foliage of shiny banana leaves and sprawling fig trees. Like most of the villages of the
Bemba and Bisa tribes, Katibunga is made up of mud-and-wattle
huts, one to a family, scattered widely among the trees and connected
by worn footpaths crisscrossing the red soil. Thick gray-blue smoke
from the cook fires inside the huts filters through the shaggy thatched

roofs, making them appear to be smoldering. Except for the old Catholic mission — a mosaic of low, misshapen rooms of crumbling bricks molded from the very clay on which it stands — the village looked much the same in the early 1990s as it had since its beginning, perhaps one hundred years ago.

As I drove alone from camp along the rugged bush track, I looked for elephants, especially Gift, through the soft mist that drifted like a bridal veil through the luscious forests. It was hard to believe that this moist world was only ten or so miles from the parched valley. At a crook in the trail I met Ronnie Hadley, a petite brunette on loan to our project from the Peace Corps. We drove our vehicles deeper into the woods to set up camp before going on to the village, which lay just over the hills. I laid out my pup tent on the soggy forest earth, matted with damp rotting leaves and worn-out mushrooms. Last night's dew dripped from the overhead thicket, leaving flower-shaped splat marks on my dusty tarpaulin. Ronnie erected her tent on the other side of our campfire — which so far was more smoke than flame.

In Katibunga we were to meet Dr. Watt, from Johns Hopkins University. PW, who grew up in my neighborhood in south Georgia, had volunteered to run our project's rural health care program in the villages. His wife, Alston Watt, had greatly expanded and improved the cottage industries.

The dilapidated bush hospital in the larger village of Mpika was the only clinic available to the Bemba and Bisa tribal people scattered through the forests that stretched for thousands of square miles near the park. For most villagers it was a three-day walk over rugged mountains to get to Mpika. The Bembas' traditional remedies — syrups of roots, berries, and owl parts, shaken with bones and mixed with ancient myths — were far more effective than Western physicians might imagine. We had seen these mysterious potions apparently cure diseases that were equally puzzling. Still, most of the Bembas, having been exposed to modern medicine, or at least having heard of it, longed for some of its magic, especially for their children. While never urging them to discard their own remedies, we offered them some of the new.

PW, Ronnie, and Grace NG'ambi, a Zambian registered nurse, were training two women from each village to be traditional birth attendants, or midwives. They would also learn AIDS prevention, basic first aid, and simple remedies such as rehydration to treat diarrhea. The Catholic priest of Katibunga had offered the mission as a dormitory and classroom for the course. Forty-eight women, wrapped in wildly colored chitenje cloths, had journeyed from all quarters of Bembaland on foot, by bicycle, and, from the most distant villages, by trucks that we had sent for them. Suckling babes were strapped to their mothers' backs or breasts with more brilliant cloths, and toddlers brought up the rear like a flock of waddling ducklings.

On sunny days for almost two months, PW, Ronnie, and Grace taught detailed lessons to the women seated on bamboo mats in the shade of the fig trees. Hand-drawn posters depicting sources of nutrition and clean water fluttered from low-lying branches. Other midwifery diagrams, of a more sensitive nature, were taped to walls inside the church, far from the eyes of village men. When it rained, red rivulets of mud gushed across the clay yard, chasing the lessons inside.

At night the women slept on straw pallets in the cozy, low-ceilinged chapel. There was hardly a minute during the night when an infant or child was not stirring, whimpering softly, or coughing. Mothers, half asleep, turned this way or that to offer a breast, pull up a blanket, or cuddle.

Most of these women had never been so far from their natal villages, certainly not for this long, and none of them had had any kind of schooling beyond third or fourth grade. More important, not one had been in a camp of only women, totally removed from their male-dominated worlds.

I had driven up to join the others for the last few days of the course and the graduation ceremony. When we reached the mission, the yard was a hive of activity: some women stirred huge pots of corn porridge over three fires, others swayed under the weight of water buckets balanced on their heads, a few shook out their colorful blankets, as children played with toys made of wire and sticks. They greeted us with a chorus of "Mopalayne" — "Hello."

Balanced on logs or boulders, we ate our porridge in upside-down red plastic Frisbees. Some well-meaning American had sent our project thousands of Frisbees to be handed out to the children as toys. But even though the Bembas are very good at playing soccer with their handmade balls, throwing Frisbees never caught on among them. However, the Frisbees made perfect dishes for porridge and mealie meal. All across Bembaland, around almost every campfire, folks could be seen eating out of red Frisbees. It was quite the thing.

We washed our Frisbees and teacups in large basins of steaming, soapy water and balanced them on the boulders to dry. At about this time PW arrived, having driven in from Mpika, and it was time for the lessons to begin.

PW, Grace, and Ronnie were concerned that the students had not completely mastered the details of female anatomy. Although they had reviewed charts and diagrams several times, some of the women remained confused about certain organs and their function. The teachers wanted to rehash this part of the curriculum, and knowing that the best way to teach the women was through song and dance, Grace had choreographed a special lesson. She asked us to sit on our mats in a semicircle around the yard.

Once we were settled, Grace directed six of the women to stand in the center of the circle. One tall, slender lady stood with her legs slightly parted and her upper arms held out, elbows bent, forearms and hands hanging down. Singing in ChiBemba, Grace explained that the woman's hands were the two ovaries, her head and torso were the uterus, and the space between her legs, the vagina. Next two other women, chanting and clapping, danced to the center and crouched down below the dangling ovaries. They were the eggs. "Each month,"

Grace sang, "the eggs grow," and with this the two women stood slightly, and the small audience cheered. "If there is no sperm from a man" (snickers at this unlikely scenario), "the eggs are discharged." The egg-dancers ducked between the legs of the center woman, rolled out onto the ground in a cloud of scarlet dust, and skipped away.

"The next month more eggs grow." The egg-dancers returned to their squatting position. "And if there is sperm . . ." — with a sweep of Grace's hands, three other dancers, trailing long cloths as sperm tails, rushed at the center woman and passed through her legs. The uterus smiled broadly. One sperm embraced an egg, the other two danced away. "One lucky sperm combines with the egg to make a baby." Loud cheers. "The baby grows in the uterus." The egg and sperm moved behind the torso. "And nine months later the baby is born through the vagina." Both dancers emerged, arms wrapped around each other, accompanied by squeals of joy. Shouts for an encore rang out, and the dancers took up their original positions. This time everyone sang along as another baby was conceived and born.

Grace told us that now all the women fully understood, and we could move on to the final lessons. During the last few days, PW had taught the new midwives as much as he could about abnormal births and how to deal with them. Each evening we and the other women cooked a supper of boiled chicken or fried fingerling fish on enormous bonfires that lit the undersides of the draping fig tree branches. Cross-legged around the fire, our faces warmed from the flames, we exchanged stories, mostly about the idiosyncrasies of men, which were amazingly similar in our vastly different cultures. Weary, Ronnie and I returned to our soggy pup tents in the weeping forest to sleep.

By the end of the week it was time for graduation. As many dignitaries as could be rounded up this far out in the bush had been invited to attend. All the appropriate chiefs were included, but only Chief Mukungule was able to make the trip. He arrived riding in the back of a project truck seated on his old DC10 aircraft-seat throne. He was joined by an official from the Department of Health, a doctor from the Mpika clinic, several members of the Mpika city council, and a representative from the Department of Labor. Sitting on a grandstand of planks balanced on boulders, the VIPs, relatives of the graduates, and villagers from all around waited for the ceremony to begin.

With a drumroll, the midwives jig-danced in single file out of the church, singing a song they had composed about their new jobs. Coming to a stop before the grandstand, they sang another song in English, thanking us for the lessons. Their angelic trilling voices lifted into the mountains, and I imagined them drifting forever as part of the mist. It was one of the most moving moments I ever had among these hills.

As PW called the name of each graduate, she sang and danced toward him, and he presented her with a certificate and a full medical bag.

Afterward as we nibbled on cookies and drank steaming sweetened tea, Ronnie whispered to me, "Delia, the women of Katibunga are giving a coming-of-age ceremony for several young girls about to reach puberty. They invited all the midwives, and they want us to come, too. Late this afternoon."

"What kind of ceremony? The Bembas don't practice circumcision."

"I'm not sure. They said they're going to teach the girls about sex and stuff. It's a traditional thing done only with women. The men aren't allowed anywhere near. They really want us to come."

THAT AFTERNOON, when Ronnie and I arrived at the mission, Grace ushered us quietly into one of the larger rooms, where we sat on grass mats laid on the floor along the walls. A few of the elder women from Katibunga, thin as dried grass stalks, filed into the room and stood before us, clapping and bowing in traditional Bemba greeting. As other village women arrived, all dressed in the colorful chitenges, they greeted the matriarchs and us in the same fashion.

Some of these women I had known for nearly a decade. There was old Mrs. Phiri, who had come asking for birth control pills after she had delivered seven babies and had had four miscarriages. There was Mary Chongo, who, because she had buried all five of her babies, had been deserted by her husband. Her ex–in-laws had arrived at her hut and carried away every pot, wooden spoon, blanket, or cloth that she owned. No other man would marry her. The project had loaned her money to buy a sewing machine so she could make and sell clothes.

After all the elders were seated on their mats, their thin legs sticking straight out, four young girls walked in and circled the room, bowing and clapping. They sat together, smiling shyly at each other. Then five women rushed into the room beating drums. They circled before us and, after several passes, squatted next to the door, the drums between their legs, and beat a rhythm that bid us all to sway and clap.

From outside we could hear a wavering chorus approaching, then a string of colorful performers, including some of the midwives, line-danced through the door and around the room. Hips and arms swaying, feet shuffling, voices trilling, they filled the room with soaring energy, sound, and spirit that bumped against the ceiling. When the opening dance was concluded, all the women sat down near the drummers except for Mrs. Phiri, who began a chant in ChiBemba. Grace whispered to Ronnie and me that Mrs. Phiri was explaining that a series of dances would follow, teaching the young girls all they needed to know about sex. That was the last thing Grace had to translate for the rest of the night.

Two dancers on opposite sides of the room swaggered to the center. One was a slender young woman dressed in a bright blouse with a chitenje wrapped and tied around her waist. The other dancer, a stouter, taller woman, had tied her chitenje in a tight knot wrapped around and around itself so that it protruded like an erect penis from her groin. Giggles and shrieks erupted all around the room.

The "man" and woman dancers circled each other, cooing and

pawing the air. The man chased the woman, and she playfully side-stepped him. He soon caught her tenderly; they embraced and dropped gently to the floor. The man touched and fondled the woman in all the appropriate places, and she reciprocated. Foreplay was slow and extended, careful and considerate. No how-to book could come close to competing with this explicit demonstration.

The mating dance was beautiful, like the union of two swans. Every conceivable position was performed for all to see. Apparently, one of the main objectives was to show a girl how to find pleasure while also giving it to her lover. I don't know about the young debutantes, but I learned a lot.

When these two dancers retired, finally collapsing into an exhausted heap, I thought the program was over. What more was there to learn? I was worn out. But they were only getting warmed up. A solitary dancer showed the young women how to find satisfaction when their men were away from home. Another taught the girls how to behave with their men during menstruation. There was a dance for cleanliness and one for cramping remedies. One dance revealed how to discreetly obtain birth control pills from the clinic; another, birth itself. The ovary, uterus, and vagina dance had been added to the portfolio. I thought of the stultifying sex education classes in American schools and of how even elephant matriarchs pass on some traditions to the young of their extended families more efficiently than we do.

Not all the dances were joyful. One swooning mother buried a dead infant. Another woman treated the wounds of a friend who had been beaten by her husband. During these poignant displays more dancers entered the stage and held hands, shielding the suffering women from approaching "men." The performance ended with all the dancers clinging together in a tight circle, chanting a melodic and tearful wail.

I felt as if a blanket were being wrapped tightly around us, pulling us together. From the youngest wide-eyed girl to the oldest seen-

it-all great-grandmother, we shared an ancient pact formed eons before words were, way back when eye contact and body postures com-
municated more than sound bites. Overused terms like "sorority"
and "sisterhood" would break into fragments of mere syllables under
the weight of the oneness in this room. Ronnie and I may have been
separated from these souls by oceans of cultural divides, by books
they had never read and jets they had never flown, but in this place at
this time, as our eyes met theirs, we were joined together, from the
first woman on earth to the last, through unbroken chains of mole-
cules like bright beads of color.

10 DELIA

MY TROOP

Individuals in the middle of a flock, school, or herd may
enjoy greater security than those at the edge.

—J. R. KREBS AND N. B. DAVIES

KICKING A SPRAY of sand behind them, the young male baboons
scampered onto the wide white sandbar that opened like a giant fan
on the edge of the lazy Luangwa River. Enormous ebony trees, stran-
gled by fig vines, leaned over the current, dipping their fingertips into
the busy swirls and eddies. I was watching the baboons from the little
straw camp I had built on the riverbank on the eastern boundary of
the park. I often lived there alone, far removed from the bustle of our
main camp.

Like kids let out of school, the baboons romped around, chasing
one another in circles, over driftwood and uprooted trees left by flash
floods. Two youngsters who had fallen behind slid down the steep
bank on their backsides and galloped across the sand to catch the
others. The adult females — some clutching small, dark infants below their bellies, some balancing older infants on their backs, all of
them scanning the bush for predators — emerged from the deep forest and sauntered at a more leisurely pace onto the beach. Several
adult males strutted along behind, swinging their heads and arching
their backs to exaggerate their size, like a bunch of fullbacks barely
able to contain their overstuffed egos and hazardous levels of testosterone. In all, the troop totaled more than 130 baboons scattered over
several hundred square yards and moving out from the trees onto the
shore.

Sitting under a *Trichilia* tree, a hardwood of such dark leaves and thick canopy that it offers one of the deepest shades on earth, I watched the baboons invade the beach for their afternoon drink and sunbath. To reach the sandbar the primates had to scamper, tumble, or slide down the steep bank on either side of my camp, so they passed all around me like a gray wave breaking on a shore.

My favorite group was the adolescent females. Sometimes these gangly teenagers joined the young males in their games of chase, but more often they sat in a loose circle near the adult females. Whenever possible they played with the infants, who occasionally wandered away from their watchful mothers. But their favorite pastime seemed to be just hanging out together, grooming one another with studied concentration, sunbathing on the beach, or having their own games of chase. I almost expected them to pull out colorful beach umbrellas, Sea and Ski suntan oil, and tumblers of iced tea garnished with mint sprigs.

But none of this behavior was idle. These females, like those of most social mammals, including lions, elephants, chimpanzees — and, in our past, humans — would remain in the same group all their lives. The bonds they formed at an early age were as strong as steel cables; only death would sever them. There were no signed agreements, but the contracts they sealed with their eyes would help them survive threats from leopards, lions, drought, and the aggressive males of their own species. They would not necessarily risk their own lives for one of their sorority sisters; they would always put themselves and their offspring first. And they would squabble with one another, competing for dominance, the best food, and the safest roosting branches. But living in a group brought its own set of benefits. If one mother saw a leopard and gave the alarm call, all had a better chance of escaping; if one found a special food source, each would have a chance to get a morsel. The more females there were in the group, the less likely it was that any individual mother or her offspring would be attacked by a dominant male — a real threat in many primate societies, in-

cluding our own. It was an ancient club — watch out for number one, but stick together for all it's worth. The Junior League was
camped on the beach.

At this moment two of the young females were grooming each
other. At first they sat face to face, each picking through the other's hair, searching for parasites and grass seeds. But the warm sun
seemed to have tranquilized one. Her head drooped to the side at
an odd angle, her arms relaxed like wet noodles, her legs stretched
out in front of her. Her troopmate moved her fingers gently through
her hair in what must have been a most comforting and relaxing
massage. It reminded me of another group of adolescent primates
long ago.

🖉 "HERE'S TO'D YA! If I never see'd ya, I never know'd ya," we
said in unison, as we clinked our tiny shot glasses filled with Coca-
Cola spiked with drops of vanilla extract. Barbara Clark, identical
twins Amanda and Margaret Walker, and I were sprawled on Barbara's four-poster bed like a bunch of throw pillows, with *Seventeen* magazines, dated June 1965, scattered among us. Her blue eyes
swimming with mischief, Amanda announced that the plan was
complete.

"Barbara, you tell your mama we'll spend the night at Deeya's,
and we'll tell our mama the same thing. Deeya, you tell your mama
you're staying at our house."

We met at 8:30 P.M. in the darkened backyard of an abandoned
house. We jumped on our bikes and, taking our hands off the handle-
bars, interlaced our arms and rode side by side down the center of
Junius Street under a dense canopy of sprawling oaks. We were not
allowed to ride our bikes after dark, and as the sweetness of the balmy
Georgia night blew through our long hair, a sense of freedom intoxi-
cated us.

At the train station, eating homemade pie filled with fat, wine-
colored blackberries, I told the others what Andy had told me: that

one grave at the old cemetery had a windowpane over the guy's face. The man was afraid to be buried in a dark casket, so he had a window built right in it.

Ga-ahl-lee! Let's ride out there. We gotta see this.

We rode in a long line out the Old Coffee Road to Thomasville's ancient graveyard, where large magnolias and oaks reached protectively over the tombs. Tendrils of Spanish moss dangled almost to the ground, caressing the headstones with every breeze. Some of the flat granite slabs had cracked and buckled into weird shapes from the maze of oak roots growing beneath them. I imagined the roots wrapping their gnarled fingers around the coffins, strangling the occupants into a second death. We parked our bikes against the dilapidated wrought iron fence and pushed open the gate.

Huddled together, we moved among the graves. A wild Cherokee rose bush grew over the top of a marble crypt and tumbled down the other side. A night breeze stirred the rambling rose, which waved its blossom-laden branches over the tomb as if blessing the dead. At each grave we bent down and scraped the moss from the ancient granite, looking for a window with a skeleton peeping through.

"Look at this. 1819 to 1822. Just a baby."

"This is the oldest one yet, 1789 to 1846." The headstone of another mound was worn to a nub, the date long since washed away by rain and time.

One of the largest marble monuments stood near the center of the graveyard. It had a big base, at least five feet square, with a column rising from it. We stooped closer, trying to read the faint inscription. Suddenly Barbara grabbed our arms. About forty yards away a dark, hunched form moved from behind one headstone and darted to another. Screaming, we ran deeper into the cemetery, stumbling over stones and roots. We reached a magnolia tree, hid behind it, and looked back, panting and clutching one another. Through the shadows and waving moss, we saw two stooped figures moving among the graves, slowly but deliberately, in our direction.

"Oh, my gosh! We can't get to our bikes from here," Barbara gasped.

"Let's climb over the fence — run through the woods," Margaret whispered. We crawled over the wrought iron railings and tore through the trees until we could no longer see the graveyard.

"Stop! Listen," Amanda said. "Let's see if they're coming."

Our heavy breathing and the chirping of crickets were the only sounds in the night air. Then we heard the crunching of leaves under faint footsteps and the parting of branches in the brush as the forms moved toward us.

"Wait just a minute," Barbara declared. "Deeya, when did Andy tell you about this grave with a window?"

"This morning. He told me this morning. Why?"

"Because — that's Andy back there!" Barbara said. "And probably Murph or Troll. They knew we'd come out here."

"Let's circle back around real quiet, get behind them. We can play the same game."

Not making a sound, we crept back through the woods toward the cemetery and climbed the fence. We found their bikes not far from ours and squatted behind a nearby crumbling mausoleum. About ten minutes later we heard footsteps coming our way.

Just as they reached the mausoleum, we jumped up and shouted, "Boo!"

Andy staggered backward, roaring, "Aahhgg!" Troll made a loud "Eeeehhh!" We sat flat on the ground, laughing. In a few seconds Andy and Troll recovered and started laughing, too. We agreed it was a draw.

A short while later we said good night to the guys, not daring to tell them our plan for staying out all night.

Looking at our watches under a streetlight, we were stunned to find out that it was only 10:15.

"What in the world are we going to do now?" Margaret asked.

"Y'all better think of something — this was y'all's idea," Barbara said.

"Let's ride to my house," I suggested. "We can tell Mama we decided to stay there 'cause I bought some new records." We knew it didn't matter which home we chose. Like the elephants, we had a constellation of mothers.

"If we hurry we can watch *Twilight Zone*," Amanda said.

And so we did. Our hair rolled up in huge curlers, we piled onto the foldout sofa bed, arms and legs flung over one another, heads resting on stomachs, hips touching. Girls being girls on a sofa bed on a south Georgia summer evening. Rod Serling tried to frighten us with some weird and mysterious tale, but nothing he said compared with our adventures in the cemetery.

AFTER WATCHING the baboon troop scamper along the beach that morning, I walked back to my cozy camp of grass and thatch. I pulled a small table and a camp chair into the shade, and unloaded all my tree books, plant presses, and drying grasses, leaves, and seedpods onto the table. Every day that I wasn't going on an elephant walk, I worked at identifying the plants of North Luangwa.

As the baboon troop moved deeper into the trees, gathering seeds and fruits, their loud *wa-hoo*s and softer chatterings drifted toward me, imprinting a vague picture of their general location in my mind. I wasn't aware that I was keeping mental track of them until I noticed a young female stepping cautiously along a branch of my shade tree. She was alone, and the rest of her troop was quite far off, probably at the lagoon, almost a mile away. She seemed tiny, with thin arms, thin legs, and big eyes, as she gingerly moved one foot in front of the other down a branch that hung near the ground on the other side of my large tree.

I did not dare look directly into her eyes. That would constitute a threat and send her galloping away. So I looked all around her, passing my eyes briefly over her from time to time, then back to my reference books. I studied a weird seedpod, turning it over and over in my hand. It occurred to me that she could identify all of these damn plants if I could just ask her down for tea.

But she wasn't interested in the flora. She was focused on me. She stretched her neck out, taking me in, then bounded toward the safety of the tree trunk. A few seconds later she advanced again along the branch as it bobbed under her weight. Finally she sat on the limb, tail hanging down, and simply stared. I followed her cue and stole more frequent and direct glances, until we were more or less looking into each other's eyes.

The next morning she came again, venturing out alone, leaving her troop in the distance. Was that a daypack on her back? Binoculars around her neck? I half expected her to pull out a journal and start taking notes on my behavior.

"Okay," I said to her aloud. "It's a great life, but it's lonely. There can be many misfortunes when you leave your troop. Just so you know."

11 MARK

MOUNTAIN ELEPHANTS

If we listen attentively, we shall hear, amid the uproar . . .
a faint flutter of wings, the gentle stirring of life and hope.

— ALBERT CAMUS

TWICE EACH YEAR, once in the dry season and again during the rains, we flew through the hot, turbulent air over North Luangwa, counting elephants. Each time the numbers told the same sad story. Even though by 1994 poaching had declined dramatically, the population did not seem to be recovering.

Studies in East Africa have shown that elephant populations can bounce back quite quickly after drought, disease, and other natural disasters, increasing their numbers by up to 10 percent each year. Throughout their history as a species, elephants have adapted to the vagaries of their environment, which kill off the very young and old but leave most of the healthy individuals in their prime to survive and reproduce.

Unfortunately, poachers first target the most reproductively active elephants because they carry the largest tusks. Poaching had dealt a severe blow to the resilience of this population, and because female elephants deliver one or two calves only about every fourth or fifth year, any recovery was likely to take a long time. It would probably have to wait until some of the young males and females had grown older, gained experience, and reconstructed their fragmented and beleaguered society. Unless the North Luangwa elephants had a trick up their trunks.

To find out whether they did and to document the population

rebound that we hoped to see soon, we needed to have frequent close contact with a number of families as they roamed between the plateau above the valley to the floodplains along the Luangwa. Though we hated disturbing the elephants, equipping some of them with radio transmitters was the only way to keep track of them, and monitoring their movements twice each week would help us protect them from poachers and yield data on the greatly reduced but still ominous poaching problem.

✐ "ELEPHANTS AT THREE O'CLOCK! About fifteen of them, headed down that ravine." I rolled the helicopter into a steep right turn, its main rotor slapping the air.

Mike Kock, a Zimbabwean animal-capture specialist, perched in the open doorway behind me, his darting rifle across his knee, the wind ripping through his red-blond hair. Delia sat on my left, a clipboard and data sheet, binoculars, and hand-held radio ready on her lap.

For several days we had been putting radio collars on elephants, but Mike was going home soon and we had not yet collared any in the mountains. In less than a minute we had descended to two hundred feet above the herd — high enough not to disturb them unduly — while we looked for a female without a calf. I chose the third cow from the back and kept my eye on her while climbing to five hundred feet, where I slowly circled at a distance, letting the elephants relax. Meanwhile Mike filled a syringe with etorphine, a morphine derivative one thousand times more potent than heroin. A single drop on your arm can put you to sleep forever, so he wore rubber gloves while preparing his syringe.

When Mike was ready, we returned to the herd and followed it down into the narrow, winding Lubonga River ravine, a jumble of sharp tree-covered ridges, sheer cliffs, and rounded peaks left by the water as it cut its way through the escarpment. The elephants immediately disappeared under thick riparian forest. We could not even see them, much less dart one. I banked right and left, following their well-worn trails and the clouds of dust rising from their huge feet through the canopy of trees. Now and then a gray, wrinkled rump and tail were briefly visible before they disappeared again in the dust and foliage. Swarms of tsetse flies and other insects launched from the foliage into the air as we swept over them. The canyon's sheer walls squeezed in on us until the rotor blades were slicing too close to the trees on either side.

"There they are — about three hundred yards ahead!" Delia shouted as I eased through a crack in the escarpment.

"Take your time," Mike said. "Let's just follow them at a distance until the ravine opens up a bit." To avoid stressing the elephants, I stayed back as far as I could and climbed to five hundred feet. Delia pointed through the windshield at a clearing about a mile ahead — a short, narrow floodplain along either side of the stream where the hills parted a bit.

The herd hardly seemed to notice us as we waffled in the sky, following slowly a quarter of a mile behind them as they headed through the trees toward the clearing. We would try to intercept them just before they emerged from the forest and then follow them onto the floodplain for Mike's shot.

At the right moment, and with the target cow near the back of the herd, I put the chopper into a steep dive, descending quickly so that we could deliver the dart and be gone in seconds. I leveled off at about ten feet above her back and slightly to her left, matched the speed of her trot, and tracked her into the opening. We were so low that Mike could have lowered himself onto her back from the skid. I could count every wrinkle as she curled her trunk and rolled her eye toward us.

"Tree! Dead ahead!" Delia shouted.

I snatched the collective lever, increasing power and pitch on the main rotor, and we lifted over a giant *Brachystegia longifolia* tree, its leaves shimmering in the chopper's downwash, my right skid skimming inches above its crown. With the clearing just ahead, I settled over the cow elephant again. In my periphery I could see Mike taking aim with his rifle.

"Clear ahead . . . clear ahead. Don't get any lower," Delia kept reporting.

I heard Mike's shot and saw the dart dangling from the elephant's hip as she broke away from the chopper. We immediately backed off to let her relax.

I relaxed a little too, sagging back in my seat as the chopper climbed.

We circled slowly in the sky for about ten minutes until she slowed, stumbled once, and then lay down. When she did, her yearling calf appeared at her side.

"Aw, man! Where'd he come from?" Mike groaned. The calf had been lagging behind its mother while we followed her; we thought it had belonged to another female.

I flew back to the bottom of the ravine, near the anesthetized cow elephant. Because of rocks and scrub brush, I could not land there, so I hovered about four feet above the ground while Mike jumped out and headed for his patient. Then Delia and I flew to the clearing some three hundred yards away and landed.

As soon as I shut down the chopper's turbine, Mike's voice came through on the radio in Delia's lap. "Get here as soon as you can. We need to process her within twenty minutes."

I grabbed Mike's darting kit with the antidote to the etorphine and followed Delia, running upslope through brush and trees until we found Mike and the elephant.

The cow sat on her haunches as if she had dozed off while reading a novel. Her calf, weighing perhaps 350 pounds, stood behind her, peeking his head out like a shy child behind his mother's skirt. Although she was immobile, we were sensitive to the fact that she could see, hear, and smell us. We approached slowly and whispered when we talked. We worked quickly, but I could not resist taking a few seconds to marvel at her soft, resinous eyes and to run my hands over her wrinkled gray skin with its own landscape of mountains and valleys. It was as tough as the bark of a tree hundreds of years old, yet I could not help thinking how fragile and vulnerable she was in a world growing too small for her kind. She sighed deeply, and big tears ran down her face.

The etorphine had inhibited her blink response, so I took off my shirt and covered her eyes to keep the sun's ultraviolet rays from damaging her retinas. Delia and I quickly began measuring the elephant's height at the shoulder and her length and taking other essential data while Mike drew a blood sample. Then we began fastening her radio collar around her neck. I was tightening one of the bolts when I heard a crash and looked up to see the calf storming over a small bush as he charged us. We jumped to his mother's other side. He stopped at her belly, trumpeted, shook his head, and kicked up some dust to make his point. Then, as though having second thoughts, he turned, screwed up his tail, and ran a few steps away, turned back, and stood watching us, flapping his ears and wriggling his trunk.

"I really wish they wouldn't do that," Mike said, shaking his head.

Moments later the calf walked up to us and held out his tiny trunk in our direction. That his mother was so relaxed seemed to convince him that we were not a threat. While we worked on fastening the collar, he followed us around, now and then reaching his trunk in our direction to sniff our scent.

We finished measuring and collaring the cow in eighteen minutes. Then, while Mike gave her the antidote, Delia and I each grabbed up an armload of gear and bolted for the helicopter.

We were strapped in our seats and I was just starting the Bell's turbine when Mike shouted over the radio: "Aaaagggghhh! Mark! Get this bloody elephant off me! Hurry!"

I immediately went to full throttle and yanked the chopper off the ground. We rose straight up, turned, and flew upslope to Mike and the elephants. The cow was struggling to stand up. Mike was crouched behind a skinny tree on the slope above her with his radio in his left hand, face to face with a much larger and very angry four- to five-year-old elephant, probably the cow's previous offspring, which had appeared out of nowhere. Mike was bouncing pebbles off its forehead to hold it at bay.

I hovered down until my right skid was nestled in the crown of the tree above Mike and turned on the chopper's antipoaching siren. Still the young elephant refused to back off. I turned the chopper left and right while hovering up and down. After several minutes of these maneuvers the brave not-so-little warrior backed off a few yards. The cacophony of noise also roused Mom to her feet. As she got up, Mike bolted down the slope, running for the clearing, with the four-year-old on his heels. I flew in behind him and again flicked the siren's toggle switch. Apparently convinced that he had saved his mother, the adolescent went back to stand at her side. She shook herself, leaving a great cloud of dust hanging in the trees, then hurried off to find the rest of her herd, her calf at her side.

We flew to the clearing, landed, and picked up Mike. Slipping his headset over his ears, he grinned. "I hope she teaches that kid some manners before he grows up."

After lunch and a rest back at camp, we returned at sunset to check the cow's radio signal. The *beep-beep* of her transmitter led us straight to her and her calves, back with their herd and support group, raising a cloud of red dust in the sunset as they trundled along a narrow trail toward the foot of the scarp and a drink of water at the upper Lubonga River. Unlike so many other Luangwa elephants that had been shot, she had risen again. From her we would learn much about how she and her society had been impacted by the stress from severe poaching, and what these secrets of the savanna might mean for us.

Mark and Delia on a ridge high above Zambia's northern Luangwa Valley, one of the most remote wildernesses in Africa.

Mark greets Cheers, one of the first bull elephants to accept us. One third of the elephants of North Luangwa National Park are tuskless because so many of those with tusks have been killed for their ivory.

When we arrived in 1986, the park's seven game scouts were demoralized and lacked the equipment they needed to do their jobs.

Retrained and fully equipped, the scouts began capturing more poachers than any other unit in Zambia did. Today North Luangwa is one of the most secure parks in Africa, and its wildlife is recovering.

Gift, a female orphan, wandered into our camp when she was only five years old. Over the years she led us to remarkable discoveries about elephants' resilience in response to stress and caused us to reflect on our own fractured society.

We radio-collared one female elephant in each of sixteen family units in order to monitor their reproductive responses to poaching. Sometimes an elephant's family members charged us as we fitted the collar.

We used toy elephants, drama competitions, and art to teach the value of conservation in village schools.

Delia performs a puppet show for village children.

Gift brings her firstborn, Georgia, to camp. Gift became a mother when she was about eight and a half years old — half the average age of first-time mothers in normal elephant populations.

Crossing the wild waters of the Mwaleshi River was only one of the many obstacles we had to overcome to reach camp.

A vervet monkey hitches a ride —and studies Delia.

Below: Searching for elephants on foot often led to close encounters with other wildlife.

Hammer Simwinga, who works for the project, introduced more nutritious crops to villagers.

Below: Cookson's wildebeest, found only in the Luangwa Valley, were often playful and curious. When we first arrived there were no roads in the park, so we did a lot of walking.

Small enterprises started with loans from the project, like this sewing business, offer goods and services that have largely replaced the poaching economy.

A sunset over the Mwaleshi River brings new hope for the wildlife and people of the Luangwa Valley.

12 MARK

THE COMMERCE
OF UNDERSTANDING

"Time" has ceased, "Space" has vanished. We now live in a
global village.

— MARSHALL McLUHAN

"THEY SAY YOU NEVER got a permit to run the project." Trish
Boulton's thin high voice, salted with a British accent, fought through
the hiss and crackle of the HF (high-frequency) radio. Trish, a soft-
spoken teacher raised in Zambia, supervised our project's educational program and ran the office in Mpika. She handled everything
from producing children's coloring books to ordering trucks from
Germany and airplane parts from America and buying mealie meal
with the fewest weevils. We'd hired her husband, Malcolm, a Brit with
an impish face and a personality to match, from a photo-safari camp,
where he had been a guide and naturalist. Now he was the project's
field manager, who kept our trucks running, spare parts and supplies
flowing, and solved just about every logistical problem that can possibly happen in the bush. I keyed the mike, watching Long Tail sweep
the ground for marula fruits just beyond the window of our radio
room at Marula-Puku.

"Says who?"

"The warden brought me the message this morning; it's from senior officials at Parks headquarters in Chilonga."

"Nonsense. Jan Zehner at the U.S. embassy arranged our permits, along with those for the National Geographic film crew, when

we entered the country. It took a year to get everything. We have them on file — and Parks must have them too." Beyond the window in front of me a great elephant turd hit the ground with a resounding thud.

This query wasn't really about permits; it was a setup by someone much more powerful than a senior Parks official.

"Okay, so what do I tell them?"

"Tell them we'll send them copies of our permits shortly."

We did that and heard nothing more. Our enemies would have to think of some other ploy to get rid of us.

🖉 THE MEDIUM-SIZE MOPANE tree appeared to have fallen across the track, blocking Tom Kotela, Isaac Daka, and the other Mano scouts from driving on to Mpika, where they were to meet with the warden, get their salary checks, and buy supplies. Three of the scouts jumped down from the truck with their axes and began cutting up the tree so that they could pass. Not easy to do, because mopane wood is almost as hard as steel and just as heavy. The local Bemba tribesmen use small homemade hatchets with thin, razor-sharp blades to quickly nip small crumbs of wood with each stroke, felling a tree far faster than a chain saw could. I know, because I once spent half a day burning up a chain saw while trying unsuccessfully to cut down a big mopane that refused to give way for our airstrip. Now, as the scouts went to work, the man nearest the butt of this tree noticed some marks made with a Bemba ax.

"Bwana Unit Leader!" he called to Kotela. "This tree is meant to keep us from touching Mpika. It has been cut." After nearly an hour they had cleared the track and driven on. Soon another mopane blocked their way and another, until finally they turned back to Mano, intending to take the longer route through Mukungule to Mpika. But that track too had been made impassable with downed trees. "Poachers," Kotela muttered.

This had happened during the early phase of our village outreach programs, when for the first time scouts had begun arresting and prosecuting big-name poachers, and it signaled the start of the inevitable backlash against the game scouts by the more determined commercial poachers and their supporters in Lusaka. The scouts had to deal with this before it became more hostile and spread to other villages. But how?

For several years before that we had struggled to keep the scouts supplied with patrol rations, food for their families, uniforms, and other commodities — all hauled at great effort and expense from Mpika, miles away. The thought came to me one short sleepless night that we could persuade the subsistence farmers at Mukungule to grow extra maize and vegetables, raise bees for honey, make vegetable oil, and provide other foodstuffs to sell to the scouts. The villagers needed cash, and the scouts could spend their salaries in Mukungule instead of Mpika. Surely this would help ease tensions between the two communities.

But convincing the villagers, many of whom were ex-poachers themselves or had worked as carriers for them, to spend their hard labor raising more crops to sell to the game scouts would not be easy. And even if they agreed, would they follow through? If anyone could get them on board, it would be congenial, silver-tongued Sugar. The person to begin with was Chief Mukungule, the oldest living tribal leader in Zambia. As was the Bemba custom, we asked for a meeting through one of the chief's retainers. Days later a message came back with the date and time.

Tom Kotela, Sugar, and I drove along the dusty track to the chief's palace on the outskirts of Mukungule village, where his head retainer, a handsome, soft-spoken man with gray hair, met us. After greeting us in perfect English, he led us into a great stand of banana trees with several mud-and-thatch huts huddled underneath. The huts belonging to the chief and his wives stood behind the n'saka, which was built on a raised red clay dais and consisted of an oval frame of poles with half-walls and a roof of thatch. Inside the n'saka the retainer invited us to sit on squat stools that seemed to put my knees somewhere just below my ears. He left us for a few minutes, then returned with another man carrying the chief's throne — the now famous row of three seats from an airliner. They placed these facing us against the opposite grass wall of the n'saka. The head retainer led the chief, a small, stooped figure with rheumy blue eyes and gray hair, wearing a blue safari suit, from his hut to the n'saka, where he sat on his DC10 throne, leaning his walking stick beside him.

"Mopalayne, Mfumu," we said, bowing deeply and clapping our hands in respect. One of the chief's younger wives knelt before us and silently held out a woven basket with freshly cooked sweet potatoes and warm roasted groundnuts, their odor filling the n'saka with a delicious musty pungency, like the warm, moist air from the deep catacombs of a termite mound. On our behalf, Sugar presented the chief with bolts of white cloth to be tied in trees at their ancestral spirit place near Marula-Puku, a bag of mealie meal, another of sugar, and a tarry plug of tobacco.

Through his interpreter-retainer, we chatted with the chief for several minutes about how stingy the rains had been and about whether his people would have enough maize to sustain them through the dry season. As I watched this wise and kindly old man, born in 1910, a tribal chief since 1928, I wished I could somehow download from his mind to mine all that he knew about his people and the subtleties of their culture.

Finally Kotela raised the touchy subject of our visit. "Mfumu, are you aware that villagers have been dropping trees across the tracks leading out of the park?"

The chief's ancient, cataract-scarred eyes shifted slightly and then settled on a place far beyond the n'saka. "I have been told," he replied simply.

"Mfumu," Kotela said gently, "it is not our purpose to punish your people for using wildlife. But unless hunting is regulated, the animals will all disappear. No one will enjoy bush meat ever again or benefit from wildlife tourism development."

In an even voice as soft as a warm breeze in the early rains, Chief Mukungule pointed out that his people were poor and that bush meat had been a tradition for weddings and funerals — and in their everyday lives — since the beginning. Some could not understand, he said, why the scouts were interfering.

Kotela gently countered that surely the chief had noticed that animals were now very far from his boma, that it took many days to find and kill a buffalo for its nyama.

The chief agreed that poaching must be controlled, but he did not know how to explain this to his villagers so that they would be satisfied.

And now it was Sugar's turn. He said that he could show the villagers how to improve their yield of maize and other crops so that they could sell surpluses to the Mano scouts and their families. With the cash they earned, they could buy mealie meal from a privately owned mill that the project would help a village entrepreneur install and buy salt, sugar, soap, and other staples from a "wildlife shop" to be built and run by villagers. With their earnings, they could purchase low-cost hunting licenses so that they could continue enjoying bush meat, so long as they did not supply the black market. This commercial interdependence with Mano, in the interests of wildlife conservation, would help foster improved relations.

As Sugar described our plans, the old chief's eyes found focus back inside the n'saka, and he sat up on his DC10 throne. "This can be a very good thing." A new light flickered in his eyes. He agreed to meet with his people to enlist their support for this idea.

"Mfumu," I addressed the chief as we stood to leave, "have you ever flown above your chiefdom, I mean in a *ndeke,* an aircraft, to see it as a bird sees it?" He seemed confused as he listened to his retainer translate, as though such a thing were inconceivable.

"When these things of which we have spoken are happening in your village, I will come with the helicopter, and we will fly to see them." He smiled, leaned on his walking stick, and offered me his hand.

A WET, A DRY, and then another wet season later, Chief Mukungule's ancient eyes shifted nervously as the helicopter rose straight up. Beneath us his boma, with its quaint thatched huts, n'saka, and banana trees, and his younger wives, their smiling faces turned skyward as they waved merrily, telescoped to a miniature below us. Behind the chief his oldest wife sat in her emerald-and-yellow-print chitenje, her forehead pressed to the window, a weak smile on her face. Even though I had explained to him that the helicopter could carry four passengers, he had chosen her alone over his younger wives to accompany him on this, their first flight ever in an aircraft.

In less than a minute we were over the heart of Mukungule village, whose huts seemed to sprout like shaggy mushrooms from the red earth, with villagers waving and scurrying antlike below. Behind the dun adobe communal meeting house, or "town hall," a large field of tall green maize stalks strained skyward in the sun. Several farmers paused from weeding between the rows, leaning on their hoes and hailing their chief as he flew by. At the end of the rainy season weeks earlier, Sugar and his farmers had carefully stepped off the width and length of those fields, calculating the number of plants in rows that would yield enough maize to supply the village plus the sixty game scouts and their families in Mano for an entire year. They were already building stick cribs to store the corn after the harvest, until it was dry enough to be shelled by hand and bagged.

Ahead a cloud of white dust rose like steam through the ragged thatched roof of the millhouse, which stood just off the village commons near the brick school. Jason Mosolo and his assistant were hard at work milling tins of maize kernels to be sold to the Mano scouts and to fellow villagers. From the air it all looked so easy, so serene. But not long after the mill had been installed, Jason had been forced to raise the price for milling a tin of maize to compensate for the rising cost of diesel. "Profiteering!" the villagers had cried as they surrounded the millhouse one morning, threatening to lynch him and his assistant. I had quickly flown Sugar to Mukungule to help explain that the rise in price was justified, that this was free enterprise at work, that the operation had to make enough money to cover its costs and allow for a modest salary for the miller and his assistant. Still the troublemakers persisted until Jason removed the mill's drive belts, shutting it down. Almost immediately a chorus of complaints rose from the village women, demanding that the mill be reopened. They were not about to go back to "stamping" — crushing corn kernels in stumps with heavy wooden poles — no matter what their husbands said. The conflict was over.

From the millhouse we flew to a broad field of yellow sunflowers, merrily nodding their heads in the breeze. Banda Mulenga and several other farmers were growing them for sale to another man who, with a loan from the project, had bought a simple hand-operated ram press, a contraption with a long lever and piston that pressed the seeds to make cooking oil; it looked like some medieval torture machine. The oil is highly prized by the villagers and game scouts alike, and Banda sold the leftover seed cake to fish farmers to feed their fish — which villagers bought and fried in black pots with sunflower oil purchased from Banda.

Using nothing but hoes, shovels, wheelbarrows, and their calloused hands and spirits, barefoot teams of men and women had hacked at the rude red earth for weeks to dig large rectangular fish ponds near the river. Sugar had brought fingerlings in plastic bags all the way from Kasama, many hours away by track and then road. At first the farmers had eaten them before they could reproduce. But now, as the helicopter hovered slowly forward, sunflowers bending below us, Sugar stood on the rim of one of the ponds, waving his clipboard at us. Below him a line of women, each with a conical basket made of sticks, waded into the shallow end and began scooping up hundreds of pounds of flapping fish. Nearby another group of women cleaned the fish and placed thick slabs of it on pole racks over smoldering fires to dry, the savory smoke filtering into the helicopter's cabin.

"*Bwino.*" Good. The old chief smiled. Sugar had timed and coordinated a lot of these activities especially for this flight, and Chief Mukungule was obviously pleased by what he saw. His senior wife sat behind him with both hands on the window ledge, gazing at her village from a bird's perspective, her weathered old face beaming.

The fish ponds proved to be such a delicious and abundant source of protein, and so profitable, that the villagers, without further encouragement, dug thirty more of them in a few short weeks. People from other villages came to see and began digging fish ponds near their homes.

Next we flew to Mary Chongo's boma. Mary, the woman who had lost all her children to diseases and had been abandoned by her husband, refused to be defined by her grief. Always on fire with life, she seemed not to have a care in the world. Below us we could see her sitting under a shade tree, running a treadle sewing machine. A group of women were cutting bolts of green fabric to make uniforms for more than sixty game scouts at Mano. Irrepressible Mary and her clutch of seamstresses stood to wave at their chief and then fell to their knees in a line, clapping and ululating in his honor.

From there we followed the Mwaleshi River, first over quiet pools and lazy water among green folds of miombo woodland, then over rills and ripples, shoals and rapids as the water hurriedly cut its way along and through folds in the escarpment, finally plunging over a series of falls and through canyons that led to the foothills near the valley floor. And then, just where the Mwaleshi began meandering through this gentle landscape, we saw a herd of elephants bathing in its blue-black waters, some squirting themselves with their trunks while others pulled up great plugs of grass along the banks. These were, I would learn later, the first elephants the chief had seen in a very long time.

As we made a wide circle around the herd, he turned his head only slightly and said to me, still watching the elephants through the side window, "*Natotela.*" Thank you.

⌒ IT WAS PRESIDENT'S DAY, and Unit Leader Tom Kotela had brought his baby girl, all decked out in a frilly new dress and coat with matching cap and booties, to the marketplace celebration in Mukungule. The delicious odor of roasting groundnuts, smoked fish, and other essences distilled from Africa's baked red earth rose into the air and mingled with throbbing music and excited chatter as Tom moved easily about, greeting and being greeted.

"Mopalayne, Bwana Kotela," Sugar greeted him. They shook hands warmly. "Ah, but your baby is looking very pretty. Where did you get such fine clothes for her? Can it be in Lusaka?"

"Ah — no. My wife even bought these very great clothes from the seamstresses in Mukungule."

13 MARK

THE KAKULE CLUB

Oft in the stilly night
Ere slumber's chain has bound me,
Fond Memory brings the light
Of other days around me;
The smiles, the tears,
Of boyhood's years,
The words of love then spoken;
The eyes that shone,
Now dimm'd and gone,
The cheerful hearts now broken!

—THOMAS MOORE

FROM OUR CAMP we could see from one sweeping bend of the Lubonga River to the next, more than half a mile of lazy water upstream and down, with gravel bars, rocky shoals, reeds, and papyrus banks, as well as scattered herds of pukus, waterbucks, elephants, and buffaloes, all bordered by a tall gallery of mixed riparian forest, primarily mopane, acacia, and *Trichilia* trees.

Every morning with the rising sun, some of the *kakules*—ChiBemba for old male buffaloes — wandered into our camp from the long grasses along the riverbank. Those left behind wallowed half submerged in mud holes, looking like black granite boulders in a backwater; still others lay farther up the bank, waterlogged driftwood cast up by the floods. All day they methodically chewed their cuds — all in no motion or slow motion. Oxpeckers danced around their bulky bodies like riveters repairing a submarine's hull, checking here, pecking there, probing at a grub, a hole from another buffalo's horn, or other tender spots.

People who have stood eyeball to eyeball with Cape buffalo bulls will tell you that they are the very definition of ornery, and unpredictable as well. Add to those qualities a sixteen-hundred-pound tank of a body, a great black boss on the forehead with ebony horns that sweep out and then up at the tips like a medieval weapon, eyes that seem permanently pink with aggression but do not see well, big ragged ears, grand piano legs, and hooves like split tree stumps. If you meet such a creature at night on a footpath, you definitely want to have a tree handy. But whatever else a bull buffalo may be, he is awe-inspiring, and after working for so many years to stop their slaughter by poachers, I guess we were glad that they finally felt comfortable around us.

Over the years we spent many hours habituating brown hyenas, lions, elephants, and other animals to our presence so that we could observe them closely without stressing them unnecessarily. When a wild creature comes close because *it* chooses to, we can see more clearly into its world; a world unclouded by fear is more transparent, more easily understood.

We labeled this small group of old male buffaloes the Kakule Club. Because their testosterone levels had ebbed, they could no longer compete for females, and they were too tired and slow to keep up with their wandering herds. They seemed to have retired near our camp, safer there from poachers and lions. They were like a group of grumpy old men hanging out together, comparing aches and pains.

For years poachers had relentlessly targeted the buffaloes, so while we were setting up our Marula-Puku Camp, these battle-scarred hulks watched warily from a distance, snorting, stamping, and shaking their heads. Whenever they chanced upon us cutting thatching grass for our cottages or gathering stones along their Lubonga River, they would storm off through the thickets, huffing like steam engines.

But as the years went by, poaching decreased in North Luangwa National Park and a circle of sanctuary began expanding around Marula-Puku. The puku antelope led the way. They began showing up across the narrow riverbed from our n'saka in the early mornings, grazing the dewy grasses as they ambled along, their fawns scampering around them. And then one morning a pair of wart hogs showed up, rooting, snorting, and farting, their piglets running around camp, tails sticking straight up like lightning rods. Finally Survivor, Long Tail, Gift, and the other Camp Group elephants began stopping by. Our camp looked like Noah's staging area for the loading of the ark.

But still the buffs glowered, stamping their feet and staring at us suspiciously, from the deep, dark *Combretum fragrans* thickets on the far riverbank. After watching the pukus, wart hogs, and elephants for a few minutes, they would turn back into the shadows and gallop away. On our side of the river we sat partially secluded in the n'saka, watching them through binoculars, wondering when they would feel safe. It was a long, frustrating business, especially after our years in the Kalahari, when yellow-billed hornbills perched on our heads at teatime and lions slept outside our tents.

One morning in late June of 1990, four years after arriving in Luangwa, I was walking along the footpath from our bedroom cottage to the kitchen for breakfast when, near the big marula tree in the middle of camp, my left foot suddenly slid away in front of me and I nearly did a split.

"Delia! Come look at this!" I yelled over my shoulder after recovering my balance.

In the path at my feet, with my skid mark across its face, was a very fresh, almost steaming, buffalo flat. Cloven hoof prints were deeply embedded in the ground on either side of the trail. At last the buffs had begun accepting us.

Every night after bathing, Delia took the hot-water kettles back to the fireplace in the kitchen, more than a hundred yards away. She hated to ask Kasokola, our Bemba cook, to come get them from our stoop first thing in the morning.

One chilly July night, after bathing in our tub in the bedroom, she picked up a flashlight and the two fire-blackened kettles and headed for the door.

"I saw buffs near camp at dusk. Why don't you leave that for morning?"

"It'll take just a minute, and I'll be careful," she said, touching my arm as she stepped around me and slipped out.

Recently a tour operator in Zimbabwe had surprised a buffalo at close range in her camp one dark, rainy night. The buff had spun around and, with a single sweep of his horns, hooked her spine out of her back. She was dead before she hit the ground.

I closed the door and began to undress for my bath. I was sitting in a wicker chair unlacing my boots when the air reverberated with the deepest growl I have ever heard. This was followed by a metallic crash of kettles hitting the ground — and then the *thump-thump-thump* of running feet on the path.

"*Maaaarrrrrk!*" I jumped up, ran to the door, and jerked it open. Delia had not run track since high school twenty years earlier, but now her flashlight was a relay baton in her hand, with round yellow marula fruits rolling like billiard balls under her feet. She was rocking and rolling as though running through a violent earthquake, eyes lemurlike in the beam of my flashlight, hair streaming back and mouth open.

Behind her was the buff that moments before had been grazing peacefully along the path. Delia had almost literally walked into his backside without seeing him, and he had spun around and voiced his surprise. Now he stood, head lowered, eyes fixed on the quickly re-treating *Homo sapiens*. Although he had chosen not to charge her, Delia had understandably not hesitated long enough to learn of his decision.

I stepped to the side as she flew through the doorway into the bedroom. "Oh my gosh! That was close." She sat on the edge of the bed for some minutes catching her breath. I held the flashlight to the bedroom window and watched Brutus continue grazing, lifting his massive head from time to time to check the door of the cottage. I gather he did not want that wild thing headed *toward* him.

The next morning I opened the bedroom door to see Kasokola

on the path through camp, fitting the lids back on the kettles before returning them to the kitchen. He chuckled all through breakfast.

The buffs' next visit came some weeks later, again in the middle of the night. The sound of something scraping the stone wall of our bedroom awakened us. A sweaty odor mixed with the sweet smell of marula fruits lay heavy on the still night air. And from just outside the window next to our bed came the sound of heavy breathing — *very* heavy breathing — mingled with the popping and squelching of fruits being trampled to a pulp. The buffalo moved along the wall until his bulk filled the window next to me. Slowly, so as not to frighten him, I leaned out of bed and looked at the side of his head and shoulders — so close I could hear him swallow. By moonlight I could clearly see the notches in his left ear, which was practically touching the window screen as he slowly cruised by, then disappeared around the corner of the cottage. We eased out of bed and tiptoed to the window as he wandered out of camp along our footpath.

The next morning he was back, with a friend who had just a stub for a tail. But they did not come into camp. Instead they stood under the winterthorn tree, staring as we moved back and forth along our trails: from the bedroom to the office, to the kitchen, n'saka, and workshop. The one with the stubby tail kept lowering his head and hooking the air with his horns. We began to call them Brutus and Bad-Ass.

Being scrutinized by Brutus and Bad-Ass became a daily ritual. And after a while they were joined by another buffalo with even less of a tail than Bad-Ass; he became Stubby. And then Nubbin joined the club, he of great boss but horns that looked to be made of wax and melting in the midday sun, running off the sides of his head.

So the Kakule Club grew, and as they gradually screwed up their courage, they began making more and more forays into camp, at first only at night, when all was quiet, but then staying through dawn and showing up for breakfast.

✍ SINCE FEMALE MAMMALS are usually bound tightly together in their natal groups, they are almost always among relatives. Living with relatives confers great evolutionary advantages, because whenever one group member feeds another's young, helps defend the territory, or in any way spends energy helping a relative survive and reproduce, the helper also benefits indirectly; the beneficiary carries some of the benefactor's genes. Thus, helpers and their beneficiaries have, over evolutionary time and partly because of these benefits, survived in greater numbers than those not giving or receiving these seemingly altruistic favors. This genetic payoff suggests a primal ulterior motive for such apparently altruistic behaviors as feeding, grooming, defending, and teaching relatives and their offspring. And even when *nonrelatives* receive such helping behaviors, research in the animal world has shown that the providers almost always get an immediate or eventual reciprocal payoff, as when, during drought, Kalahari lions from different, unrelated social groups get more to eat by cooperating to kill larger prey than they could bring down alone, or when unrelated human neighbors work together to build a fort for their common defense or raise a barn with the expectation that the ones being helped will soon offer help in return.

Males would benefit by remaining in the natal group, except for one big drawback. If they bred with their female relatives, they would produce genetically unfit offspring with anatomical and behavioral defects that would make them less likely to survive. So most male mammals — elephants, lions, baboons — are forced to leave their birth groups.

One of the most dangerous times in a male mammal's life is that period when he must leave the sanctuary of his mother's birth group and strike out on his own. Almost as soon as male lions begin developing a mane at about two years of age, older males that have emigrated from other prides kick them out. On their own in unfamiliar terrain, young males suffer severe disadvantages compared with their sisters who stay in their home pride. These solitary males are at higher risk from almost everything in their environment: wandering around on their own, they can be beaten up or killed by older, stronger individuals or coalitions of territorial males; they are less successful in bringing down large prey; and initially they do not know where to find food and water in their strange new lands.

Males who are especially good at risk-taking — for example, those who travel as far as it takes to fight strange males for the best territories — are generally the most successful; that is, they leave more offspring to the next generation than males who slink around their old homesteads trying to avoid the immigrant males while staying close to their mothers. So natural selection has consistently favored and promoted the genes for risk-taking in males of almost all mammalian species, including our own.

Males have many more sperm than females have eggs, making eggs a valuable and limited commodity, probably the most sought-after and fought-over natural resource of all. Males, and even their sperm cells, compete with each other, fighting for females and their eggs, and the most aggressive males are often the most successful breeders and providers. Throughout the natural world risk-taking, aggressive males have generally left more offspring and genes, generation after generation. For the human animal, this has been our legacy as well.

But such behavior carries costs. Besides the obvious disadvantages of death, injury, and starvation, there is loneliness. Since most male mammals leave their home territories and groups, they do not spend their lives in close proximity to relatives. In many species the only company they keep are the females they seek, and even then they are often rather quickly displaced by other more competitive males. But in some species, wandering males form loose, temporary groups. The Camp Group of male elephants — Survivor, Long Tail, and Cheers — were an example of such a free-form alliance. By just hanging out together and feeding near each other, they accrued some group-related benefits. It is more likely, for example, that several pairs of watchful eyes will spot a poacher before a single pair will. But as harmonious as these groups can sometimes be, if a receptive female comes prancing by it quickly becomes "every bull for himself."

When males get older and their testosterone levels drop, they see each other less as competitors and more as cohorts. Males like our Kakules, who could no longer successfully compete for females and dominance in their herds, and the aging Kalahari lions we once knew, who were no longer strong enough to hold a pride, seemed to be aware of their solitude. Old lions often would stand on a termite mound or dune top, looking far across the landscape for minutes at a time, "cooing" into the wind, inviting social contact among pride-mates who were no longer there to hear them. And sometimes they would meet and hang out with other older males, even former enemies, just to be with someone, anyone, rather than spend one more minute alone. Years ago in the Kalahari we even knew a solitary bull wildebeest who, whenever he saw us driving along his section of the fossil riverbed, would plod right behind our Land Rover as it trundled along. Presumably this somehow made him feel less alone, though our truck hardly resembled a wildebeest. Individuals of a social species will do almost anything to avoid being alone in an empty desert — or in a river valley full of lions and poachers. Far away from their relatives for most of their lives, many male mammals are at first aggressive, adventuresome competitors, then finally find themselves alone and, perhaps, lonely.

Just a Farmer
Just a Builder
More than a Father
More than a Man

I learned of my father's death when I flew to Mpika for a village development meeting. One of our friends met me at the airstrip to give me the news. Alone with my thoughts on the flight back to camp, I was cruising through quiet air with beautiful thunderheads stacked around when I felt him beside me, sharing our romance with Africa one last time.

Ahead a storm was brewing clouds too big for the sky, towering pinnacles of vapor turning pink, purple, red, and blue-black in front of the setting sun. Below the clouds a crimson rain streaked down to the green and gentle hills going to sleep in the dusk along the edge of the escarpment. Wisps of vapor, like an old man's white eyebrows, perched over each peak.

A curtain of gray rain began pouring from a big thunderhead ahead on my left; another stood to the right. Between the storm cells a slip of lighter sky promised a way through. But it suddenly grew darker, and then closed off. I urged the plane forward; flying blind as spikes of lightning flashed on either side, rain hammering my windshield.

I kept the nose of my craft pointed toward where the lighter patch of sky had been, until finally my wings tore free from the ragged tatters of cloud. Ahead, shafts of golden sunlight were spilling and spreading like puddles of melting butter over the malachite green of the valley floor. Then I saw a rainbow — no, I swear to God, a *double* rainbow — arching from the hills of the scarp to the Luangwa River, with our camp directly beneath its center. Then I *knew* Dad was beside me.

"This is for you, Dad!" My cheeks wet with tears, I shook my fist at the sky as I shot the gap between the massive black shoulders of the two thunderheads. The rainbow reappeared, two dazzling ribbons of color.

I did not want to land, so I wandered around, cloud to cloud, watching the rain spill over the hills. Then I flew aimlessly along the sinuous, rain-swollen Mwaleshi River. I flew lower, and then very low, among the dead trees on the plains west of the river. Banking and twisting, I tortured the plane through a series of tight turns, daring the branches to pull me out of the sky.

"See the buffalo, Dad? Over there! And the wildebeest, and the snowy egrets near that round waterhole."

I hurried across the Mwaleshi to the plains, where I knew I would find elephants. As I crossed the river, the sun came out one last time before it slipped below the Muchinga Mountains. It turned the water to sparkle and the plains the most brilliant green that ever was. A herd of elephants hurried under the plane, some wheeling, shaking their heads in threat.

The sun setting beneath the storm was one of the most beautiful sights I have ever seen in Africa, but I did not regret not having my camera. I knew I would remember it better than a photograph could.

Ahead, along one of the turns in the river, and a few feet below the plane, stood a sward of tall *Phragmites* reeds, their feathery, cream-colored heads nodding to the crimson sunset.

I dipped my starboard wing, easing the Cessna lower, until its wingtip sliced through some of the tall, wavering heads. A stream of down followed the airfoil skyward again, turning to fiery incandescence before the dying sun.

I landed and strolled to the brow of Khaya Hill. Distant thunder grumbled over the purple scarp while a stream murmured from the meadow below. All around me were the beautifully honest, clean, clear truths of Nature, the truths my father had taught me. I knew that so long as I was in a wild place, he would always be with me.

I drove back to camp, parked the truck, and walked to the river's edge, where I sat down in the grass near the Kakule Club. Just another aging male hanging out in the park with his cronies.

14 DELIA

TOO MUCH SUGAR

The day is done, and the darkness
Falls from the wings of Night,
As a feather is wafted downward,
From an eagle in his flight.

— HENRY WADSWORTH LONGFELLOW

The mountains are no more fixed than the stars.

— ANNIE DILLARD

THE SQUAT BLACK HF RADIO, our link to the rest of the world, sat on a wooden table in the open reed hut next to our cooking area, where it chattered to itself throughout the day. Except during scheduled conversations, we kept the volume low. Still, now and then we could hear the Catholic nuns at an isolated mission checking on the welfare of their even more remote sisters, or a guide from John Coppinger's safari camp on the Mwaleshi River ordering marmalade or beer from Lusaka — which was actually a secret code. For years safari companies could not operate in North Luangwa because of the poachers. Now John had established rustic yet elegant reed-and-grass camps offering old-fashioned walking safaris that meandered by herds of a thousand buffalo. His clients watched small herds of elephants, no longer timid, bathe in the rivers. His camps were remote, and between visitors the guides lived alone and became somewhat lonely. When John was sending a tourist group that included a pretty single woman out to one of the camps, he would tell the guide over the radio that he was including "marmalade" with the supplies. Or if it had been a long dry spell between tour groups, we would hear one of the safari guides begging John to send some "marmalade" his way.

At six-thirty every morning and four-thirty every afternoon we "did radio" with Trish Boulton at the project office in Mpika.

Soon after one of my trips to Fulaza with Sugar, Trish informed me one morning on the radio that she had bad news. Sugar was in the Mpika hospital, she said, in very serious condition. He had been diagnosed with diabetes and had slipped into a coma. I sat down hard on the old safari chair. Is there anything we can do? I asked. Can we fly him to Lusaka? Trish said no; the Cuban doctors, doing the best they could in Mpika, did not want him moved. We agreed to do radio again at noon.

Kasokola, who was cutting up onions on the table nearby, asked what was wrong with Sugar. He didn't know about diabetes, so I tried to explain.

"He eats too much sugar for his condition, and he's been under too much stress. He has gone into a deep sleep, and they can't wake him."

"What is stress?"

"You know how Sugar is, he worries too much. He's always upset about things not going well."

Sugar was no better at noon, and at four-thirty we got the news that he had died. I thought of his serious nature, of his determination to help his people. We would never be able to replace him, and I wasn't sure we could succeed without him. I walked to the river's edge, my face streaked with tears. I could hear the baboons barking in the distance and wished I had my own troop to call.

15 MARK
CHIPUNDU PRIDE

If I had a hammer.
— PETE SEEGER

WORRY RODE SHOTGUN on my drive from Marula-Puku Camp to Chipundu village that June morning in 1993. Sugar had been essential to our work with villagers. A Bemba himself, he had a magical way of reaching people, a knack for describing a sunflower press so poetically that the people could see a new future in his words.

His final performance had been at Koluba village, a tiny settlement of perhaps a dozen scattered mud huts surrounded by maize and sorghum patches, perched near the brow of the escarpment not far from the western boundary of North Luangwa Park. Except for a footpath to Mpika, miles to the west, the village was almost completely cut off from the outside world, and it was notorious as a staging area for some big-league poachers. Sugar had paced back and forth in front of a gathering of men on the bank of the nearby stream, calling and waving his arms like a circus barker, selling them on the need to build a rudimentary road and a pole-and-stick bridge so that they could haul their maize and other produce to market.

As news of Sugar's death spread from village to village, the Bemba people took it with their customary fatalism: "Ah, Bwana, again it seems we have been Bemba'd," a man said to me. "It is our way."

LIKE MOST AFRICAN TRIBES, the Bembas have not had an easy history. In the early 1800s in Lubaland, west of Lake Tanganyika in what is today known as Congo, King Mukulumpe ("the great for-

124

ever") ruled their ancestors. In his *Short History of the Bemba,* P. B. Mushindo relates that one day, according to legend, a villager brought before the king a woman with ears like an elephant's. Mumbi Makasa claimed to be the daughter of a man named Liulu ("heaven") and the queen of the abeena-Ng'andu, the crocodile clan. But because of her unusual appearance, her many brothers and sisters had despised her from birth.

Despite the woman's very large ears, King Mukulumpe found her beautiful, and he married her. She bore him three sons, including one ChitiMukulu fwamamba UmuLuba ("rude basket made of leaves"). He and his brothers grew up to be thugs, hurting and killing many people. Their hearts hardened by their father's frequent punishments, ChitiMukulu and his brothers sought permission to leave Lubaland in search of their own country. Mukulumpe gave each of them an elephant's tusk, spat on them to bless them, and gladly sent them on their way.

ChitiMukulu and his brothers, along with a large following, roamed for many years in search of a place to start a colony of their own. In their travels they mostly subsisted off the land, but occasionally they plundered settlements along the way. They also paused for extended periods to cultivate many of the plants they needed for subsistence, some of which are still found in Bembaland today.

Boldly adventurous as well as industrious, they crossed the Lwapula River at the border of today's Congo and Zambia; over some years, they traveled about four hundred miles south, establishing villages as they went. Eventually ChitiMukulu began worrying that he and his brothers would die without leaving heirs. Mukulumpe, their father, had forbidden them to bring any of their sisters with them, and according to Luba custom, only a sister's son could be an heir — a custom adopted to ensure the integrity of the royal bloodline. So ChitiMukulu sent Mumbo, his cousin, and some carriers back to Lubaland to kidnap Bwalya Chabala, ChitiMukulu's sister, who was also Mumbo's half-sister, to be the mother of their successors.

Bwalya came willingly, but on the way back, while the others were fetching firewood and water, Mumbo and Bwalya made their own "fire." Soon after arriving at the boma of Chief ChitiMukulu and the others, Bwalya was found to be pregnant. Mumbo admitted to being the father of her unborn child. Upset that Mumbo had sullied their royal bloodline by impregnating his own half-sister, ChitiMukulu and his brothers banished him from the clan and renamed him Kapasa of the Membe ("male private parts") clan. His totem relations were to be the Nkashi ("female private parts") clan. Bwalya's baby died from neglect soon after it was born.

ChitiMukulu and his band of Bembas continued exploring from Lake Bangweulu all the way across the Luangwa River to today's border between Zambia and Malawi. But industrious Bisa people were already living there, and by the 1830s they were organizing caravans of a hundred or more carriers to transport ivory, gold, copper, and slaves to Kilwa, Zanzibar, and Mozambique Island on Africa's east coast, where the goods were traded to the Portuguese and Arabs. Bisa carriers returned to the interior with manufactured items, including bolts of cloth and dinnerware, for their own use and for trade with other neighboring tribes. Although they occasionally used donkeys as beasts of burden, human carriers transported the bulk of the goods, and since being a carrier was vital to trade and commerce, it was a respected and valued occupation.

Meanwhile the Arabs, not content with their coastal enterprise, and especially hungry for more ivory and slaves from Africa's interior, began extending their commercial interests inland, setting up outposts along the traditional trade routes used by the Bisa, Yao, Nyamwezi, and other tribes. By trading guns for ivory and slaves, the Arabs fomented conflict among inland tribes and then took advantage of the consequent political instability. Robert July describes this period in his *History of the African People:* "As time passed, the system fed upon itself — more guns and an ever-rising demand for diminishing supplies of ivory led to increased raiding and slaving with consequent breakdown of village life and the rise of bands of rootless adventurers all too ready to add their measure of violence to the turbulent times."

With guns obtained from Arab traders, the Bembas forced the Bisas east into the Luangwa Valley and west past Lake Bangweulu. ChitiMukulu's people eventually dominated the huge tract of land now known as the Northern Province of Zambia. And then in the late 1800s, the British arrived, along with other foreign governments that began colonizing the continent. The Bemba, no longer dominant, were dominated instead. The British brought with them even more sophisticated weaponry and transportation than the Arabs had used, exacerbating tribal conflicts and the slaughter of elephants and other wildlife. Western medicines led to declines in human mortality rates; that decline, along with immigration, spurred the growth of human populations. To conserve the dwindling wildlife, the British in Northern Rhodesia (now Zambia) enacted laws requiring hunters to have licenses and limited the number of animals that could be shot.

In 1963 Kenneth Kaunda ended fifty-two years of British rule with a largely bloodless revolt that led to the establishment of the independent state of Zambia. But to promote unity among the country's seventy-four tribes, Kaunda discouraged the expression of almost all tribal traditions. Instead of being freed, the Bembas and other tribal people were once again stifled. Kaunda also strongly discouraged capitalism and free enterprise, promising citizens that the state would provide free education, health care, and other fundamental community needs. But as well intentioned as these policies may have been, few services were actually delivered, and corruption flourished — including commercial poaching.

Highly organized poachers, their middlemen, and corrupt officials took over where the Arabs and colonists had left off, controlling and plundering the resources that the local people needed to sustain themselves and improve their lives. In the 1970s, '80s, and '90s, Bemba communities were once again subjugated by outsiders, this time by commercial poachers who often paid them little more than a kilo of meat for carrying a hundred pounds of ivory, skins, and other contraband sixty miles or more over the Muchinga Mountains to Mpika and to nearby Tazara, a village and railhead from which contraband was smuggled aboard trains north to Dar es Salaam and south to Lusaka, Zimbabwe, and South Africa.

By 1985, poaching of all wildlife species had escalated to the point that it was a national institution. The economy of Zambia had crashed with the loss of copper exports as the primary foreign-exchange earner, and many high-level civil servants and military personnel had turned to the slaughter of rhinos, elephants, and other wildlife, often using government equipment. I met contract pilots who told of flying air force helicopters into the bush to transport tusks, rhino horns, and meat, their decks awash with blood; honorary rangers (unpaid volunteers such as ranchers or farmers who provided petrol, food, and transport to scouts) who were threatened for stopping an official Mercedes, its trunk full of tusks, at a checkpoint; and too many other examples of corruption to mention. During our countrywide search for a study area, we found that only two or three of Zambia's nineteen national parks contained viable populations of large mammals.

But when, in 1992, Zambians elected their first truly democratic president, citizens were able, for the first time in decades, to engage in free enterprise, with the hope of bettering their lives. Suddenly there was a surge of interest in the new businesses our project was helping to start. People in many parts of Bembaland were asking questions, coming to see, wanting to participate — even in Koluba and other remote, hardscrabble poaching hangouts.

𝒮 SUGAR HAD BEEN the best at answering these observers' questions. But now he was dead, and as I drove through the rocks and rubble of the Muchinga Escarpment headed for Chipundu village that morning in the dry season of 1993, I worried that unless we could quickly replace him with someone as capable as he, all our work could be undone.

Alston Watt, our community service adviser, had proposed hiring a Zambian named Hammer Simwinga, the son of a medical practitioner, who had training in small business and agricultural development. Even though he was supporting Kasonde, his wife, their three young children, and two AIDS orphans, Hammer traveled from his rural home to our office in Mpika to meet us. I immediately noticed that his entire being radiated, like the sunflowers he would plant, and that his aura of good will defined him more clearly than any of his physical attributes. He could not finish a sentence without laughing, and his most important goal was service to others. In him I saw a new dawn for our work with villagers and a better understanding between them and us. We hired him on the spot.

From that day on, Hammer rode his motorbike from village to village distributing fingerling fish in plastic bags for new fish farms, sunflower seeds and presses, chili pepper seeds to ward off crop-raiding elephants, plans for new beehives, soccer balls and crayons from America for the "Sister Schools," bolts of cloth for sewing co-ops, tools for carpenters, medical supplies for clinics and the traditional birth attendants, and much more — all in the name of wildlife conservation. Like a modern-day Johnny Appleseed, he left a wake of renewed hope, pride, and prosperity behind his bike wherever he traveled.

This morning I was to meet Hammer for the second time in Chipundu, where he had been working with farmers to grow more crops with better yields and to hold the village's second Field Day, an agricultural fair. Sugar had tried to organize such a fair a year earlier, but no one, not a single farmer with a single fruit or vegetable, had shown up. It had been one of Sugar's biggest disappointments.

At the outskirts of the village I turned onto a better track and began passing the mud huts of villagers I knew, including that of Miriam Malenga, who always greeted me as though ready to celebrate life for any reason. I could not help but feel happy whenever I saw her.

But today her reed door was closed and her cooking fire was cold, as was the case with the other bomas I passed. And where were all the children who usually flocked to the track when they heard our truck approaching? I drove on, worried that some catastrophe had befallen the village or that perhaps they were all at a funeral for the latest victim of AIDS. I crossed the stream and continued up the hill toward the center of the village. Ahead were villagers, lots of them, crowded around the common ground near their school.

As I stopped the truck, I heard gumba music throbbing not far away, and a flock of women and children, clapping and singing, skipped toward me, Miriam among them. She took my hand and dragged me through the crowd to an open-air market. Set up on the commons were stands made of reeds, sticks, and grass, each festooned with brightly colored squashes, gourds, pumpkins, shocks of corn, bunches of bananas, pans of groundnuts, combs of delicious black honey, bolts of boldly colored chitenje cloth, bottles of sunflower oil, and trays of kapenta (dried fingerlings).

"Mopalayne, Ba Owen!" people called to me.

And then Hammer walked toward me, handsome in his dark slacks and blue-and-yellow print shirt, his eyes sparkling, smile warm and unassuming. He took my hand and curtseyed respectfully in the traditional Bemba greeting, though he is in fact from the Nyamwanga tribe. "Hello, sir."

That morning in Chipundu, Hammer and I held hands for a long time, as is the custom in that part of Africa.

He and Alston Watt would continue to establish village enterprises throughout the region, eventually benefiting an estimated twenty thousand people.

16 DELIA

A PRESENT FROM GIFT

Each instant of life
one after the other
came rushing in
like priceless gifts.

— ANNA SWIR

Perhaps there aren't any grownups anywhere . . . Grownups know things . . . If only they could send us something
grownup . . . a sign or something.

— WILLIAM GOLDING

FOR NEARLY THREE YEARS we had watched the little orphaned
elephant Gift as she danced her jig in camp or wandered alone on the
grassy plains. She was now eight years old, barely an adolescent. It
would be another seven or eight years before she would be mature
enough to have a calf of her own. Another three thousand days of being alone, with no sisters, aunts, or cousins.

One morning Patrick Mwamba came to me once again in the
stone office cottage, where I analyzed elephant data.

"Madame, come see. The baby elephant, the one you call Giftee,
has got a baby."

"That's impossible! Where did you see her?"

"By the hippo pool."

Patrick and I scrambled into the truck and drove to the hill overlooking a clear pool in a bend of the river. Scanning with binoculars,
we looked in all directions, but Gift had disappeared. After searching

for her for several days, Mark and I finally found her feeding near our airstrip. Hidden deep in the mopane brush, standing next to Gift's belly, was a tiny dark gray calf. Walking first one way and then the other, Mark and I tried to get close enough to see if the calf belonged to Gift or if it also was an orphan who had taken up with her. Finally we saw the wee infant suckling. At about eight and a half years old, Gift was a mother! Mark and I looked at each other, stunned.

Before the onslaught of poaching in Luangwa, elephant females had their first calf when they were about sixteen. Gift had reproduced at half that age. In the 1970s females did not ovulate until they were on average fourteen years old; the earliest age recorded for first ovulation was eleven years. Gift must have ovulated when she was about six and a half years old. Nature does not often cut the age of first ovulation in half. We thought this had to be some strange anomaly, perhaps because Gift lived alone in a male world.

The calf's pointed forehead indicated that she was a female, and we named her Georgia. They often ambled into camp together, looking more like young sisters than mother and offspring. Since Gift showed no fear of us, Georgia accepted us right away and, with her ears and trunk flopping about, trotted at her mother's side down the footpaths between our cottages. As Gift fed, Georgia would stand under her mother's belly and look up at us with swimmy, curious eyes, as though wondering if we were somehow part of their missing herd.

Researchers in East Africa had learned that in normal unstressed populations of elephants, allomothering — care given by female relatives other than the mother — greatly enhances calf survival, and the young ones learn a lot about mothering from older aunts or sisters. Relatives even assist in the removal of the birth sac from newborns. Adolescents, although they are not lactating, practice nursing infants before they have their own first calf. They defend calves, play with them, touch and teach them. They help newborns step over roots and gently help them stand when they fall down. When a distressed calf makes a squeaky cry, an avalanche of females rushes to its aid. Georgia had no one but Gift.

As often as we could, we hiked around the hills near camp with Gift and Georgia, observing how this single mom who had no female support group was coping with raising a calf. Gift was not a good mother. After the age of five she had not been part of a unit, so since then she had not experienced the frequent touching and gentle care ordinarily shared among family members. Gift rarely touched her calf and often hardly seemed to notice her.

In the first weeks of its life, a calf normally stays very close to its mother, usually within a foot of her, and sometimes leaning against one of her large legs as if it were a tree trunk. When it is a few months old it will begin to venture farther away, but if it strays too far, the mother or another female — one of many aunties — will follow it. Not so with Gift and Georgia.

One morning when Gift was feeding on fruits in camp, Georgia, now about three months old, experimented with feeding nearby. She was just beginning to eat grass on her own, but it seemed to take a lot of concentration. Georgia tried pulling up the stalks, but she could not wrap her trunk tightly enough around the grass to pull the stems from the ground. Eventually she sank to her knees, turned her head to one side, and nibbled on the grass. Meanwhile, Gift walked quickly from our kitchen area to Kasokola's cottage, about forty yards away. She stood out of sight of Georgia, on the opposite side of the hut.

Suddenly Georgia realized that she had lost sight of her mother. Squealing loudly, she dashed around camp, her little legs pumping, trunk wriggling. She trotted right up to us, stared at us for a few seconds, then ran toward the office cottage, in the opposite direction from her mother. We backed up so that we could see Gift. The young mother continued to feed on marula fruits, completely ignoring the shrill cries of her calf.

Kasokola, slinging dough from his fingers, rushed out of the kitchen, and together we watched Georgia scurrying one way and then the other, screaming the entire time. I had the urge to chase her toward her mother, to somehow usher her in the right direction. But we dared not interfere for fear of making the situation worse.

Finally, Gift nonchalantly walked toward the workshop, where Georgia could see her. The calf trotted to her mother's side and stayed very near her until they both ambled out of camp several minutes later.

"This Giftee is too 'moveous.' Both these elephants need a proper mother," Kasokola informed us as he went back to the bread dough.

Gift's mothering skills seemed to improve slightly over time. One morning when Georgia was five or six months old, Mark and I stood in a small stand of mopane trees near our airstrip, watching Gift and Georgia pulling leaves and branches from the mopane shrubs, stuffing them into their mouths, and munching loudly. Occasionally they would disappear in the thick brush.

The air was stagnant and hot, and single-minded tsetse flies swarmed around us, biting our arms and legs. Each bite was as painful as a bee sting and made us twist and jerk in a strange antifly dance. We cut small branches from the trees and waved them about as fly swatters. Losing sight of the elephants, we stepped around a large termite mound to look for them. Gift, her ears flapping and trunk extended, pounded the ground as she charged directly toward us from only twenty yards away. This was no jig. We had accidentally gotten too close, and Gift, who now seemed very large, was defending her calf. Mark and I stumbled backward. When she was ten yards away Gift settled down, throwing her trunk our way one last time before continuing to feed. Georgia, who was five feet behind her mother, flapped her tiny ears wildly at us. She lifted her trunk and let forth with a shrill squeak. From then on we gave them a wide berth.

꧁ BESIDES OBSERVING Gift and Georgia on the ground, we watched them, as well as the radio-collared elephants, from the helicopter. The bird's-eye view increased our ability to see newborn infants, group composition, and the specific vegetation types they frequented. One afternoon as we hovered near a small elephant family, we noticed a small female with a tiny new infant. As with many of the families, there were more infants than adult females in the group.

"Wait a minute. Gift's infant could explain everything," Mark said. "Maybe Georgia isn't a fluke. Since the adult females have been killed, maybe the adolescents are breeding." Mark banked the chopper in a tight turn, putting my feet against the horizon and my stomach near the floor, and we flew back to camp.

As Cheers chomped on fruit just outside the window of our office cottage, we scrolled through years and years of data. We had aged and analyzed 255 different family groups. Of these, only 27 percent were normal in the sense that they included enough adult females to account for the number of infants present. All the other families had more calves than adult females — but there were enough *subadult* females to account for the calves. The adolescents must be breeding.

Now we had a theory to explain the mystery of too many infants per adult female, but we had to get proof. Every day we took off in the chopper, soaring over the elephants and observing the families. We confirmed that in less than two decades poachers had shot 93 percent of the elephants, mostly adults, and that female adolescents between the ages of eight and fourteen were giving birth to more than half (58 percent) of the calves born.

Apparently, elephant females are biologically able to ovulate and give birth earlier than had been observed. Perhaps when the elephant population is stable, the presence of numerous adult females suppresses early ovulation in younger females, as is the case for some other mammals. In what biologists refer to as a density-dependent phenomenon, the age of reproduction is correlated with the number of elephants. After the mature females were shot, the drastic reduction in population density may have triggered hormonal changes in the younger females, stimulating early-age ovulation. This inherent ability to reproduce as adolescents might allow the elephant population to recover from the decimation by poachers. The elephants were playing their ace.

There were more surprises. After poaching, one quarter of the family units consisted of a single mother and one calf. In the 1970s, before poaching, families consisting of only two elephants made up a mere 3 percent of the total. So as it turns out, the torn and frag-mented elephant society produces not only more aggression and gangs, but also single moms and adolescent mothers.

Standing on a sandstone bluff, Mark and I watched a young soli-tary female and her tiny calf as they moved along the still waters of the Lubonga. The pastel colors of the rock face danced in the clear water. Then I noticed that our own reflections, although we stood higher, were close to those of the elephants, even touching their shoulders. It seemed as if we were drifting with them, neither species knowing where the downstream current would lead.

✑ IN THE DAYS when Georgia was still a small calf, we looked up one morning to see her and her mother walking boldly up to the low grass fence of the kitchen boma. Mark and I stood on the stoop watching them forage only a few feet from the cooking fire. Gift swept her trunk back and forth along the ground, making loud sniffing noises as she searched for fruits. Once she found one, she deftly curled the pointed tips of her trunk around the fruit and tossed it un-derhand, so to speak, into her mouth. Georgia was not quite so adept at this task. Her rubbery little trunk seemed to twitch about like an unattended garden hose until she finally located a fruit. Having watched Mom, she curled her trunk toward her mouth and let fly. However, the marula missed not only her mouth but her entire head, bouncing off somewhere behind her. Patiently she found another one. This time it sailed between her stumpy legs. Again and again she tried, fruits glancing off her body in all directions and rolling across the ground. Finally she scored a hit and chomped loudly.

From the porch we watched the two little elephants leave camp and wander along the river. Four years later Gift presented another calf, which we named Gem. She had no family, so she was starting her own. Gift turned out to be appropriately named, for she taught us more about the altered reproductive biology of North Luangwa elephants than did any other elephant. Perhaps her early motherhood was unconventional in elephant society, but it was the only hope for the elephants of Luangwa to recover. Little by little, "panono, panono," one elephant at a time, the great herds may return.

By nature, Nature gives.

17 DELIA

A DANGEROUS DINNER

Come let us draw the curtains,
heap up the fire, and sit
hunched by the flame together,
and make a friend of it.

— HUMBERT WOLFE

KASOKOLA AND I STOKED UP the wood stove hotter than it had
ever been. "We must get it really hot," I said. "Much hotter than to
cook a chicken."

The cooking area in our camp was a rambling hodgepodge of
structures made of various materials, all stuck together in a row. The
stone cottage had a roof of homemade tiles formed from a slurry of
bark fiber, cement, and termite mud. Inside were two rooms: the
storeroom, which was very important since we journeyed to Lusaka
only two or three times a year, had wall-to-wall shelves stocked with
tinned beans, peaches, peanut butter, large canisters of flour, rice,
powdered milk, sugar, tea, and coffee. The other room had two tables
for peeling and kneading, an old-fashioned cupboard where pottery
dishes and glass jars were neatly shelved, and the freezer. African baskets, dried peppers, onions, and garlic hung from the rafters.

Jutting straight out from the cottage was a long porch, covered
by a thatched roof; here we washed dishes on a heavy wooden table
and clothes under a spigot. A solar pump drew water from a well by
the river. At the end of the porch, stuck on like an afterthought, was
the cooking hut, a round structure of reed half-walls with a thatched
roof. Steaming, blackened kettles perched on a grid above an open

fire that always burned cheerfully on the stone floor of the hut. An iron wood stove squatted near the fire; its chimney, topped by a little hood like a cocked hat, passed through the thatched roof. Every morning smoke belched from the stack as the old, retired male buffaloes lounged nearby.

The cooking area was almost in the center of the camp. No matter where we were going or what we were doing — returning from an elephant walk or a chopper flight — we passed by the kitchen, where Kasokola was always ready with a wave or a cup of coffee. This was the heart of our camp, the place where we ended up sitting on the wash table or around the fire, grabbing the steaming kettle for coffee, adding firewood, or watching elephants or buffaloes. Cheers and Long Tail or Gift and Georgia were often nearby, because a giant marula tree not only shaded the kitchen but also peppered the ground with fruit.

A fire marshal would never have approved of the chimney poking through the thatch or the open fire blazing on the floor beneath it. Rural Zambia had no fire marshals or building codes, of course, but on the advice of one of the Bembas we had insulated the chimney with bark from a baobab tree, which he assured us would not ignite no matter how hot the chimney became.

However, we had never before cooked a roast in our wood stove. Generally we don't eat meat, and our gas freezer, an old kerosene jalopy from our Kalahari days that never really froze anything, usually held only whole wheat flour and cereals to protect them from weevils, roaches, and ants. But when two very generous sponsors came to camp, we purchased an assortment of meat and transported it from Lusaka, a twenty-hour drive over potholed roads and rutted bush tracks. After the sponsors departed, there was meat left over and we invited our staff to share a pork roast with us. With three buffaloes grazing nearby, Kasokola put the roast in the oven at four in the afternoon and began peeling potatoes for dinner. I rummaged through the vegetable basket, searching for an edible month-old cabbage.

"So, what do you think, Kasokola? Is it going to rain soon?" Toward the end of the long, dry season, questions of rain flavored every conversation on the continent.

"That, madame, very much depends on the weather," he replied.

As Kasokola was putting potatoes in a pot and I was scraping the rotted, stinky leaves off a head of cabbage, Gift and Georgia walked up to the woodpile about ten yards from where we stood. The Camp Group males had eaten most of the marulas, but Gift must have remembered that sometimes the odd fruit rolled under the woodpile. With her trunk she picked up one piece of firewood after another, moving them aside and sniffing around the ground until the woodpile was spread out in a mess more than twenty yards wide. Georgia stood nearby.

"I hope she's going to put it back together again," Kasokola said.

Gift found no fruits, so she and Georgia walked down the main footpath and fed on tall grass by the river. I watched them pulling the long stalks, complete with roots, from the ground and swatting them over their backs to shake out the dirt. Then they stuffed the grass, roots and all, in their mouths.

I returned to the stone office cottage to continue writing an elephant report. Outside I could hear the *whack, whack, whack* of the elephants slapping grass on their backs. Now and then I checked on them through the window, and after an hour they disappeared into the long grass. I lost track of time but finally looked up to see the faint glow of a peach-colored sunset behind the flat-topped acacias. Then I heard a scream.

"FIRE! FIRE! FIRE!" Kasokola wailed from the kitchen.

I grabbed the large fire extinguisher in the office and ran. Small orange flames lapped at the chimney stack that poked through the thatch of the cooking hut. Mark was already spraying the fire with another extinguisher, and when he emptied it he grabbed mine. The flames had doubled in height and were roaring over a quarter of the roof. In a few seconds Mark exhausted the second extinguisher, and for an instant the fire went out, just vanished. My eyes darted back and forth. Suddenly the fire jumped back to life. Kasokola pushed another extinguisher from the workshop into Mark's hand, and again he covered the roof with white spray.

By now the staff, who had been bathing in the river, had run over from their camp, towels wrapped around their waists. They immediately set up a bucket brigade, taking water from the spigot and passing it to Mark, who threw it on the fire. The entire roof of the small cooking hut was engulfed in tall flames that reached hungrily into the marula tree.

"It's going to burn the porch roof!" I screamed. "Help me move the table!" Kasokola, some of the others, and I grabbed the long heavy table and dragged it out from under the roof. Sparks and burning embers shot wildly into the sky and rained down on us. If the other roofs caught fire, the entire camp could burn. I joined the bucket brigade, and in spite of the intense heat blasting our faces, we slung one bucket after another toward Mark.

A few small flames spread to the ten-by-fifteen-foot porch roof. Then *swush,* in seconds the entire roof exploded in flames thirty feet high. Instantly the great limbs of the marula and *Pericopsis* trees began to burn. No longer able to get to the spigot under the roof, the men ran thirty yards to the workshop to fill each bucket. But the raging fire shrugged off the water until the burning roof sagged against the exposed wooden beams, then fell against the door of the cottage.

I heard a roar behind me. I whirled around and saw flames racing through the dry grass toward the office cottage. Our data, our records, our journals were stored under thatch. Two of us grabbed shovels and beat at the base of the flames, which reared five feet high. Black soot and hot smoke choked our throats. The shovel quickly became too heavy for me to lift, but there was no time to grab anything else. Turning my face away, I darted forward, swatted the flames five or six times, then jumped back when the heat threatened to consume me.

Then the worst happened: the wind began to blow, sending a torrent of living sparks, thousands of hot, burning embers, through the air toward the rest of the camp. A red-orange glow lit the sky and reflected spectacularly in the lazy river, which ignored the frenzy, flowing leisurely past the turmoil.

I yelled for someone to help me kill the grass fire. Kasokola ran over with a large tarp and dragged it through the fire line, racing back and forth next to the flames. The tarp smothered the flames, but here and there they bounded back. I ran behind Kasokola and beat the up-starts to death. Finally, only twenty yards from the office, only a few yards from the solar panels, all the flames disappeared. We hurried back toward the main fire.

"The whole camp's going to burn — we gotta get this roof on the ground!" Mark shouted, as the wind continued to send sparks high into the air. The guys grabbed chains, threw them around the burning posts, then hooked them to the hitch on the Unimog, our huge all-terrain vehicle. Mark drove forward, pulling the flaming posts out from under the burning roof. The entire structure — blaz-ing roof, rafters, and posts — crashed to the ground in a tornado of sparks and fire.

The flames burned lower now but still lapped at the trees and the rafters of the stone cottage. Within seconds the ends of the rafters began to burn, leading the fire inside the kitchen to the shelves and tables. Two men tore the screens from windows and crawled inside, smoke pouring around them. The Bemba men quickly passed buck-ets of water through the windows to douse the flames. The window shutters and door were ablaze, but the men stood their ground, pitch-ing water to the ceiling and against the door.

Patrick Mwamba pulled the buried water pipe out of the ground, held it up like a fire hose, and sprayed the flames. Dense black smoke billowed out of the windows. I worried that the men in-side would be asphyxiated.

My hair was singed, and we were all coughing and drenched

with sweat. The grass roofs had almost burned themselves out and lay in two huge smoldering piles of red ashes on the ground. A few small flames continued to flicker from the kitchen rafters, but they were soon drowned with water.

Searching for more fuel, the fire lapped at the branches of the marula tree above our heads. Before we knew what he was doing, Kasokola had shinnied up the tree and beaten out the flames with an inner tube. We looked around anxiously for any more flames jumping from the piles of debris. Smoke poured from the remains of the collapsed roofs, but minutes went by and there was no more fire.

"I think we've got it," Mark said finally.

My lovely, lopsided bush kitchen was a blackened pile of rubbish. We walked around, pulling out a burned pot here, a blackened tray there. I found my red enamel teapot, with hyena tooth marks from the Kalahari, crushed and blackened, sitting on the fire grate. Kasokola, shaking his head sadly, lifted the remains of his favorite pan from the wreckage.

And then we remembered the pork roast.

The thatch of the cooking hut had collapsed on top of the wood stove, burying it completely under a pile of charred rubble. Mark grabbed a rake and pulled away the burned debris. Underneath a layer of black ash and smothering remains, the iron stove glowed cherry red from the intense heat. Its dainty little feet had collapsed, and the stove sat flat on the ground, legs sticking straight out. Shielding his face from the heat with his arm, Mark pried open the oven door with the rake. A black-crusted blob, all that was left of the roast, rolled out and bounced across the ground, hissing like a hot cannonball.

Balancing the roast on the end of the rake, Mark carried it to the wooden table we had saved from the fire. Someone handed him a machete, and he sliced away the charred layer of crackling. Inside, the pork was white and succulent. Perfect — Julia Child could not have done better.

We ate our dinner as planned, in the n'saka by the river, smoke still belching into the night from the blackened remains of my precious kitchen. No one had been hurt, and the rest of the camp had been saved. Reason enough for a feast, and we were all hungry. The potatoes, of course, had not fared as well as the roast; we could not even find their carcasses. The Bembas brought a huge pot of mealie meal from their camp, and we sat by the river, plates in our laps. We decided against having a campfire.

✒ WE HAD SO MANY important things to do that it took more than a year to rebuild the kitchen. But eventually the structures were constructed much the way they had been before. Now and then I teased Kasokola about the recipe for pork roast: *"Sprinkle roast with garlic salt, stoke fire, burn down kitchen, serve hot."* But he took it very seriously, and if I jokingly suggested having a pork roast for dinner, Kasokola shook his head. "Ah, but-ee, that meat is a very dangerous thing."

18 MARK

WILDLIFE DRAMA

She would make her eyes see more today than they
ever did before.

—JULIA MOOD PETERKIN

HIDING IN THE TALL dry grass, two poachers stalked noiselessly toward an elephant feeding not thirty yards away. Unaware of the danger, the big bull reached down with his trunk, tore off more grass stems, and lifted them to his mouth, his ropy tail flicking contentedly.

Ka-Boom! The elephant's knees buckled at the shot. He pitched forward, driving his tusks into the ground and balancing on them for a moment. Then he hauled himself upright, and charged. The poachers fired again, but the elephant seemed determined to kill before he died. He quickly gained on one of the fleeing poachers, but just as he was about to crush the man, he stopped. His massive body convulsed, and he rolled onto his side, shivering in his death throes. In seconds the poachers began hacking at his tusks with their machetes.

But the tusks were as limp as rags — because they were, in fact, made of twisted cloth bound up with strips of bark. The tail was indeed a rope, and the machetes were wood.

The elephant itself was propelled by two schoolchildren, bent over and swaying under a gray sheet, their black spindly legs poking out beneath the cloth. Three other classmates played the poachers in this wildlife drama, which had taken Hammer weeks to arrange. The prize for the most original, creative, and best-acted skit among various village schools would be a safari into the North Luangwa Park, where the winners would get a chance to see real elephants for the very first time in their lives — even though none lived more than thirty miles away.

The poachers separated the fake tusks from the cloth body and began stealing off with them. But suddenly a tall boy ran in from the grassy perimeter of the Mpika playground. He wore a radio headset made of plastic cups, and, with his right arm and hand held high over his head, he twirled a staff with a horizontal stick attached, its ends painted white to simulate a helicopter's main rotor. His billowing chitenje mimicked the chopper's fuselage, and close behind him were three "game scout" passengers dressed in bits of green khaki.

The chopper circled, swept in, and landed as its pilot squatted down. The game scouts, brandishing their wooden rifles, leaped out and gave chase, tackling the poachers, handcuffing them, and then marching them to the magistrate, who held court from a school desk on another part of the playground. After they were sentenced to two years at hard labor, the poachers were led to jail behind a bench in yet another corner of the yard. There students held a sign reading: POACHERS DON'T STEAL OUR ANIMALS!

With the criminals safely locked up, one of the game guards solemnly stepped to the center of the stage area, stood tall, and declared: "Our wildlife is our heritage! We must protect it for future generations!" The crowd of teachers, students, and villagers from more than fourteen communities — all once notorious for harboring poachers — rewarded the players with rousing applause. Hammer beamed like a proud father.

After the poacher had apparently served hard time, he was led out of jail by a chorus of singers chanting

> "A dream of judgment!
> Away with poaching!"

The singers covered him with a white sheet and took him to the mattress, where he lay down as though sleeping. Next an orator stalked to the bed, stood tall, and shouted to the gathering: "As you can see, our friend Shaka, the convicted poacher, is fast asleep, and he has a dream. In his dream people tell him of the importance of nature." A boy wearing a cardboard mask of a kindly face advanced and stood over the recumbent Shaka. "But he did not listen and instead continued poaching."

At this point the chorus again chanted:

> "A dream of judgment!
> Away with poaching!"

In the next scene Shaka was up to his old tricks. Carrying a toy homemade rifle, he stalked and shot three students who were crawling on their hands and knees, pulling up grass as they pretended to be grazing animals. He hacked at their carcasses with his hands, and the chorus sang:

> "Every time,
> I see the poachers
> killing animals,
> I do cry. [gesture of wiping tears from their eyes]
> Up on the mountains
> Up on the hills
> Behind the rivers
> Up in the sky.
> Every time
> I see the poachers
> killing animals,
> I do cry."

After several stanzas, the poacher went to sleep under his sheet again. This time in his dream he saw a stern vision of justice — portrayed by a boy wearing a cardboard mask. His knees knocked as the chorus chanted:

> "A dream of judgment!
> Away with poaching!"

Justice dragged Shaka, howling and still wrapped in his sheet, away for good.

Another skit showed tourists paying money at a gateway into the park, then seeing elephants, zebras, and puku likenesses as they walked on safari. The money was given to a schoolmaster, a doctor, and a merchant, to show how revenues from wildlife tourism would benefit the community. While this was going on, another student paraded with a sign that read: OUR WILD ANIMALS ARE WORTH MORE ALIVE THAN DEAD! DON'T POACH!

In still another performance, a player asked:

"Is it wrong for an elephant to be born just like you?
  Tell me, is your mother died [dead] like an [poached]
      elephant?
  No! She is born like you, she had a mother like you, she
      prays like you.
  Tell me why her mother died.
  Why? Because of *you*, you selfish *you!*

You want her ivory,
Understand my position and love it
For my mother's death.
What is wrong, selfish *you?*
Yes, selfish *you!*"

The chorus sang:

"Trees are important
  Animals are rare,
  Minerals are precious,
  So look after them.

  Zambia's our territory,
  Zambia's our land.
  Air is delicate,
  Hold tight for life.

Minerals are precious,
So look after them."

After watching the skits from fourteen villages, a panel of judges chose Mwamfushi village primary school as the winner for their depiction of the helicopter and dreaming poacher. We were pleased, because for years Mwamfushi had harbored some of the worst poachers.

Early the following Saturday morning, the students, together with teachers and parent chaperones — more than twenty in all — piled into the open back of our Unimog truck for their safari trip into the park. Three hours later, covered with red dust from the track, they arrived at Marula-Puku, where Delia met them with cookies and orange squash.

From the camp, Hammer and I drove the students south through the plains along the Mwaleshi River, where a thundering herd of almost a thousand buffaloes stampeded across the track in front of us. Farther on, at the confluence of the Mwaleshi and Luangwa rivers, we crept quietly to the bank above the water to see more than four hundred hooting, honking hippos, which made the kids giggle. While we lunched with the hippos Hammer quietly huddled with the children, explaining that someone could shoot and kill one of these beautiful animals only one time and benefit from doing so only once before it was gone forever. By keeping the animal alive, the people would benefit from it many times during its life by showing it to paying tourists. In this way, he told them, the animal could be worth much more to them alive than dead.

After lunch we drove through the mopane woodlands, looking for elephants. Wart hogs, zebras, waterbuck, and even a pride of lions showed themselves. But when I climbed onto the back of the truck to give them a little lesson on the habits of these animals, a little girl in a blue dress looked up at me and pleaded: "May we please see an elephant?"

Sadly, I explained that since poachers had killed almost all of

North Luangwa's elephants, we might not be able to see one that far from the sanctuary of Marula-Puku.

The sun was setting on the Muchinga Escarpment, so we turned around and began the long drive back to Mwamfushi village. As we drove north through mopane woodlands past the turnoff to Marula-Puku, I looked back through the cab's rear window into the Mog's bed. Most of the passengers were now wrapped up in their blankets against the relentless tsetse flies and billowing dust. But the girl in blue clutched the side of the lurching truck, her head sweeping back and forth, diligently scanning the landscape.

We were barreling around a turn in the track when suddenly he was directly in front of us, blocking out the mountains of the Muchinga and the setting sun. I slammed on the air brakes as Long Tail, the huge, tuskless bull elephant who often hung out in our camp, towered over our nine-foot-tall, eight-ton truck, shaking his head, flapping his ears, and blowing like a sounding whale.

I quickly switched off the Mog's diesel, leaned out my window, and warned my passengers: "Be perfectly quiet and still." And they were.

Long Tail shook his head and blew again, a cloud of dust snapping from his ears as he curled up his trunk to take our scent. And then, not fifteen feet from the little girl in blue, whose mouth hung open and whose eyes looked to be the size of billiard balls, he wrapped his trunk around the branch of a mopane tree, stripped its green leaves, and stuffed them into his mouth.

✍ THE NEXT MORNING, as we stood up from the breakfast table, I said to Delia: "Today I'm taking you somewhere special."

We packed a picnic basket with a couple of bottles of Boschendal wine, some smelly cheese from the bottom of the fridge, camp bread, resolidified chocolate, and other goodies saved too long for a special occasion. We tied up our sleeping bags and drove to the airstrip. There we put everything in the back seat of the chopper, climbed into our seats, and buckled up. Just before lifting off, I pulled a bandanna from the pocket of my vest and blindfolded her.

We took off and flew west toward the Muchinga Escarpment. At the scarp wall I pulled up the collective lever, adding more power, and we climbed to more than three thousand feet. We flew for another ten minutes, and as we passed directly over a mountain peak I told her to take off her blindfold. Almost two thousand feet below us and slightly to the left of the chopper's nose, a pristine river flowed through the miombo woodland until it reached a great tear in the western wall of the Rift Valley. There it plunged over a series of waterfalls, each like a giant stairstep, dropping nearly two thousand feet in a mile. With no roads, no villages, no development of any kind, the scene looked the way much of Africa did not so very long ago.

At the base of the first major waterfall, at the downstream edge of its plunge pool, the river flowed around a large dome of rock before pouring over the next falls. I had wanted to land there for a long time, but the rock was usually inundated with raging whitewater. On a recent flight, I had seen that the river had ebbed, exposing a nub of the boulder.

I lowered the collective, and we began descending.

"I don't see where we can land." Delia sat tall in her seat, her head against the Plexiglas.

"See that little rock right below the upper waterfall?"

"We can't land there — it's *tiny,* and there's water swirling all around it!"

"Just wait a minute; it'll get larger."

"Mark Owens, if we crash, you had better be dead, or I will kill you myself."

"Trust me."

A hundred feet above the river, I circled the upper waterfall, checked the wind, and began the landing approach, coming in from downstream, flying directly into the turbulent air. We came to a full-power hover over the rock, a dizzying cauldron of whitewater boiling and surging all around.

I slowly lowered the skids until they contacted the rock. But as I eased the helicopter down, it began to tilt back. I rose back up to a hover and tried landing in a slightly different place. This time the aircraft rolled to the left. Finally I turned the ship ninety degrees, held the controls off against the crosscurrents of air, and felt around with the skids until they nestled onto a dry, level spot. I slowly dropped the collective and cut the power. We popped the doors and stepped out into a cool, refreshing paradise.

The river thundered over the falls above us into the crystal-clear waters of the large pool at our feet, surged around the boulder, and then, a few feet downstream, plunged over the next falls, and the next, and the next. After the heat and tsetse flies of the valley, the refreshing breeze tinged with spray tingled on our cheeks and noses. Paradise flycatchers and Nysner lories flitted among the crowns of tall *Uapaca kirkiana* and *Combretum imberbe* trees standing along the banks of the pools, their lower branches draped with wisps and wigs of lichen. Thick, brilliant green mosses covered the rocks at their feet.

What had looked like a boulder from the air was really the back of a larger outcropping that had once formed a ledge across the river. Over time the rushing water had cut it down along both banks, so during the lowest flows of the dry season this small spot was left high and dry. In the rainy season the outcropping was submerged and hammered with a maelstrom of wild water that had augered deep, perfectly round hydraulic holes in the rock along the pool's edge. Those same floods had rounded the back of the outcropping so that it quickly dropped off on the downstream side. We walked hand in hand along its steepening back until we could see over it to the pool below the next falls.

Protected from crocodiles and hippos by the succession of waterfalls, we stripped at the edge of our pool and plunged into the cool, swirling water. For the rest of the day we swam, sunned, snacked, and swam again.

After the sun disappeared behind the peaks, I built a small fire. Its smoke, carried by a laminar flow of air over the rock, crawled like a white snake along the camber of the outcrop for about fifty feet, then plunged over the side to follow the river as it descended through the gorge.

Delia surprised me with a tin of the smoked oysters we kept for special occasions, or sometimes just to give us a sense of celebration.

As we sat back to back, she sighed.

"Mark, we can't go on keeping umpteen balls in the air and living on two to three hours of sleep every night. Let's let Hammer, Malcolm, and the rest of the guys handle the day-to-day running of the project so we can focus on our elephant research."

"That's a great idea. Why didn't you think of it before?"

"Really? Do you mean it?" She sat up and searched my eyes as though she could not really believe what I had said — because I had agreed to this so many times before. And always before, something, usually poachers, had gotten in the way. This time I was determined not to let that happen. We toasted our new direction with glasses of wine, and then, after the fire had died to coals, we spread out our sleeping bags and crawled inside. We lay on our backs listening to the sounds of the river and staring speechless at the full moon rising over the trees.

"Mark! I swear this rock is moving."

"You've had too much wine. Go to sleep." I pulled her close. And the rock really did move.

19 DELIA
When I Close My Eyes
I See Elephants

Find expression for a joy, and you will intensify its ecstasy.

— OSCAR WILDE

FOR YEARS I HAD had a little grass camp on the banks of the Luangwa River, from which I staged elephant walks on the east side of the park. Every woman should have her own camp.

Now it was to become home for Mark and me so we could concentrate on the elephant research. We would continue to work with Hammer on the village projects, but we could now turn over much of the logistics to Malcolm, Trish, Rex, Anne, and the rest of the team. First, though, Delia Camp, as everyone had called it, in spite of my insistence that its name was Nyama Zamara, had to be rebuilt. It had never been a fancy place, consisting only of my tent, a flat-topped grass shelter for cooking, another hut for storage, and a reed shower stall with a glorious view of the river. Now, after several years, the thatch was ragged and disheveled, making the small huts look like old haystacks. Bornface Zulu, my companion and guide on the elephant walks, assembled a team of workers from the villages to rebuild the camp. While he and his crew set to work building new huts, I continued to identify plants and age elephants. Mark stayed on in Marula-Puku, using the chopper to locate the elephants, until we could rebuild the shelters.

One morning, as I squatted to measure an elephant footprint on a sandbar, I heard the *whop-whop-whop* of the helicopter to the west. I switched on my radio, and Mark's voice crackled.

"Hey, Boo, I'm on my way to pick you up. I want to show you something."

I grabbed my daypack and trotted toward the riverbank. Just as I reached the edge of camp, the chopper settled onto the landing spot we had cleared. The freshly cut grass spiraled up in the rotor wash and blew around like a green blizzard. Lowering my head and shielding my face from the debris, I ran toward the chopper and hopped in. The glistening river and emerald lagoon fell away below us as we lifted.

Putting on my helmet, I asked over the intercom, "So what's this about?"

"Just wait. You're not going to believe it." He smiled at me. Flying over the rain-drenched plains, we spotted herds of zebra and buffalo as we flew north.

"There. Look up there." Mark pointed through the bubble window to a large green plain that sprawled for miles between two rivers.

Elephants — hundreds of elephants, long meandering lines of elephants — moved across the grassy savanna in a mass of gray, swaying bodies. It was a congregation of elephant families, melded together on the vast succulent plains, where they munched rich grasses. It was a scene once common in Africa, but we had never seen it before. North Luangwa had not seen it for years. During the poaching war the elephants had avoided the plains, where they were easy targets.

Small families of four to six elephants and many single moms with tiny infants kept their identities as distinct units. They did not quite mingle with other groups, but the family units fed within fifty yards of one another. Surviving orphans, who made up 9 percent of the population, still foraged alone, but they were *close* to other elephants. For a social animal to be rejoined with such a massive herd after years of being alone must have eased some longing. I risk being anthropomorphic, but I choose to believe that some type of joy spread among those souls. Youngsters frolicked about on small meadows; teenage bulls sparred with their tiny tusks; older, tuskless males, like Cheers, strutted their stuff with hunched backs and streaming scent glands.

We flew on and on, watching and counting more than five hundred elephants, taking notes and photos, recording the GPS readings and habitat types. But mostly I allowed myself to absorb this glorious moment and all it meant for the earth.

Five hundred elephants congregating on a plain was not confirmation that the Luangwa population had suddenly recovered from the slaughter. Only fifteen years earlier twelve thousand elephants would have gathered on this same plain. Indeed, our aerial censuses still showed that the total number of elephants had increased only slightly. But it was a good sign that they felt secure in the open terrain and that at least some aspects of their lives could return to normal, which might translate into more successful reproduction and the beginning of a recovery.

We tracked them from the air every day. We located the radio-collared families and noted their positions in relation to other groups. One day we landed near the herd and camped in a dense clump of trees next to a small stream. There we were able to age 260 elephants. Their energy, sounds, and pungent smells hung thickly on the hot air, and at night, instead of a few calls drifting on the wind, a chorus of trumpets resounded across the valley.

All the camp elephants had left Marula-Puku, and we guessed that they had joined the assembly. On every flight I searched for Survivor, Cheers, Gift, and her offspring. I imagined Long Tail attempting to impress females, Stumpie picking fights with other males. When elephants interact with one another, sometimes their facial scent glands secrete so much moisture they seem to be crying. I wished I could have seen the faces of Gift's calves, who had spent all their lives in their own small family, when they encountered five hundred elephants moving together through the grass.

After we camped with the elephants, Mark dropped me off at Delia Camp and returned to Marula-Puku to enter the data on the computer. I ate cornbread and cabbage alone on the riverbank, watching the hippos and listening to the barks of the baboon troop in the distance. Something about seeing the elephants joining with their own kind had made me happy but had also left me melancholy. The Southern Cross seemed dimmer than usual, its stars lost among the strays of the Milky Way's tail.

Later, when I closed my eyes to sleep inside my little pup tent, I saw elephants behind my eyelids, and I knew that in the morning they would still be there.

The new grass huts grew every day like birds' nests. Soon the men had completed the pole frames and raftered ceilings and had built a corral of thorn bushes as a hyena-proof hangar for the chopper. I counted the days until Mark and I could live here with elephants.

20 MARK

A DANCE WITH SURVIVOR

Wonders happen if we can succeed
in passing through the harshest danger;
but only in a bright and purely granted
achievement can we realize the wonder.

— RAINER MARIA RILKE

EARLY ONE MORNING I left Delia in her new, unfinished camp on the Luangwa and flew back to Marula-Puku, where I ate breakfast in the n'saka. Shortly I would begin loading the Unimog with drums of jet fuel and other supplies we needed to live at Delia Camp.

At Marula-Puku the ground was covered with a carpet of yellow marula fruits, so I had plenty of company around my table. The Kakule Club buffaloes lazed about the kitchen area, some sleeping, others still stuffing themselves. On the footpath near our office cottage Survivor, the young bull elephant with the hole in his left ear, plugged fruits into his mouth, his ears sweeping back and forth contentedly. Years earlier, in the midst of the intense struggle against ivory poachers, he had been the first elephant to sense sanctuary in our camp, the first to accept us. But then, mere yards from here, a gang of poachers had shot and killed one from his group, and for months, while the elephants avoided camp, we thought it had been him. Now he was still somewhat shy, less inclined to come as close to us as he had before, curling his trunk and sometimes his tail, holding up a foot, and even mock-charging when we came too near. But as he came into camp to feed every day, his fear of us was slowly ebbing.

After finishing my last mug of coffee in the n'saka, I got up to walk to the office. Survivor was still standing across the footpath, sweeping his trunk over the ground in search of fruits, and I walked slowly toward him, subtly asking him to move aside. He merely cranked up his tail slightly and continued feeding, the hollow *swoosh* of his breath sounding through his trunk as it swept the ground. He watched me carefully, easily, with his left eye.

I was within thirty feet of him. We had not been this close in a very long time, and I was not sure how he would react. He turned directly toward me and raised his trunk, his eyes a little wider, his tail a little more curled as he lifted his left front leg and held it off the ground, rocking forward and back, unsure of what to do. I raised my right hand and reached out to him. He stepped toward me, laid his ears back, raised his head, and arched his trunk forward. I reached as high as I could, until the tip of his trunk was only a foot or two from my fingers and I could feel his breath. Then, like two dance partners we pirouetted around each other for perhaps half a circle. It lasted only a few seconds, just long enough for me to feel again a rare and special bond and an awe that I have felt only when close to sensitive creatures of other social species, whether lions, brown hyenas, Cape hunting dogs, or elephants. As though realizing that he had done something foolish, Survivor snatched back his trunk, blew out my scent, and shook his head until his ears flapped. Then he turned and walked away.

◈ As we strolled along the tree-lined boulevard from our hotel to the conference center one morning in November 1994, the caress of the sweet Florida sea breeze against my cheek seemed seductive after the dry heat of Africa. Our studies of the North Luangwa elephants, one of the most heavily poached populations in Africa, had shown not only how devastating poaching had been but also how well the ivory ban was working. The ban had lowered the black-market price of ivory and had thus severely curbed poaching, giving the elephant populations an opportunity to recover. Because of our research work, Delia and I had been invited to join six people from Zambia's Department of National Parks, the Anti-Corruption Commission, and the Ministry of Tourism as that country's delegates to the United Nations Convention on the International Trade in Endangered Species (CITES) meeting in Fort Lauderdale. For eleven long days and nights, with delegates from 112 other nations, we listened to lectures and paged through a thick catalogue of briefs describing the threatened or endangered state of listed species — including *Loxodonta africana,* the African savanna elephant — before voting on whether or not each species could sustain a resumption of trade.

Despite the devastation by heavy poaching, Zambia still had one of the largest elephant populations, so the collective voice of its candidates would carry considerable weight in the debate on whether to continue a strict moratorium on the trade in elephant products. Some countries, such as Zimbabwe and South Africa, wanted to resume the ivory trade, claiming that they needed money from the sale of tusks to support conservation. But historically the legal trade had been used to cover an illegal one. In fact, before the ban, up to 90 percent of the ivory sold legally on the world market was actually from illegally shot elephants. In other words, if you bought ten ivory bracelets at any shop in the world, nine of them would likely have come from poached elephants.

Because the ivory ban was so hotly debated, the elephant vote was left until the very last day of the conference. Tensions among delegates in the ivory "working groups" were running high. At one point a Tanzanian delegate demanded that delegates from Burundi, who were lobbying to sell their stockpiled ivory, explain how they could have such a stockpile when the country had no surviving elephants.

The night before the vote, our delegation stayed up until early morning writing Zambia's position paper. The next afternoon, Henry Mwimwa, National Parks' astute chief research officer, read it to the CITES General Assembly. In the paper our team argued strongly that the moratorium on the ivory trade should be extended, not just for two years but for up to ten, to give elephant populations time to recover; we suggested that dissenting nations with less than 2 percent of the continent's elephants were trying to establish a trade policy that would jeopardize the other 98 percent of the elephants. The convention voted with an overwhelming majority to continue the ban until the next CITES meeting, in two years.

Shortly after the CITES meeting, our testimony citing the results of our studies and their implications for elephant conservation were read before a United States congressional hearing attended by major international "ivory interests," some lobbying to resume the trade. These groups began intensifying their efforts to undermine our work.

WE HAD JUST sat down for a midmorning tea break by the river in Marula-Puku when a truck with government license plates rolled to a stop near our radio room. Two Zambians, city-dressed in slacks and dress shirts, got out. A cold cramp knotted my gut when the one with a twisted smile and a pit bull's face introduced himself as Romance Musangu, chief of security for the highest office in the land. He was "one of the Big Boys from Lusaka" that Talky, our informant, had warned me about, maybe even *the* kingpin in the web of officially sponsored commercial poaching that had targeted the park. He and his "assistant" had come to "visit" the North Luangwa Conservation Project.

Government dignitaries had often visited before; over the years we had entertained the minister of tourism, the director of wildlife, members of Parliament, numerous permanent secretaries, and local tribal chiefs. Only months before I had flown then president Chiluba to several villages during his reelection campaign. We kept our host government up to date on our activities at all times.

But this visit was different. Musangu wanted to see everything, including our office, bedroom, dining, and kitchen cottages. His eyes lit up when he saw our trucks, the motor grader, and especially the Cessna. When I rolled back the heavy door to the helicopter hangar, he gasped, "Ah, but that is a very beautiful machine!" He seemed to be making a mental inventory of everything he saw.

We invited the men to stay for lunch — what else could we do? — and while they sat in our n'saka by the river, I excused myself briefly and hurried to the kitchen, where Delia was chopping onions. I took her firmly by the arm and led her into the pantry, where we could not be seen.

"Be very careful!" I hissed. "These guys are not our friends. I'll explain later." Her face masked in fear, she tried to ask a question.

"Later! Just be careful, that's all! Let's just feed them lunch and try to get them out of here." I hurried back to our guests with a tray of cool water and orange squash while Delia and Kasokola broiled a chicken in a three-legged cast-iron pot, boiled cabbage, beans, and onions in gravy, and steamed mealie meal to make nshima.

Over lunch, Musangu's narrow eyes held mine in conversation, but I had the feeling he was seeing way beyond me to the camp buildings strung out along the river, as though making a mental map of its layout. Soon after they finished eating, they drove hurriedly out of camp, as we stood on the riverbank wondering — and worrying — about the meaning of this strange visit.

Two days later Talky arrived from Mpika in one of our project trucks. I had not seen him for a long time and was immediately concerned that he would jeopardize our clandestine relationship — and his own security — by showing up in camp where our Zambian workers would see him.

We had barely sat down in the n'saka before he began: "Sir, you and Dr. Delia are in very much danger. You can be put in prison or even killed anytime from now." Without touching the tea I had fixed him, he leaned forward in his chair and went on to tell me that high-level officials in Lusaka were upset because the project had shut down poaching and they could no longer get ivory or game meat from North Luangwa. Working through Banda Famwila, the Parks regional field commander in Mpika, they were planning to put an end to the project one way or another.

"Look, we've been through this sort of thing for years," I said, trying to brush off his warning.

"No, sir, this time is different. You must take care. Believe me. Bwana Musangu is a very powerful man. He even reaches the very top." And he named other officials who had been mentioned many times by our friends in the Anti-Corruption Commission. Then I knew he was right to worry.

I decided not to tell Delia of Talky's warning, at least not until she had had a little time to enjoy her new camp. We were scheduled to fly to the United States on leave in a few days; maybe I would tell her then.

21 DELIA

GRASS HUTS AND
LEOPARD STUMPS

When it is dark enough, you can see the stars.
— CHARLES BEARD

MY TENT SHOOK. A lioness was slithering along the back wall, bumping the canvas with a swishing sound. An entire pride — ten lions — had walked into Delia Camp, where several Bembas and I were finishing up the straw huts. As usual, I had camped some distance away from the men. As usual, I regretted that decision.

Bornface and I had first seen the lions about a week before, lying along the riverbank at sunrise, their paws hanging over the edge, folded neatly. Heads swinging in unison, back and forth, back and forth, they had tracked us from about two hundred yards away as we built the camp. It was a group of females with their cubs. And since these lions had a social system similar to that of the East African lions, they were probably close relatives who had been together since birth, raising their cubs, hunting, hanging out on the beach — a typical mammalian social group. As with the female baboons and elephants, the lions derived advantages from being in a group of close relatives: as a team, the cats could bring down larger prey, communally suckle their young, defend a larger territory. And the fact that they were related meant that all these advantages were bestowed on their kin. No adult males were in sight. They would come and go, as male lions are wont to do, fighting for tenure, showing up for supper, or to copulate.

164

We came upon the lionesses again when Bornface and I walked to the lagoon one morning to watch a pair of fish eagles. The lions had climbed up on a good-size termite mound. It was about eight feet tall and fifteen feet wide at its base, but not nearly large enough for ten lions. The cats made a game of it, like kids playing king of the hill. There was not a square inch of the white, dusty hump that was not covered with paw, tail, or chin as the cats perched on the top, clung to the sides, and curled about the bottom.

And now, at eight-thirty at night, I listened to the lionesses pacing back and forth behind my tent. The lazy moon would not rise until after ten o'clock, so camp was dark except for my little flashlight beam bouncing around the shadows, illuminating one blond body after another. Ears erect, tail lashing about, each one walked about ten steps east, whirled around, and walked back again, sniffing the ground like a bloodhound. As always, the cats wore their thoughts on their tails: agitated, alert, definitely curious, probably hungry. This was not good. One lioness could topple my tent with a single blow; ten could demolish it like tissue paper — with me wrapped inside. They were not simply passing by, satisfying their curiosity. They were focused on my tent.

I sat in my small folding safari chair for more than an hour, listening to the lions, loving it and hating it at the same time. Meanwhile, the hippos sounded as if they were having a small war down by the river. Their loud splashing sounds and territorial roars mingled with the soft footfalls of lion paws. Great night out.

One lioness stopped just outside the flimsy gauze window. I stood inside, just out of view. She lifted her huge head until her nose was only one foot from my stomach. Nothing between us but cheap canvas — not even the rip-proof variety. Not daring to shout for Bornface, I waited. The frames of the new huts stood around my tent like reed-and-pole skeletons in the dim light.

I heard a muffled sound — like a cough — from the direction of the men's camp. The lionesses jerked their heads in that direction and trotted toward the noise. As soon as they left, I called out: "BORNFACE. CAN YOU HEAR ME? THERE ARE LIONS OVER HERE."

"Yes, madame," came the reply. "They are here also."

"What should we do?"

"We'll come to you once they leave our place." I could hear the men shooing the lionesses with shouts and saw their flashlights playing in the darkness. In a moment he continued, "We are coming to you, Dr. Delia."

I waited anxiously, and in a few minutes I could see a tight wad of men wobbling toward me, shining their lights in all directions. Finally they reached the door of my tent, and I stepped out. The tightness in my chest loosened — *my pride*, my side, had arrived.

"Thanks, guys. Is everybody okay?"

"Yes, madame, but these lions are very dangerous. They have been circling our camp for many times now."

"Let's move your camp over here," I suggested. "We can set your tents up inside the new huts. It'll be safer."

Scouring the bushes with our lights, we went to their camp, grabbed armloads of gear, and carried it back to my area. Looking for the lionesses all the while, we rigged the men's tents inside the pole frames, which were at least partly secured by the incomplete reed walls. The moon had risen by now, and we built a bonfire. The lionesses were nowhere to be seen, but we guessed they were still nearby, watching us with their keen amber eyes. For curious creatures this commotion was too good to miss.

When we had settled down in our tents, I listened for the sounds of soft paws plodding through the brush, but the only night noises were the throaty chuckles of hippos. Then, just when all was quiet, the lions walked into camp again. They stood no more than fifteen yards from my tent, and all ten bellowed forth with full roars. I laughed with the hippos now that I felt safe and thought of other lion times.

Among the shadowy dunes and white-hot sands of the Kalahari we had studied lions for more than seven years. Following their low-slung tawny bodies through the long grass as they hunted or watching them from behind a tree as they raided camp, we got to know the lionesses of the Blue Pride. We had our share of exciting moments with the lions, but what we remember best are the quiet times: the long hours of waiting with them for the Kalahari heat to break, for the slow-moving sun to finally sink behind the dunes, when the lions would begin their night shift. Many late afternoons found us waiting with the lions in some isolated spot, sharing the same lean shade of a twisted thorn tree, all of us lethargic, torpid, lightheaded, comatose. The Kalahari heat is a great equalizer, reducing all creatures to a sluggish heap.

At first we would sit in the truck with the windows open, under a tree close to the lions, and wait for them to stir. But the shade of Kalahari thorn trees is as thin as lace, and the sun always burned its way through the roof of the truck. Soon we would open the doors quietly, begging for a breeze. Then, if the lions' shade was better than ours, we would drive over and park near them, opening the doors as wide as they would go. Inevitably the lions would rise slowly, one by one and, as if they were sleep-walking, stagger over and plop down in the shade of the truck, lined up like so many throw rugs. Eventually, after years of sun-waiting, we found we could slide out of our truck and sit on the ground near them.

Late one afternoon the temperature seemed stuck at 120 degrees, and the air was almost too hot to breathe. Mark and I slid out from his side of the truck, away from the lions, and sat on the white sand. Happy, Blue, Sassy, and Chary of the Blue Pride were sleeping under a scraggly acacia bush about thirty feet away. Not a tail or an ear twitched as we moved to the ground. No one cared. The sand did not seem much cooler than the truck, but when we dribbled water from the canteen over our heads, the slight breeze brought goose bumps to our skin. As we wet our T-shirts and breathed in deeply, the moisture on our chests reached inside to cool our bodies. The lionesses had not had a drink of water for six months, getting the moisture they needed only from their prey or wild melons. I wished we could pass the canteen around the circle.

After a few minutes Happy stirred. She lifted her head and, through half-closed lizardlike eyelids, gazed at the truck. Nothing in her features expressed surprise or even awareness that we had entered her space on the sand. She worked her rough tongue over dry lips several times, then stood and took a step toward us. We were quite unprepared for this, and our bodies must have tensed slightly as we stared at her. She walked toward the truck and seemed to be heading for the rear bumper, which would take her on a path no more than two yards from us. We didn't move as we watched her giant paws lift and drop in the loose sand, her large head hanging low and relaxed. At one point her paw landed no more than an arm's reach from Mark's boots. She never looked at us but strolled to the back of the truck and stretched out under the bumper, her face turned away. I could count the individual hairs of her ear tuft. Turn up the heat; we will stay here forever. What does comfort matter with a lion at your toes?

Over the years we discovered that the social system of Kalahari lions was somewhat different than that of lions elsewhere. Yes, they lived in tightly knit prides of lionesses with their cubs and various consorts of unrelated males fighting for possession of the pride every few years. But when severe drought hit the desert and most of the large-bodied prey scattered into herd fragments over thousands of square miles, the prides of mothers, grandmothers, sisters, and female cousins disbanded. No longer able to find hefty gemsbok or stately eland, they hunted smaller prey — hares and guinea fowl — in pairs, then finally solitarily. Sassy, who for years had slept, groomed, and played with her pridemates every day, now stood alone on the dune top cooing into the harsh wind. Before the drought Spicy or Happy would have answered her call and sidled up to her, and the two would have rubbed their long bodies together from nose to tail.

But now no one answered her *coo*, and Sassy fed that night on wild tsama melons and old bones. Eventually the former pridemates dispersed over hundreds of square miles, some of them never seeing each other again, as far as we knew.

Years later, when the rains came again and the grasses greened, herds of two thousand springbok and five hundred gemsbok dotted the plains once more. Wandering lions came together and formed groups in order to bring down the large prey. But, breaking all rules of lion society, they did not necessarily rejoin their relatives. Raking in strays from the distant dunes, a female here, a female there, they came together to form new prides. Sometimes — many times — when you're out in the desert in need of a friend, any group is better than none.

   SLEEPY-EYED, but more enthusiastic than ever to finish the huts of Delia Camp, the men and I roused ourselves before dawn. They crawled quietly over and through the pole frames, securing the crossbeams and rafters with strips of bark. One stalk at a time, they wove the bright red and green reeds tightly into very strong walls with twine. They tied long grass stems into thick bundles and threw them higgledy-piggledy onto the rafters, where one man straightened and fastened them into a rather floppy thatch.

As the days went by, each Bemba wove his imagination into the tying, twisting, and thatching, so that the huts acquired their own bush character. It was impossible for the men to simply bind a reed into place. Using bark, Jackson Kasokola made large cross-stitches on every two feet of wall, adding a bold geometric pattern to the exterior and interior. Bornface added his signature by bending reeds into arches and lashing them to the hip roofs. Patrick Mwamba outdid everyone by braiding three different species of grass stalks together into long garlands that framed the windows and doors.

We stood back to admire their handiwork. The bedroom hut, only five yards from the high riverbank, encircled a massive *Trichilia* tree. On three sides it was made of golden bamboo stalks held together with ropy red bark in large X patterns. The third wall, facing the river, had a large open window that offered a view of the slow-moving current and the distant shore. The branches of the tree spread like arms across the room and served as shelves for the water basin, books, and binoculars. A colorful cloth woven and dyed by Bisa women was draped across the bed, which was shrouded in an enormous mosquito net.

The dining and office huts were also built around large trees overlooking the river. I radioed Mark that at last the camp was finished and he should come home. He answered that he would be there by late afternoon.

✍ I PLANNED a candlelight dinner: smoked oysters on crackers, a mock cottage pie made from baked beans, seasoned with piri-piri sauce and topped with mashed potatoes, and bread freshly baked in the black pot. By midafternoon I had completed the preparations. Sitting on the riverbank, I watched my favorite soap opera: the troop of baboons, who were scattered across the beach on the opposite shore.

A young female sashayed away from her troopmates toward a small, shallow pool tucked behind an old fallen tree, which formed a formidable fort against crocodiles. The Luangwa River swarms with one of Africa's highest densities of Nile crocodiles, but this little unnamed pool was a safe place to drink, and Ms. Baboon knew it. No doubt she had known it all of her life, having learned it from her elders.

Hesitating only briefly, she knelt to drink, her backside sticking up, tail elbowed down. After a few moments, she sauntered back toward her troop, which was moving slowly into the forest. As she left the beach, she passed an old stump tucked under a shrub and overgrown with dried grass. It looked very much like the straw-colored mane and head of a lion peeping from the undergrowth. But this stump had mimicked a lion's head for years, as long as I had been here, so neither the baboons nor I were fooled. None of the troop members wasted precious foraging moments by stopping to investigate the harmless stump and establish whether it was carnivore or grass. Knowing that a lump is not a lion reduces stress.

Suddenly, several of the baboons halted on the edge of the trees, forming a tighter group. Using my binoculars, I saw a strange form hunkered low to the ground under a bush. A few of the baboons began barking alarm calls. Some of the others rushed over to the mystery bump, while two large males bounded back and forth to get a better view. Long moments — precious feeding time — were spent as they shouted and sprang about, gathering data but also presenting a confused target to the possible predator. At last it became apparent that the lump was a freshly fallen tree limb bent in a weird leopardlike shape complete with spots of bark.

As the commotion died down and the primates moved on, the landmark was unconsciously sketched on their mental maps and mine: "This bump is not a leopard but a tree limb." Never again would they have to stop and investigate that fallen branch. Knowing that a limb is not a leopard is part of being home.

If this troop were suddenly transported to a different valley or a distant forest, all of the baboons would have to draw a map of the new neighborhood in their minds. Lion-looking stumps covered with weeds would have to be investigated one by one and plotted on their charts — and Africa's bush sprouts many, many stumps pretending to be lions. Diagrams scrawled in some primitive, wordless language would register: this waterhole dries up early; this floodplain has good grass during the rains. The survey would take years, as they roamed and searched for the closest Starbucks or the best salad bar in the unfamiliar suburb. Mapping one's range is an expensive endeavor, costing precious time and energy, high risks, and unpleasant emotions. In a new place the sense of security felt by Ms. Baboon as she knelt to drink at the familiar pool would be lost. She would rarely feel safe from lurking predators or lingering starvation. All of the troop members would be a bit more jumpy, and they would probably enjoy less quality beach time together. Mothers might be less attentive to infants; males might fight more often; adolescents might disperse sooner; single moms and gangs of young males might become more common; families might break apart. Of course, baboons and most other animals are smart enough not to leave their homes in the first place unless they are forced to do so.

However these concepts are formed in the mind, research has shown that being aware of the riches and dangers of the home range is one of the most ancient and primitive of all animal sensations. Feelings born of mapped spaces and familiar faces make a place into what we call home, and it has been a deep part of almost every creature on Earth, including ourselves, for a long time.

🖉 MARK ARRIVED in the late afternoon. I showed him around the newly constructed huts, pointing out Jackson's artwork and Bornface Zulu's hip roofs.

Later we sat at our little dining table, our faces reflecting the candlelight, and watched the ripples of the river swish against the faces of moonlit hippos. Every minute of our lives, every lion we had seen, every campfire we had shared, seemed to have led us to this place at this moment. The poaching had stopped, the village programs were working well, and the elephants were poised to make a comeback. Buffaloes, hippos, and elephants had been sighted in areas where they had not been seen in twenty years. We had a great staff living in Mpika and Marula-Puku to manage the project. Perhaps we could breathe more easily and laugh more often. We talked about how we would locate the radio-collared elephants and follow them on foot. We planned to dart and collar more of them. As the moon shadows embraced the river beaches and stretched their arms toward our shore, an elephant trumpeted in the distance.

Clinking our enamel mugs together, we toasted the elephants. We had no way of knowing that after nearly a quarter of a century, this would be our last night in the African bush for a long, long time.

22 DELIA

CAMP ARREST

I envy the animals two things — their ignorance of evil to
come, and their ignorance of what is said about them.

—VOLTAIRE

"WHAT'S THAT?" I sat upright, my eyes searching the strange dark
room. The clock read 4:30 A.M. A phone was ringing. Why? We had
lived without telephones for more than twenty years. I hated their in-
trusive ring-anytime-they-please sound.

Mark leaped from the bed. I ran after him into another room
and switched on the light. Yellow and cheerful, my mother's kitchen
on plumb and nelly street in Americus, Georgia, popped into view.

"Yes, Malcolm," Mark answered, "I hear you. Go ahead." I slid to
the floor, my back against the cabinets, and stared at Mark. Malcolm,
our project manager, would not call at 4:30 A.M. unless something really bad was happening.

After our night in Delia Camp, we had left as scheduled on our
annual leave in Europe and the States to raise money for the project.
As we learned from Malcolm's call, a few days later, at ten in the
morning, his wife, Trish, who supervised the educational program,
heard a commotion outside their house in Mpika and ran to a window. A large flatbed truck loaded with armed men roared into their
yard. Brandishing AK-47 automatic rifles and wearing an assortment
of patched-up drab green fatigues and scruffy boots, they jumped
from the bed of the truck and jogged into positions surrounding the
house. Trish picked up her baby son and ran to the front door and
locked it. Ronnie Hadley, who had shared the sacred dances of the

Katibunga women with me, was also in the house. Malcolm was in Lusaka on a supply run.

One of the men banged on the front door. Trish handed the baby to Ronnie and motioned for her to take him to the back room. Trish stepped onto the porch and demanded to know what they wanted. The man said he had orders from the field commander of National Parks, Banda Famwila, to hold everyone on the project under house arrest and seize its equipment. Trish, a Zambian citizen, knew most of the local game scouts by name. They often came to her house or the project office for fuel allotments, patrol food, or medicines. But she did not recognize the man who stood at the door or any of the others.

"Do you have a warrant?" she asked.

"No, we do not need a warrant. We are on official business."

Calmly but firmly, she told him that they could not put one foot inside her house without a warrant. "Zambia is a country with laws," she said, and stepped inside and locked the door. He shouted that he would return with official documents, then drove away, leaving the ragtag posse patrolling the garden. Malcolm returned to Mpika that afternoon to find his house surrounded by armed guards.

At about the same time that these men surrounded the Boultons' house, Hammer rode his motorbike to the project's office — a cream-colored building painted with dramatic gold and black patterns — and found strangers milling about the doors. The keys for the trucks, the checkbook, the documents — everything he needed to conduct the village projects — were locked inside, but another band of men refused to let Hammer enter.

✍ FOR YEARS the game warden and others had warned us that Field Commander Famwila, working in league with his superiors in Lusaka, would try to end our project so that they could return to elephant poaching. Now that the villagers had become fish farmers and millers, the smugglers had no one to hire to shoot the elephants. The illicit trafficking of ivory had dwindled to a trickle. For their dirty business to continue, the project had to be stopped. Famwila and Musangu had obviously planned this illegal seizure for some time; the game warden, the magistrate, and most of the senior game scouts, all of whom had worked closely with our project for years, were in Lusaka for a meeting. As soon as we left for the States, the commander moved to end our project and take over all of its assets.

After hearing this news from Malcolm, we phoned the American ambassador to Zambia and explained what had happened. He knew our project well, having visited our camp and the village programs. Ambassador Kutchel was also well aware of our long-standing difficulties with Famwila and Musangu, but this time they had gone too far. Ronnie Hadley was a Peace Corps volunteer seconded to the project, and she had been put under house arrest by a band of paramilitaries. The ambassador firmly demanded that the Zambian authorities release Malcolm, Trish, their baby, and Ronnie. The senior bureaucrats with whom he spoke apparently knew nothing about the illegal seizure and house arrest, which made it seem even more likely that Famwila, Musangu, and several other higher-level officials were acting on their own.

Night fell in Mpika with Trish, Malcolm, Ronnie, and the baby huddled inside their small brick house while armed men skulked through the garden, trampling the poinsettias and moonflowers. No one slept except the guards. The next morning they refused to allow Malcolm or Trish to go to the open market for supplies for the baby.

My mother had been quietly offering us food, coffee, and soft smiles since the first phone call. "John Pope is Jimmy Carter's best friend, and I've known John all my life. I could get you a meeting with Jimmy."

Several hours later we sat next to former president Carter on his living room sofa in Plains, Georgia. Open on his lap was a large picture album, showing our village outreach programs, our game scout assistance, our elephant research. He nodded as we told him about the illegal ivory trade and the corrupt individuals who had been put out of business as poaching decreased. My mother looked on, rocking gently in a chair across the room.

"I know the president of Zambia," the president said. "I can't promise anything, but I'll do what I can."

THE NEXT NIGHT at 11:00 P.M. a truck rushed into Marula-Puku. Rex Haylock, the general manager for the project, and his wife, Anne, sat up in their bed. They were now living in our camp as they prepared to take on more of the logistical problems so that we would be free to study elephants from Delia Camp. The driver slammed on the brakes only feet from their cottage windows, and twelve men piled out, eerily backlit through the dust swirling in the headlights as they waved their weapons and shouted. Rex hurried out to meet the men, and Patrick Mwamba, Jackson Kasokola, Bornface Zulu, and the other Bemba tribesmen, many of whom had worked with us for ten years, crept from their cottages and watched quietly from the shadows, holding their axes loosely at their sides.

The group leader curtly told Rex and Anne that they were confined to camp and that if they attempted "escape," they would "be restrained." After demanding food and lodging for his men, he and two others pushed their way into our stone and thatch cottage and began rummaging through files and journals. The only documents that interested them were the truck maintenance records. An hour later they shrugged their shoulders and returned the data books to Anne.

AFTER THAT first phone call, we had not slept. We wanted to go back to Zambia immediately, but the ambassador advised that since a few high-level officials had taken such extreme — and illegal — action against our project, it would not be safe to return. Calling everyone who could help, we secured as much support as possible to free our friends and the project. Five embassies were now involved.

On the third day of the house arrests, some out-of-town friends
— one Zambian, one Canadian — who were totally unaware of these
events, arrived at Malcolm and Trish's house for a previously scheduled party for the baby's first birthday. The guards promptly put
them under house arrest as well and impounded their vehicle.

A few hours later an American embassy diplomat phoned Malcolm to say that a truck was on its way from Peace Corps headquarters to free Ronnie and drive her to Lusaka. He added that the next
morning officials from the American embassy and the British High
Commission would arrive by plane to demand the Boultons' release.

That afternoon the Peace Corps representatives drove into the
yard. Presenting official documents, complete with stamps and signa-
tures, they told the guards that they were taking Ronnie and her belongings. The guards still did not have a warrant, so they did not try
to stop the officials as they escorted Ronnie, who had helped train
the midwives of Katibunga and knew many of the babies by name,
through the garden gate laden with flowering bougainvillea and honeysuckle.

The next morning a large prop plane swooped low over the tiled
roofs of Mpika. Malcolm ran outside and told the guards that American and British diplomats had arrived and that he was going to the
airfield to collect them. He drove off before they could say a word.

At the airstrip an entourage from the two embassies as well as a
Zambian attorney disembarked from the plane. Malcolm drove them
and several policemen to the office of Field Commander Famwila and
told him that everyone was to be released. His bluff was over.

The diplomats then flew to Marula-Puku and secured the release of Anne and Rex. Malcolm called us to say that all of them were
safely in Lusaka.

⚬ THE ZAMBIAN GOVERNMENT was not responsible for the
attempted takeover of our project. Only a few corrupt but powerful
individuals from the Chiluba administration were involved. Several

years later, in a concerted effort to clean up corruption, President Mwanawasa fired many dishonest civil servants and jailed others, including some of those who had sought to destroy our project. But in 1996, when this incident occurred, those men were still in office. We had worked closely and extremely well with many Zambian officials for years, so we did not want to speak out against the government in general. The Ministry of Tourism, which had issued permits for us to conduct the project for ten years, said we could continue our work. Even after all that had happened, Malcolm, Trish, Rex, and Anne were prepared to return to Mpika and Marula-Puku, and Hammer wanted to go on working with the villages. However, the U.S. ambassador advised us that since the people who orchestrated the illegal action were still in powerful positions, it would not be safe for us to return to Zambia.

All was set to continue, but when Malcolm and Trish returned to Mpika they found that Famwila had illegally seized much of our equipment, including trucks, the grader, radios, and computers. Hammer found that the project office was once again locked. Mpika is in the far north of the country, and there was no one to stop Famwila.

Every day we spent hours calling across the Atlantic on lines hissing with static, trying to reclaim the project. The police confiscated some of our equipment from the field commander and held it for us, but some of it disappeared. Now that Malcolm, Trish, and the others were safe it was more difficult to get the embassies involved. Weeks went by, then months. While the village farmers waited for seeds and the game scouts waited for diesel fuel, negotiations between international attorneys and officials bogged down over words and phrases. It became impossible for Malcolm, Trish, Rex, and Anne to conduct the project, and eventually they had to leave to find other employment.

Many of the farmers and small business people we had helped no longer needed outside assistance, but some still needed logistical support and loans, and hundreds of others had asked to join the programs. We were sure Hammer could continue to expand the village work, but we could not find him. As far as we knew, there were no trucks or even bicycles to support the village work — all had disappeared. We tried again and again to reach Hammer by fax, phone, and mail, but we could not get through.

It seemed that the ivory dealers had finally succeeded in closing down the project. I imagined Mary Chongo needing fabric for her sewing business but having no way to transport it from Mpika. The school in Fulaza would need books and paper. The midwives would need supplies, the farmers new seeds, the millers more diesel, but there was no way to help them. Famwila could continue to supply guns and ammunition to the villagers who did not have other jobs.

Like Gift, our dreams and efforts had become an ivory orphan.

23 MARK

ADRIFT

See? See? That's what you'll get! There isn't a tribe for
you anymore!
— WILLIAM GOLDING

I HAD NOT BEEN BACK to the farm where I grew up for years.
Now, driving a rental car and pulling a U-Haul loaded with the bits
and pieces of our lives in Africa, we turned onto County Road J-6.
It had been paved long ago, and the farmers had taken down most
of the fences and plowed out the hedgerows bordering their fields,
which now crowded the asphalt on either side. Without hedgerows,
farming is closer to the bone, for every square foot of arable land that
would otherwise serve as windbreaks and wildlife habitat is tilled.
The gusty wind whipped up clouds of topsoil from plowed fields this
spring day, casting it into the sallow yellow sky.

As we crossed the railroad tracks and drove along the county
road I slowed down; everything seemed somehow familiar but foreign at the same time. Our neighbors' fields were smaller than I remembered, and their farm buildings closer together — as though the
land had shrunk.

On a low hill across the fields near Swan Creek stood Fulton
Union Church, white and pretty; when I was a kid, its steeple seemed
almost near enough to our house that I could have hit it with a baseball from the yard. We stopped at its small, tidy graveyard to share
some memories with my parents and other relatives buried there.

Standing at the foot of Dad and Mother's graves for the first
time ever, I felt the lead weight of despair and a perfect darkness

where their light had always been. But I knew at once, as though they had willed it, that this shadow, this drought, would be washed away by fresh drops of rain sweeping across my landscapes, my rivers and forests. I knew that I would never again watch a skein of geese headed south in an autumn sky or see fresh snow on a meadow or the lights in an old farmhouse at dusk without remembering my father's crooked pipe and impish smile and my mother's sweet, sad eyes and soothing embrace.

And then we drove on home — or where home should have been. Our old farmhouse had been razed, as had our workshop and the windmill that Dad and I had climbed. The woods where we had run in summer thunderstorms had been cut to little more than a huddled clump of maple, oak, and hickory trees. It took a minute to recognize this place where I grew up. I felt numb and melancholy as Delia and I walked hand in hand to the Gullywhumper — only to find it dry, its frogs and salamanders long gone. Someone had cleared the creek of trees and shrubs, and it was now a lifeless, muddy canal that looked fatigued by the load of sediment it carried. A few hundred yards away, across a field of stubble, a constant stream of traffic on the Ohio-Pennsylvania Turnpike cut through the carcass of the farm I had worked as a boy. The big old maples were gone from our front yard, and the wind whistled through the spare ribs of the old barn. Delia and I strolled into its cavernous interior and looked up to the high oak beams I had walked in my bare feet; for a moment I could see again the fresh stacks of sweet-smelling hay forty feet high and hear the echoes of laughter as I jumped with my brother and sisters from the oak beams into piles of cow feed on the barn floor. But then a gust of cold wind swept it all away.

Like the poached elephants of Luangwa, Kalahari lions in drought, and so many Americans, my siblings, and most of my extended family, were scattered. We received a warm welcome from an aunt who lived nearby, but there was nothing to hold us here, and for the first time since settling in the Kalahari Desert of Botswana more than twenty-two years earlier, we were without a home. We still planned to return to Zambia as soon as it was safe, and we had made repeated calls to the American embassy in Lusaka to try to determine whether it was. But in the meantime we had to find a place to live.

So we headed west, camping along the way, looking always for horizons that reminded us of Africa. But every time we found a likely valley, we also found a major road or a railroad passing through it, the rumble of the trains and traffic smothering the wild sounds coming from the countryside. Sometimes in the quiet just before dawn, I imagined that I could hear the thunder of hooves on the plains or the full-bellied roar of a lion splitting the night, or see platinum elephants crossing a river in moonlight. And as I rose every morning in yet another strange place, I found myself, coffee mug in hand, looking up to the mountains and ridgetops, imagining that the great horizons of Africa stretched beyond. I felt twisted, cracked, and dry, like the roots of a tough desert plant ripped out of the hardscrabble ground. How could we not go back to Africa? How does one decide not to breathe?

If we could not return, we wanted to find a last piece of wilderness in this country, but as we searched state by state, valley by valley, we gradually realized that there is no true wilderness left here — or anywhere else on Earth. In the more than two decades that we had been in Africa, the last of it had disappeared.

We would have to settle for second best by finding a troubled piece of *former* wilderness, one that we could begin to restore in what remained of our lifetimes. We would work to heal it, and it would heal us, make us whole and complete again, make us feel at *home* once more.

One day in the early fall of 1996, we turned onto a narrow gravel road that followed a creek bottom north for several miles to an old farm. It was near a crystal-clear lake and included a cabin on a meadow at the foot of the Rocky Mountains. The feet of too many cattle had stomped the meadow to dust and rounded down the creek's once proud banks; a complex of ditches leading to the creek had drained the marsh, and large bald spots showed where the forests had been clear-cut. But we bought "Thunder Mountain Ranch" and immediately started dismantling the web of barbed-wire fences, picking up and hauling off generations of junk, and restoring the marsh. We also began working to recover the grizzly bears that had roamed the mountains. In her way, Nature began rewarding us. As I later wrote in my journal:

> This evening the larches, sun-splashed and dazzling in their golden cloak of autumn, stood proudly forward on the rocky shoulders and ledge lines, looking down from the mountains on our new home at the edge of the meadow. Early snows on the high peaks and crags were pink cotton as the sun lay down for the night. The full moon rose through a blush of alpenglow into the sky above Windy Pass and sat on my left shoulder as I headed across the creek for the warmth of our fire, the new frost crisp under my steps. I cannot help it: I am falling in love with this new land, bewitched by its marshes, moose, mosses, mushrooms, and moons, its great horned owls hooting from deep in the dusk. A coyote calls, and then others, until their yips, yaps, and yowls fairly nip at the edges of the marsh. And finally a wolf's long, mournful song rises from the larches at the base of the mountains and soars across the valley. It is alone. I pause to savor the echoes of its last call until they are lost among the peaks and then head for the house again. But, in the gathering darkness, deep behind my soul, someone, something, whispers "Africa."

24 DELIA
THE STONES OF MY STREAM

My right and left arms round the sides of two friends and I in
the middle;
Coming home with the bearded and dark-cheeked bush-boy
... riding behind him at the drape of the day;
Far from the settlements studying the print of animals' feet ...

— WALT WHITMAN

If we have no peace, it is because we have forgotten that we
belong to each other.

— MOTHER TERESA

MARK AND I FOUND A PLACE of our own and mapped a territory, somewhere between snowfalls and moose tracks, but like any
new home range, it didn't feel quite right. Most of the stars were different, some upside down, some missing altogether. With no Southern Cross, the sky seemed cut off at the knees. Leopard-looking
stumps hid in grass clumps and peered at us with carnivorous eyes.
For years now I had had no troop, no female group, as the women of
Katibunga did. I wasn't even close to having the social support that a
baboon or lioness has. I saw elephant families moving slowly through
the gray space between the trees, but when I opened my eyes they
were gone. We wondered how Gift and her small family were faring.
As tiny as they were, they would still be targets for poachers. We kept
trying to reach Hammer but finally gave up.

After growing in strength and maturity in distant waters, a
salmon must return to the exact estuary where she hatched — a

thousand miles through the open ocean, hundreds of miles of her native river, against the current of her natal tributary. Instinctual maps made partially from memories of the stones of her stream guide her homeward. At every bend and fork, without hesitation, she must make the correct decision and swish on toward her childhood address.

Could it be that like all the animals we had studied, in the end we just wanted to find our own troop and our home? Are we all salmon searching for our streams?

Months after leaving Zambia, we received this letter:

Dear Mark and Delia, Greetings from Zambia, Mpika District, which has been your African Georgia. It has started getting much warmer. It could be that Luangwa Valley influence is slowly getting control of our plateau winds. Probably these are early signs of the begging of the rain season.

How are you "guys?" It's sad the team is no longer here any more. At times I wished I could as well leave. But alas am not British or Scottish. I have to learn to take the pain courageously.

I always get consoled as every week reports reach us at our homes that places like Nkobe and Mukungule, a place which is relatively populated with people, wildlife has finally forced its way. To us as former NLCP staff its great achievement.

For weeks I tried to contact you by fax and email everything was difficult. Apparently every single item has been taken over by the "big boys" from Lusaka who have been "biting" the project complete hastily from people we loved so much and worked with. It was now the last storm which for sure we could not survive this time. No ways I had to surrender. I would not be bought to their side and I made a decision which is very costly. No job and no income with a wife I find it hard. Mark, Are you not coming soon?

It's painful to be here in Mpika and continue to see what was rightly under our project, equipment, buildings, etc completely under strangers — reaping where they never sewed. Believe me Mark I always hold back my tears. Because I know what it took for the project to be what it was. And how I loved the bike you bought me. It is no more.

I and Albert struggled to hang on with the community development programme. No one, however, cared for the continuing of the programme. Big guys were here but no one dared to introduce us nor could we have any audience. NLCP concept can't die that way. It is a model to be applied in community based conservation programmes.

Now at home this time waiting to hear from you. Don't feel I have lost hope and trust in what you have done to our park and the people here. The revolving fund which was the backbone of our success and continuity, to our surprise we were told there was nothing. I am only waiting to hear from you for further instructions. All the villagers did not want to see the project die.

Thanks. God bless.
Hammer.

We wrote to Hammer immediately, assuring him that we would continue our support for the village projects. He replied that he no longer had an office but worked under the banana trees the way we did in the beginning. Prince Bernhard of the Netherlands paid for a new motorbike for him.

A few months later he wrote again: "The established work structure still exists despite all what has happened. Activities in the communities are still going on and we are a focal point in development for our District. Some of the activities are tuck shops, cooking oil making, farming of fish, bee keeping. Women clubs are still active in sewing and baking industries."

Bit by bit, from the other side of the world we helped Hammer rebuild the village programs. He wrote applications for grants and raised funds from organizations such as Harvest Help, which supplemented our support for farmers. Hammer and his colleagues wrote their own charter, formed their own project. The news spread, and many other villagers asked to join their programs. Grace NG'ambi, using her special dance, taught the women of Nabwalya to be traditional birth attendants like those of Mukungule. Hammer moved back into the project offices. From its simple "one-man, one-woman" beginning the project had grown to reach the people of fifty-two villages. Fifteen hundred households had sustainable industries such as sunflower presses or beekeeping. Agriculture had been improved, and food security for families had doubled in some areas. There was a new school in Chilyaba, and there were supplies for the clinic in Nkomba. Sixty percent of the participants were women. Zambians were running the project, teaching each other fish farming and beekeeping. The beauty was they almost did not need us anymore. That was what we had wanted all along.

One afternoon Gift's daughter Georgia, who was less than nine years old, delivered a calf right in our old camp. So at the young age of sixteen, Gift, who would normally be giving birth for the first time, had three kids of her own and one grandcalf. From being a solitary orphan who wandered alone and could only watch elephant mothers and daughters from a distance, she was now the matriarch for a family of five. Kasokola would have said, "Panono, panono."

🐘 LYING IN A MEADOW under a mountain dusted with spring snow, so far away from Luangwa, I felt as if I were in a raft drifting on a shoreless sea. Under Hammer's leadership the village work had soared, and once again the elephants were safe. Our dream had spilled over, and again we found ourselves in the wild surrounded by vast beauty. Yet the space around us seemed as empty as the gray place where elephants hide.

In my mind I saw the baboons scampering across the river beach. I remembered the young female who often left her troop, scampered into my camp on her own, and watched me identify plants. One morning when the other baboons were nearby, I had a chance to watch her leaving the group. It was not a matter of walking away with cocky confidence. She stole a few steps in my direction and then looked back, as if reassuring herself that they were still there. When they moved away, she bounded back toward them and stood nearby for a few moments, torn between curiosity and camaraderie. Finally, she corraled the courage to jump into my tree, but she listened intently to their calls. She always knew exactly where they were.

I walked to our cabin and telephoned my childhood friends the Walker twins, Margaret and Amanda. I said, "Here's to'd ya. If I never see'd ya, I never know'd ya." It had taken all my life to understand what that means: baboons, elephants, and people belong with the ones they truly know. We need more than strangers around us. Mark and I had studied the significance of social systems of other species for decades, but in doing so, we had left our own families. And what we learned was that it is not so much that the troop is incomplete without some of its baboons or human beings, but that the individual baboons or human beings are incomplete without their troop.

Margaret and Amanda flew west to visit me, and a few days later we stood on the edge of the sweeping meadow. I pointed out that the white-tailed does had left their small herd and were almost evenly scattered across the field, each standing alone. This meant they either had had their fawns or would soon, I explained. The three of us spread out across the meadow and walked quietly through the lush grass shadowed by mountains. Minutes later we found twin fawns — their soft coats spotted with white — curled tightly in the grass. As instructed by their genes, they lay motionless, their huge brown eyes reflecting the sky. This strategy of stillness, along with their lack of odor, prevented predators from finding them. As long as we kept a few feet away, the fawns would not bolt, and their mother would return safely to them. Margaret and Amanda froze in awe, their hands covering their faces. Twins from my troop intertwined with twins from Nature.

My raft drifted closer to a shore. More friends, old and new, came to see the elk and cougars and us. Slowly a new group formed, loose at first, and wobbly, but becoming more solid with shared smiles and ski trails. Because most people are as scattered as desert lions, one can find plenty of strays in the dunes; all you need is a net to bring them in. To be complete, we need Nature and our troops, but both are slipping away beyond our reach. We must save what wilderness we can because it was our first home, and without it we will never fully understand who we are. Like Gift, we must put our troops and our families back together again. Like Kalahari lions at the end of drought, we must form a new pride.

Yawning cardboard boxes and crumbled newspapers surrounded me as I unpacked some of our stored belongings, many of them wedding presents we had not seen or touched in twenty-five years. Gingerly I opened the carton labeled DELIA'S THINGS. Wrapped in yellowing tissue paper was the china horse Grandpa had given me when I was ten. Nestled among old letters was the wristwatch he gave me when I learned to drive in the pecan orchard. I held them against my heart and then placed them on my shelf. They are the stones of my stream.

I remembered the last time I saw Gift and Georgia. Of course, I had no way of knowing that it would be my final encounter with them. I was driving to my camp from Marula-Puku and had just forded the Lubonga River. The grass was nearly as tall as the truck, so I could not see very far on either side. Suddenly they stepped into the track ahead of me, and I switched off the engine. Without hesitating, Gift walked gracefully to my open window. The still, hot air drifted with her movements — an elephant breeze. She was so close I could not see the top of her head, but by leaning slightly, I could see into her gray eyes, fringed with long lashes. Her trunk, usually so curious and busy, dangled loosely. I could have reached out and touched her, but instead I sat very still. How did I know to memorize her face, to make note of the "smile lines" creasing her cheeks, to notice that her eyes always seemed sad? Notes that will have to last me a lifetime. She stood there for only a minute or two and then glided by like a big ship. Georgia followed her, slightly farther away, glancing at me with her moist, deep eyes. It was a fine goodbye.

No elephants move through the thickets here, but the soft footfalls of deer and elk can be heard along the creek. The moon touches my face with the same light that smiles on the distant lionesses in the long grass. The stars are out of place, but soon they will become oriented to my new place until I am familiar to them. Time has allowed me to map my new space, and the honking of the Canada geese brings spring as heartily as the sparrow weavers' trill.

I lay on the warming ground until I could no longer feel where I ended and the earth began. The oneness I share with Nature, the women of Katibunga, and my own troop makes me whole. I pushed myself up from the ferns that were rallying with all their might for spring and dusted the last of the snowflakes from my sleeve. Impotent in this new season of warmth, the cold crystals fluttered through the air and literally disappeared before my eyes. As I emerged from the woods at an easy pace, the large meadow opened before me, offering a walk in any direction.

Maybe someday we will return to Marula-Puku and Fulaza, but that is not really important. What matters is that Gift keeps having babies, that Hammer is distributing seeds, and that the winterthorn still sings.

MARK

EPILOGUE

AS OF THIS WRITING (2005) the work we began in 1986 to conserve the wildlife in and around North Luangwa National Park by
offering villagers alternatives to poaching is nineteen years old. Hammer Simwinga, whose heroic and selfless efforts sustained and pre-
served the North Luangwa Conservation Project (NLCP) during the
attempted seizure by corrupt officials, has founded his own offspring
organization, the North Luangwa Community Conservation Development Project (NLCCDP). In 2004 villagers in the Mpika area chose
our project and NLCCDP as the model to follow for future wildlife conservation and wildlife-based remote rural development programs, and it is being replicated in other parts of Zambia.

On September 20, 2005, the National Geographic Society and
the Owens Foundation for Wildlife Conservation cosponsored an
evening with Hammer Simwinga and the best-selling author Alexandra Fuller at the National Geographic's auditorium in Washington,
D.C. To get to America, Hammer had traveled more than eleven
thousand miles, battling automatic doors, escalators, and hotel key
cards like a Bembaland version of Crocodile Dundee. Then he rode
horses in Idaho; saw bears, elk, bison, and the scenic grandeur of the
Tetons; was interviewed on National Public Radio; toured the nation's capital; and ate his way across the country. Then he saw his
name in lights on the National Geographic building.

"Ah," he said. "First I am an American cowboy, and now this! I can be telling stories for the rest of my life and never finish."

For more than an hour on his night, he, Alexandra, and Senior Editor Oliver Payne enchanted the audience with descriptions and impressions of village work and wildlife, which Alexandra had written about for the *National Geographic*'s September feature issue on Africa. And then Hammer returned to Zambia to continue the project.

⚘ ELEPHANT POACHING in North Luangwa decreased by more than 95 percent from 1986 to 1996. The Frankfurt Zoological Society (FZS), our funding partner for nineteen years, stepped in to continue elephant research and support for antipoaching programs, and Marula-Puku is now the home of Hugo van der Westhuizen and Elsabe Aucamp, who are managing those programs. NLCP is now one of the most secure parks in Zambia. In fact it is so well protected that the Conservation Foundation of Zambia is working with FZS to reintroduce black rhinoceros.

Gift and her family still stop by at Marula-Puku, as do Cheers, Long Tail, and Survivor — who not only eats the marula fruits but harasses the staff as well. More and more elephants can be seen walking along the rivers of the Luangwa Valley. Although Gift's grandcalf died, she and her three offspring are now the beginning of an extended family.

Sadly, Tom Kotela has died, but Mano Unit, under the leadership of Samushi Kamuti, has consistently been chosen as the best in Zambia at the wildlife officers' annual parade. For the past two years the scouts have been given more sophisticated paramilitary training so that they can handle any threat from poachers.

Isaac Daka, one of the top game scouts in Zambia, is now the unit leader of Chikwa/Chifunda, from which he and his officers are ably protecting the eastern flank of the North Luangwa Park.

Chief Mukungule has died, but his successor enthusiastically supports the community-outreach work of Hammer and his colleagues. One morning before he died, the old chief watched a group of elephants on the outskirts of his village for the first time in many years. He wrote us a letter thanking NLCP for making that possible.

Mary Chongo continues her sewing industry under the tree next to her home, though she recently wrote to say that she has worn out her Singer treadle machine. The traditional birth attendants trained by Dr. Philip Watt still practice in their villages, and the Owens Foundation recently funded the training of another group in Nabwalya. The small school in Fulaza is still operating, and villagers recently wrote to ask for help expanding it. In all, more than twenty thousand Zambians benefited from job training, agricultural assistance, small business loans, improved education, and rural health care provided by NLCP. To turn away from poaching and embrace the conservation of their wildlife resources, the people of North Luangwa needed only a new direction and a bit of help and encouragement.

Malcolm, Trish, Rex, and Anne now live and work in Tanzania, where they have set up a company converting crop wastes to a charcoal-like fuel as an alternative to cutting down forests for firewood.

In exchange for a large subsidy from the European Union, the Department of National Parks and Wildlife Services has been privatized in order to stamp out corruption; it is now known as the Zambian Wildlife Authority. Many of the senior officers have been replaced, including those who engineered the illegal seizure of NLCP. In fact, President Mwanawasa and his administration have fired or jailed many former officials, including the previous president. The new government is also making admirable strides in the conservation of its wildlife resources and the proliferation of community-based conservation projects.

It will take many years for the elephant populations of Luangwa to build back their former numbers after the severe poaching of the 1980s and '90s. They need room to grow, which will require a secure habitat, and they need time to grow old, to learn the lessons of life and pass them on to their young. A continued — and strengthened — United Nations moratorium on the international trade in ivory is crucial, at least until poached populations are reestablished.

But it is perhaps no more important than the need to stem the growth of the human population. In most of Africa, as in other parts of the world, human populations are now so dense that unrestricted hunting, even for subsistence purposes, especially with modern weapons, would quickly deplete the wildlife, bringing many animal populations to extinction. Unless human numbers are in balance with those of neighboring wildlife populations, the decline of wildlife will continue to be a hard reality. Despite the ravages of AIDS and a plethora of other diseases, Africa's populations continue to outstrip the carrying capacity of the continental resource base — as is the case in many other places on Earth. So long as this growth in human numbers continues, the misery for both human and wildlife populations will grow exponentially.

Elephants, buffaloes, and other animals are expanding farther and farther from North Luangwa, repopulating areas where they have not been seen in decades. The elephants and hippos have recovered from poaching to such an extent that their crop raiding has become an increasing problem. Hammer and his colleague, Moses Nyirendu, and their team have encouraged farmers to ring their fields with chili peppers and beehives, which seem to be effective ways to ward off the giant herbivores.

WHILE WE CONTINUE to support our project in Zambia, since returning to the United States in 1996, we have been working to recover remnant populations of grizzly bears and wetland habitats in the Pacific Northwest. For information on the Owens Foundation for Wildlife Conservation, contact our Web site, www.owens-foundation.org, or write to us at P.O. Box 870530, Stone Mountain, Georgia 30087.

APPENDIX

SUGGESTED READING

ACKNOWLEDGMENTS

INDEX

APPENDIX

The North Luangwa Conservation Project

A Multidimensional Community-based Approach
to the Conservation of Natural Resources

NLCP REFERS TO the project as founded and designed by Mark and Delia Owens in 1986 and directed by the Owenses until 1997, and to the community outreach work that continues to the present as an offshoot of the original NLCP model. The project included the following programs:

Microbusiness Development and Employment Opportunities
Agricultural Assistance
Rural Health Care
Conservation Education
Wildlife Law Enforcement
Wildlife Research and Monitoring
Tourism Development

NLCP was a multifaceted project designed to satisfy the basic needs of rural people living on the outskirts of Zambia's North Luangwa National Park and to restore and manage a depleted natural resource — the local indigenous wildlife — so that eventually it could benefit the people and the local economy. By 1985 highly organized commercial poachers had severely depleted the park's major wildlife species, including 93 percent of the elephants and all of the black rhinoceros. Our wildlife censuses revealed that two thirds of the park's area had been depopulated of its large mammalian species; had the slaughter been allowed to continue, the other third would have been killed off within five or six years. Poaching and the black-market wildlife trade made up the primary economy of the area. Poaching and working for commercial poachers were the only ways local people could benefit from the national park, which the Zambian government at that time did not have the financial resources or political will to protect or manage. Criminal elements and corrupt officials from outside the communities hired shooters to kill elephants for about ten dollars each; the organizers could get up to two hundred dollars a pound for the ivory. They hired villagers as carriers and paid them as little as two pounds of meat to transport hundred-pound loads of contraband meat, ivory, and skins on their heads up to sixty miles over the mountains to settlements along the Cape-to-Cairo Road. Poaching was not only illegal, it was also dangerous, unsustainable, and not very profitable for local people. It also eroded the moral fabric of entire communities. Poachers took children as young as ten out of school to work as virtual slaves and took young girls away from their families in exchange for favors.

Conceptually, NLCP was not an attempt to conserve North Luangwa National Park through the development of ecotourism in the short run. That approach was not possible because wildlife populations had been depleted to extinction or near extinction, and the area was not secure enough or the infrastructure developed enough to sustain visits by large numbers of tourists. Instead, we sought first to empower villagers and their communities economically and with improved health care, education, and security. At the same time we bolstered wildlife law enforcement so that the animal populations could recover and once again become a sustainable resource. The age-old symbiosis between wildlife and people could be recatalyzed only after the animal and human communities had been independently restored. NLCP conserved wildlife by helping villagers develop legitimate alternatives to poaching and by helping them realize direct and indirect *sustainable* benefits in exchange for conserving their natural resources. NLCP made a deal with them: "We will invest in you if you will invest at least sweat equity in yourself and if you will help conserve your wildlife." The project expected a measurable return: the repopulation of wildlife and improved quality of life for local people, including a reduction in the numbers of poachers in each village.

None of the assistance was a handout: the NLCP loan fund for startup enterprises operated much like those from commercial lending institutions, except that they were interest free. The loans were to be repaid so that we could invest in and help others from the same community. Any tangible or intangible assistance beyond what might be expected from a "good neighbor" was made conditional on an in-kind investment (usually labor) by the recipient in order to reinforce the self-help concept and to ensure that the enterprise would be self-sustaining. This concept was at first difficult for villagers to understand and accept. For decades foreign assistance programs had consisted of grants-in-aid, which did not require recipients to invest in themselves or to be accountable for the money they received. Eventually most of the local people understood the concept of self-help, and when they did, the pride they felt in their own accomplishments was truly remarkable.

INDIRECT BENEFITS OF NLCP PROGRAMS TO LOCAL PEOPLE

The direct financial benefits of tourism and associated jobs as well as other business opportunities coming from the park could not be realized until the wildlife populations were revitalized and until NLCP had built a rudimentary physical infrastructure, including roads, bridges, and airstrips. In the meantime the project stimulated indirect benefits to the local people *on behalf of the park and its wildlife,* including jobs, business opportunities, and community development through improved health care and education, for example. These programs, which were not directly related to the park and wildlife, were generated by and subsidized with resources from outside the area. The programs were expected to become self-sustaining and/or supported by entities within Zambia in ten to fifteen years.

These NLCP programs offered villagers alternatives to poaching and also demonstrated to them the value of wildlife conservation. Program administrators and their assistants were specifically asked to find creative ways to repeatedly reinforce the notion that opportunities and resources were being made available to villagers on behalf of the wildlife community in and around the park. For our pilot programs we initially selected fourteen villages near North Luangwa National Park that were known to harbor hardened commercial poachers.

Wildlife clubs are one of the most important tools for reinforcing the link between conservation and the programs offered in the villages. Initially, through NLCP, these clubs were a forum for discussing personal and community needs within the context of conservation and for assessing a community's available talents and resources to address those needs. But under the North Luangwa Community Conservation Development Project (NLCCDP) the clubs have become much more: they are now repositories for loan funds, training facilities, and the spearhead for expanding programs into other communities — all on behalf of wildlife. When villagers request that the project start a program in their community, they must first form a wildlife club and pay a fee to join it. They are charged an additional fee if they miss a meeting, and they lose their membership if they miss more than three meetings. The fees tend to weed out those who are not in earnest about addressing community problems. Each member's money is held in a sort of savings account until he or she decides, with the help of project advisers, on a worthwhile business enterprise. Then the money, in conjunction with a low-interest loan, is used to develop that business. Members of long-established clubs share their skills and training with the new initiates, which makes it unnecessary to hire more and more vocational trainers.

Because women are more likely than men to remain in their home community, NLCCDP requires that 68 percent of the members of each wildlife club be women before the project will set up a program for a village. Thus women have become economically empowered in developing businesses, and many are assuming leadership roles in their community for the first time. This elevated social status has made other opportunities more readily available to women, including access to family planning techniques.

MICROBUSINESS DEVELOPMENT AND EMPLOYMENT OPPORTUNITIES

The Village Approach to Microbusiness Development

Meeting with tribal leaders. According to tribal protocol, we asked the village headmen to request a meeting with the chief and his elders. At the meeting we and our Zambian community development officer explained that NLCP was a wildlife conservation organization commissioned by their government to help villagers find alternatives to poaching in and around the national park, so that their wildlife would return to benefit all their people. Because of poaching, few large wild animals were left in these areas, and in some cases people had been reduced to eating mice and other rodents for meat. We asked the chief and elders for suggestions on how we could best work with them and the villagers to improve their agriculture and community infrastructure and to stimulate job opportunities and sustainable commerce as alternatives to poaching. After the chief gave us his endorsement, he then instructed his elders and headmen to arrange meetings with interested villagers.

Explaining project objectives to villagers. In each village, after being introduced by the headman, we explained that NLCP was not an antipoaching entity, even though we were offering substantial assistance to wildlife scouts, and that no one was forced to participate in the programs we hoped to develop with them. We explained that we were there primarily to assist any and all villagers who refrained from poaching, including reformed poachers, and that we *represented* wildlife conservation interests and the national park, that we were speaking to them on behalf of the beleaguered wildlife community. We reiterated many times that our programs were designed to help them turn away from poaching by developing legitimate employment and business opportunities, so that more of them could again benefit from their wildlife as the populations recovered.

Assessing skills and interests. We began by surveying villagers about their interests, skills, and formal training. Even in the most remote areas we found some young men who had left their villages for training and had returned as mechanics, electricians, cobblers, carpenters, or farmers; and women who could sew, make crafts, garden, or in other ways provide goods and services to their communities.

Documenting available resources. We helped villagers survey the raw materials and other commodities available for use in microindustries.

Choosing appropriate small industries. After local interests, skills, levels of training, and resources were assessed, the NLCP revolving fund administrators (including local Zambians) screened applicants for interest-free loans to pay for additional training, acquisition of basic equipment, enrollment in small-business management courses, and advice from outside experts on the development of appropriate small industries.

Businesses were considered appropriate for loans if they met the following criteria:

Readily available resources and nearby markets. Because of the expense and general lack of transportation, NLCP emphasized the development of microindustries that used local raw materials to produce items or commodities that could be sold or traded locally.

Low startup costs. NLCP concentrated on industries that required low initial capital investment and simple machines. Spare parts and other support for the industry had to be readily available in Zambia, preferably in Mpika. NLCP did not encourage industries that relied on tractors or other large equipment that required high maintenance or imported spare parts.

Minimal environmental impact. NLCP did not encourage the raising of livestock other than rabbits, guinea fowl, and other small domestic animals. Large livestock require a lot of grazing land and represent substantial losses when killed by predators, which intensifies the conflict between humans and wildlife, leading to the destruction of the latter. Our objective was to *reduce* that conflict so that both wildlife and people could prosper in a harmonious synergy.

Satisfaction of basic needs. Industries supplying basic products immediately needed by villagers were encouraged. These included the following:

1. *Sunflower seed presses.* These provided jobs for many local farmers. The press operator purchased the seeds from the farmers, produced the oil with the press, and then sold the oil to villagers and game scouts or at the open market in the central village. The roughage (cake) from the pressed seeds could be used as feed for farm-raised fish, chickens, rabbits, and other small livestock.

2. *Maize-grinding mills.* The mills provided jobs for the millers and a service for the community. Grinding mills, even simple ones, require diesel fuel and some spare parts, so they were not the most appropriate industry for remote villages. However, we agreed to sponsor several mills in some of the larger, more easily accessible villages because they relieved scores of women of the task of grinding maize by hand — laborious, time-consuming work. The women were thus freed to start businesses, become more economically independent, and assume greater responsibility in the community.

3. *Fish farms.* The fish farms provided jobs for operators and a good source of protein for villagers who purchased the fish. The larger villages and the game scout camps provided good markets for the fish.

4. *Carpentry shops.* One village had six trained carpenters; supported by an initial loan for tools, they made and sold furniture locally, including desks that the project purchased for schools as part of the Conservation Education Program.

5. *"Wildlife" shops.* These provided a living for the shopkeeper and a much-needed service to villagers. Before these general stores were established, people in many villages had to walk for two to three days to purchase basic items such as matches, soap, cooking oil, and cloth. Wildlife clubs started by villagers sponsored some of the first shops with NLCP loans.

6. *Sewing.* Using foot-powered treadle sewing machines, women and men

were able to make clothing to sell to villagers, merchants in the central village, and game scouts. Making uniforms for the scouts catalyzed other forms of commerce between the game scout camps and local communities, improving relations that had been strained by clashes between poachers and the scouts' antipoaching activities.

7. *Beekeeping.* Beekeepers were taught at first to house their bees in wooden box hives instead of cutting down trees to access the honey of wild bees. Further experimentation resulted in environmentally sound hives made from mud and small amounts of cement. The beekeepers could eat the organic honey themselves and sell it to others, and the bees helped pollinate some crops. In some cases beehives were used to ward off crop-raiding animals, including elephants and hippos.

8. *Shoemaking.* Villagers made sandals from old tires and sold them locally and at the marketplace in Mpika.

9. *Mousetrap making.* Villagers made mousetraps from scrap metal and sold them to other villagers and to the expatriate community in Mpika.

Entrepreneurial loan program. Each year NLCP offered each village a 1-million-kwacha (this figure fluctuated with the U.S. dollar–kwacha exchange rate) entrepreneurial loan fund. Individuals applied for loans from their village's revolving fund and bought equipment, training, transport, and other support for startup industries. For example, a villager could apply for funds to purchase a sunflower-seed press and have it transported from Lusaka to his or her village. After the industry was up and running, loans were to be repaid in quarterly interest-free installments. If the loan was not repaid or if the borrower was in arrears, the delinquent sum was subtracted from the 1 million kwachas available to that village for the next year. This requirement created peer pressure for loans to be repaid and on time; only 15 percent of the borrowers defaulted. The project was both strict and lenient, insisting that payments be made but allowing extra time for repayment during drought and other hardships as long as the person was earnestly trying to repay the loan. All payments were returned to the revolving fund to support other worthy proposals.

Training. After a villager received his or her equipment, the community development officer provided free training in using it and periodic retraining. Many villagers did not understand the fundamentals of operating a for-profit business. NLCP taught them how to factor in production costs so they could set a fair market price that allowed them to realize a profit and how to do basic accounting so they could track the progress of their businesses.

Employment Opportunities

NLCP hired many local people — up to one hundred at a time — to accomplish its objectives. Villagers were hired as community service experts, agriculture experts, teachers, drivers, mechanics, road and airstrip construction workers, camp staff, research assistants, and secretaries. These jobs boosted the local cash economy and constituted an indirect benefit from the national park to the people. The project also offered valuable training, so that when the indirect-benefit phase of the project was over, people who had developed skills and training would be more likely to find jobs elsewhere.

AGRICULTURAL ASSISTANCE

The aim was not only to improve crop yields but to introduce crops, such as legumes, that required little or no fertilizer and were good sources of protein and in general were more nutritious. Proposals requiring tractors or other motorized machinery were not funded or encouraged because the equipment could not be supported in remote areas.

Expert advice and training. Zambian agriculture experts who were full-time employees of the project visited all villages to offer training, workshops, and in-field advice on what crops to plant, how to fertilize them with compost, how to use mulch, protect crops from wildlife, and harvest and store them with the least waste.

Agricultural fairs. Village fairs were encouraged so farmers could learn about new crops, farming practices, and markets for their produce.

New crops. Wherever appropriate for local soils, climate, and food preferences, new crops were introduced that could be fertilized adequately by composting and by rotating crops to avoid depleting soils of nitrogen and other key nutrients. Soybeans, groundnuts, peas, beans, and other legumes were emphasized because of their relatively high protein content and their nitrogen-fixing ability. Chemical fertilizers were too expensive and difficult to obtain and apply, as well as environmentally offensive. Villagers were not encouraged to grow crops that would have to be transported long distances to market. Some novel ideas that were tried included drying mushrooms for sale and planting chili pepper crops around maize and soybean fields to protect them from elephants, hippos, and buffaloes.

Markets. The project helped farmers find new markets by encouraging the government-paid game scouts as well as project employees to purchase produce from them.

Fruit trees. Very few fruit trees had been planted in the area, so growing bananas, guavas, avocados, and mangos was encouraged and supported.

RURAL HEALTH CARE

This program emphasized disease prevention and the use of basic remedies and treatments. Complicated high-tech equipment such as X-ray machines, though much needed, were not offered because they were too expensive and too difficult to operate and maintain. Instead we trained villagers in simple first aid, lifesaving techniques, and family planning, so that they could assist others in remote locations with simple, easily obtainable, effective remedies.

Under-five clinics. Because dehydration from diarrhea is one of the leading causes of death among children in remote rural areas, NLCP periodically provided transportation for medical personnel from Mpika to outlying villages, where clinics were held. The project also sponsored a nurse who traveled to villages to teach basic rehydration methods.

Training of traditional birth attendants (TBAs). Perhaps the most successful program in the NLCP Rural Health Care Program was the training of two women from each of twenty-four villages to be traditional birth attendants, or midwives. A volunteer American doctor and a Zambian nurse taught the course in a remote village mission, where the forty-eight women stayed for two months. Along with midwifery, they were taught first aid, AIDS prevention, family planning, nutrition, sanitation, and early childhood development. Refresher courses were offered periodically.

Donation of medical supplies. In cooperation with AmeriCares, an American medical organization, NLCP donated medical supplies worth $1 million U.S. dollars to Zambia. The supplies were flown from the United States. Smaller donations of medical supplies have been sent periodically since 1997.

CONSERVATION EDUCATION

Another indirect benefit from the national park was our NLCP Conservation Education Program, which served schools in the fourteen target villages. The program employed a full-time educational officer, a qualified Zambian teacher who worked closely with the government's Ministry of Education. Although the program emphasized conservation education, its services went far beyond that, offering curriculum development and basic materials to remote schools that in some cases had never seen such things before. NLCP was often the sole provider of these items.

The following were some aspects of the program:

Conservation education. The project's education coordinator traveled to each school at least once a month to present programs on the value of conserving natural resources and to offer basic lessons in the natural sciences. The officer also taught lessons, met with teachers, planned future visits, assessed the school's needs, and provided materials.

Educational materials. The project provided such items as floors and roofs for the school buildings, desks, chalkboards, textbooks, paper, pencils, notebooks, crayons, posters, maps, globes, and soccer balls, many of which were shipped from the United States, Australia, Canada, and Europe. The project also paid for teachers' salaries and housing.

Bookmobile. NLCP provided a five-hundred-volume mobile library that was made available to schools through the conservation education coordinator.

Sister School Program. The project set up an exchange program between American schools and remote Zambian schools. The children exchanged letters, materials, stories, reports, artwork, and a lot of joy.

Curriculum. The NLCP education coordinator wrote a conservation education curriculum and produced teacher packets for all the area schools that included wildlife conservation workbooks, activity books, and board games. The program was coordinated with Zambia's Ministry of Education.

School construction and maintenance. The project built a school for one village and hired villagers (including some ex-poachers) to make bricks and help with construction. Some of the roofing sheets and window frames were paid for by ADMADE, a government program that returned revenues from safari hunting to villages. The project also built a house for the teacher and bought desks from NLCP-sponsored carpenters. In some other villages the project paid for school maintenance and repairs.

Drama and art competitions. NLCP provided many extracurricular activities for the schools, including sports and drama and art competitions, which otherwise would not have been available. Winners were occasionally taken on "safari" into the national park, where they could see wildlife, a treat that the children had never experienced.

INTEGRATION OF PROGRAMS

To jump-start a cash economy, we tried to develop synergy among businesses and programs so that they could buy from and sell to each other. For example, newly equipped carpenters in the jobs program made desks for the schools served by the NLCP Conservation Education Program (the project paid for the desks); game scouts bought food and clothing from the newly trained farmers and seamstresses; farmers who grew sunflower seeds sold them to the sunflower press operators, who in turn sold the oil to the villagers or game scouts and sold the pressed cake to fish farmers.

DIRECT BENEFITS OF THE NATIONAL PARK TO LOCAL PEOPLE

Villagers living in Game Management Areas (GMAs) around the park benefited directly from the park or its GMA in sustainable legal ways, most notably from tourism, hunting, and park-related government jobs.

TOURISM

Well-managed tourism in the national park can benefit local people directly in the following ways:

Jobs. Safari companies hire local people as drivers, safari guides, construction workers, road crews, cooks, staff, management, and biologists.

Markets for agriculture. Safari companies buy produce from local farmers.

Markets for arts and crafts. Safari companies take tourists to villages where they can purchase locally made arts and crafts such as baskets, clothes, and wood carvings, and products such as organic honey from local people, thus providing a market for these goods.

Infrastructure improvements. Any improvements to infrastructure, such as park roads and bridges for tourism, also benefit local people. NLCP built new airstrips, roads, and bridges and improved roads all the way from Mpika through several villages to the national park, which benefited all the people in this area.

It is often pointed out that tourism cannot financially support national parks, and that is almost always true, even in well-developed countries, because only the government has the resources to manage the parks. It is also stated that a national park cannot provide a living to all the local people in an area. But this argument ignores the value that many local people place on the park as a place that preserves their heritage. So long as a threshold number of people are able to make a living from the park, they will have an incentive to conserve it. More than anyone else, local people deserve to benefit from the park — but in ways that will not diminish the resource. We believe in the world heritage concept: that because ecosystems are interrelated, they belong to and sustain everyone, and it is therefore the responsibility of all the peoples of the world to help protect them.

HUNTING

As in most other countries, hunting is not allowed in Zambia's national parks, but it is allowed in Game Management Areas and surrounding open areas. NLCP worked to sustain lawful hunting for villagers in the following direct ways:

Establishment of the Mukungule Game Management Area west of the park. As commercial poaching declined, recovering wildlife populations began spilling out of the park into the GMA. With wildlife regulations and routine game scout patrols in place, legitimate local hunters increasingly benefited from this expanding resource.

Transportation of licensing officers to remote villages. Prior to that service, villagers from isolated settlements had to travel for up to three or four days to reach one of the larger villages where licenses were sold — and the allotment was often sold out by the time they arrived. As a result, many villagers hunted without licenses. Illegal subsistence hunting declined when transportation became available, making it easier to get licenses. Hunting regulations and other wildlife laws, including those pertaining to quotas and licensing, are very important for the restoration of depleted animal populations. In the near term there is a need to augment, but not necessarily replace, the benefits from hunting with more nonconsumptive uses of wildlife.

After depleted wildlife populations have recovered sufficiently to allow professional safari hunting, local people can benefit from programs that return revenue and meat products to them, as well as from associated jobs. NLCP assisted neighboring safari hunters by supporting antipoaching operations in their concessions and by assisting game scouts and villagers in those areas. The project did not, however, support the trophy hunting of at-risk, threatened, or endangered populations because that practice targets the most genetically fit and reproductively active individuals — the very ones whose reproductive performance is needed for the recovery and sustainability of the population. In general, when trophy hunting is allowed, the wildlife resource must be closely monitored and regulations strictly enforced.

Improved relations between game scouts and local communities. NLCP encouraged the scouts to buy local produce and products rather than importing goods from distant markets.

Park-Related Government Jobs

Government jobs contribute revenue to the local economy. A viable national park provides jobs, opportunities, and revenue to local people. When NLCP was founded, there were only seven game guards living in one camp near the park's western boundary to patrol and protect the whole park. Using local labor and materials, NLCP revitalized seven additional game guard camps by building forty-eight traditional houses for more than fifty scouts. The Zambian government hired the new officers and paid their salaries, which greatly stimulated the local cash economy.

Wildlife management provides jobs and revenue. Prior to NLCP the game scout camp had no vehicles, and no vehicles or machinery were assigned to the park itself. NLCP supplied aircraft, trucks, tractors, trailers, fuel tankers, and a motorized grader to support the game scouts' work and maintain the park. This fleet of vehicles provided jobs for drivers, mechanics, and workshop managers. Other management activities provided jobs for radio operators, secretaries, wildlife research assistants, and biologists.

Wildlife Law Enforcement

In 1986, when NLCP began, the seven game scouts of Mano Unit had only one functioning rifle and a single round of ammunition to protect NLNP. The scouts had not been paid for months and did not have uniforms, boots, patrol food, trucks, fuel, medicines, compasses, camping equipment, or almost anything else needed to do their jobs. Morale was low, and the scouts themselves shot wildlife inside the national park for their own consumption and for sale.

Working under the auspices of the Department of National Parks and Wildlife Services (NPWS), NLCP revitalized the law enforcement program to protect the park from further devastation. While NPWS supplied additional scouts, NLCP covered much of the costs of law enforcement, including those associated with transportation, construction of housing, roads, and airstrips, as well as patrol food and other assistance.

The purpose of NLCP's assistance was to build infrastructure, provide transportation, and equip and supply enough game scouts to field patrols throughout the park and its surroundings. NLCP personnel did not accompany game scouts on patrol and were in no way involved in law enforcement except through financial and logistical support. We considered it essential to gather information on poaching from local villagers and from aerial reconnaissance, then quickly transport the better-equipped and -supported scouts to areas were poachers were active. At the same time we worked to increase the number of man-days spent patrolling each month to boost the presence of law enforcement officers on the ground. The use of aircraft and the construction of rudimentary roads, bridges, and airstrips were crucial to this effort.

Some of NLCP's contributions to law enforcement from 1986 to 1996 were the following:

1. Refurbishing of seven game scout camps and construction of a new one west of the park.
2. Provision of uniforms, general equipment, transportation, and radio communication.
3. Construction of roads, bridges, airstrips, and an operations center to facilitate antipoaching patrols, including a jail to hold captured poachers.
4. Payments to village operatives who gathered undercover information on the locations, plans, and movements of major poaching figures.
5. Airlifting of scouts into poaching areas with fixed-wing aircraft and a helicopter, and day and night aerial reconnaissance missions to detect poaching and locate poachers.
6. A grinding mill and a miller (an ex-poacher) for Mano Unit game scout headquarters.
7. A tractor and trailer, trucks, fuel, and vehicle maintenance for game scouts.
8. A park-wide radio communication system.
9. Promotion of commerce between scouts and villagers to enhance community relations.

WILDLIFE RESEARCH AND ECOLOGICAL MONITORING

The wildlife populations in the park were surveyed, monitored, and researched, and the relevant results and implications were presented to Zambia's National Parks and Wildlife Services.

NLCP's ten-year study of elephants in NLNP included biannual aerial censuses to monitor population density; determination of the ages of 60 percent of the herd, using the footprint technique for aging (Lee and Moss 1995 and Western, Moss, and Georgiadis 1983) to establish the age structure of the population; and the radio-collaring of one individual in each of sixteen family units to study range movements, habitat selection, social behavior, and reproductive biology. Reports on population density, distribution, and habitat selection relative to poaching pressures were submitted to NPWS. Scientific data are being published in technical journals.

NLCP hired a full-time botanist to conduct a two-year research project that produced the first vegetation map of NLNP, quantified the impacts on mopane woodlands by repeated forest fires (mostly set by poachers), documented trends in woodland/grassland competition, identified fungus species, and documented their importance for wildlife and human communities.

TOURISM DEVELOPMENT
The NLCP staff contributed to the writing of the government's official Tourism Management plan for NLNP. The plan emphasized low-impact tourism that included low-cost park visits for Zambian citizens. With the decline in poaching, several operators established successful safari operations within North Luangwa.

The goal of NLCP was to make its programs as self-sustaining as possible. The hope was that village entrepreneurs would continue to operate their own cottage industries and that the project itself would continue under the supervision of local Zambians after the expatriate NLCP directors and staff left the area.

🖉 As of 2006, the project is twenty years old and so successful that its model for community-based wildlife conservation is being adopted elsewhere. Hammer Simwinga and Moses Nyirendu's nongovernmental organization, the NLCCDP, is benefiting more than 1,500 families in fifty-two villages. The most successful microindustries continue to be beekeeping, fish farming, sunflower presses, general mercantile shops, and improved agricultural methods. Of course, the more remote villages have problems with transport, which has limited the productivity of some of their industries. However, the local people are still enthusiastic, and the project continues to attempt working in these areas.

Those programs that depend on foreign financial support and are not economically self-sustaining, such as conservation education and rural health care, are not as active as they were and are in need of additional sponsorship. The training of traditional birth attendants has required comparatively little outside support and the program continues today, though it too needs help. And help may be on the way. Hammer and Moses are already working with the Zambian Wildlife Authority to develop the oversight and the community infrastructure needed to receive and wisely spend future ecotourism dollars. The North Luangwa is becoming a bright new destination for people wanting a back-to-nature walking safari.

In our opinion, a project such as NLCP can be successful in many parts of the world. It must be seen as a very long term multidisciplinary endeavor that requires the cooperation of the national government and the local people and at least initial foreign financial support.

SUGGESTED READING

Barnes, R.F.W., and E. B. Kapela. 1991. Changes in the Ruaha elephant population caused by poaching. *African Journal of Ecology* 29: 289–94.

Bradshaw, G. A. 2005. Bringing down the gods: human violence, trauma, and their effects on elephant communities. Dissertation, Pacifica Graduate Institute, Santa Barbara.

Bradshaw, G. A., A. N. Schore, J. L. Brown, J. H. Poole, and C. J. Moss. 2005. Elephant breakdown. *Nature* 433: 807.

Douglas-Hamilton, I., and O. Douglas-Hamilton. 1992. *Battle for the elephants.* New York: Viking.

Eltringham, S. K. 1982. *Elephants.* Dorset, Eng.: Blandford Press.

Eltringham, S. K., and R. C. Malpas. 1980. The decline in elephant numbers in Rwenzori and Kabelega national parks, Uganda. *African Journal of Ecology* 18: 73–86.

Hanks, J. 1972. Reproduction of elephant, *Loxodonta africana,* in the Luangwa Valley, Zambia. *Journal of Reproduction and Fertility* 30: 13–26.

———. 1979. *A struggle for survival: the elephant problem.* Cape Town: C. Struik Publishers.

Ivory Trade Review Group. 1989. *The ivory trade and the future of the African elephant.* Interim report for the second meeting of the CITES African Elephant Working Group.

Jachmann, H., P.S.M. Berry, and H. Imae. 1995. Tusklessness in African elephants: a future trend. *African Journal of Ecology* 33: 230–35.

Laws, R. M. 1966. Age criteria for the African elephant (*Loxodonta a. africana*). *East African Wildlife Journal* 10: 251–72.

———. 1969. Aspects of reproduction in the African elephant, *Loxodonta africana. Journal of Reproduction and Fertility* Suppl. 6: 193–217.

Leakey, R. 2002. *Wildlife wars.* New York: St. Martin's Press.

Lee, P. C. 1987. Allomothering among African elephants. *Animal Behavior* 35: 278–91.

Lee, P. C., and C. J. Moss. 1995. Statural growth in known-age elephants *(Loxodonta africana). Journal of Zoology* (London) 236: 29–41.

Lewis, D. 1985. Population density of Luangwa elephants. *Report to Zambian National Parks and Wildlife Services.* Lusaka, Zambia.

McComb, K., et al. 2001. Matriarchs as repositories of social knowledge in African elephants. *Science* 292: 491–94.

Moss, C. J. 1988. *Elephant memories.* New York: William Morrow.

———. 2001. The demography of an African elephant *(Loxodonta africana)* population in Amboseli, Kenya. *Journal of Zoology* (London) 255: 145–56.

Owens, D., and M. Owens. 1992. *The eye of the elephant.* Boston: Houghton Mifflin.

———. 2005. Single mom, only child. *Natural History,* 22–25.

———. In press. Early age reproduction in female elephants after severe poaching. *African Journal of Ecology.*

Poole, J. H. 1989. The effects of poaching on the age structure and social and reproductive patterns of selected East African elephant populations. In *The ivory trade and the future of the African elephant,* vol. 2. Ivory Trade Review Group, prepared for the seventh CITES meeting.

———. 1996. *Coming of age with elephants: a memoir.* New York: Hyperion.

Poole, J. H., and J. B. Thomsen. 1989. Elephants are not beetles: implications of the ivory trade for the survival of the African elephant. *Oryx* 23: 188–98.

Renewable Resources Assessment Group. 1989. The impact of the ivory trade on the African elephant population. Report to the Ivory Trade Review Group for the second meeting of the CITES African Elephant Working Group.

Western, D., C. J. Moss, and N. Georgiadis. 1983. Age estimation and population age structure of elephants from footprint dimensions. *Journal of Wildlife Management* 47: 1192–97.

ACKNOWLEDGMENTS

HAMMER SIMWINGA is a hero not only to us but also to the village people for remaining true to the ideals of our work, for keeping those ideals alive despite the dark forces of corruption, and for carrying on in service to wildlife and to his fellow man. To this day he continues the village programs that offer many people near North Luangwa Park a better living through improved job opportunities, higher-quality agriculture, and better health care, so that they can afford to conserve their wildlife. Moses Nyirendu and Albert Chilambwe have also played major roles in ensuring that these programs continue, and Grace NG'ambi ably teaches basic midwifery and medical skills to the traditional birth attendants. We are deeply grateful for their contributions and loyal friendship.

Our love and heartfelt thanks to Mary Dykes, Delia's sister-in-law, who has worked long hours seven days a week for years to administer the Owens Foundation for Wildlife Conservation, based in Georgia. Mary bought and shipped to Africa everything from paper clips to airplanes, radio-tracking collars for elephants, and educational and medical supplies for villagers. Among many other tasks, she organized the Sister School Program and raised funds. Mary put the foundation at the center of her life, next to her family, and we would be lost without her. Her husband, Bobby Dykes, Delia's twin brother, kept our computers working and cared for our photographic material. In the early days Helen Cooper directed the Owens Foundation and supervised everything stateside. She and her husband, Fred, have helped us in many, many ways over the years.

We are grateful to the former governing officials of Zambia who gave us permission to create the project and conduct elephant research and, even more, to the current administration under President Mwanawasa for its efforts to eliminate wildlife-related corruption. We especially thank the dedicated game scouts of Mano Unit, who, outnumbered and outgunned by poachers, regularly risked their lives under the most difficult conditions to protect the wildlife of North Luangwa and, at times, us. Former Manu unit leader Tom Kotela, another Zambian hero, now gone, was remarkably courageous in resisting corrupt officials to stand with the project against commercial poaching, as were Martin Mwanza (deceased), Isaac Daka, Gaston Phiri, Samushi Kamuti, John Mosolo, Monday Mukwaya (deceased), and many others. Isaac Longwe, formerly the warden of Bangweulu Command, counseled and assisted us in countless ways for years. We appreciated the support of the honest, hard-working members of the Department of National Parks and Wildlife Services, and its Ministry of Tourism. Bornface Zulu, David Chile, and Godfrey Chikalipe assisted with field research. Thanks to Paul Russell, Norbert Mumba, Clement Mwale, and Charles Lengalenga at the Anti-Corruption Commission for their friendship in dark hours, and for their dedication and diligence in curbing ivory smuggling and associated corruption. They saved a lot of elephants in North Luangwa and in Zambia as a whole. There are no words to adequately thank these people. We literally owe our lives to some of them.

For more than thirty years Bob Ivey and Jill Bowman have been loyal friends, confidants, and our oasis in desert storms. They have always been there when we needed them, and we owe them a great deal for their unfailing support.

Jackson Kasokola (deceased), Mumanga Kasokola, Patrick Mwamba, Mwaba, and Harrison Simbaye (deceased) worked by our sides for more than ten years, doing everything from building airstrips to darting elephants. Along with Bornface Zulu, Milford, and our other Bemba staff, they will not be forgotten.

Our effort in Zambia could not have succeeded without the volunteers who dedicated years of their lives to assisting us. We thank Alston Watt for improving the village work tenfold; Dr. Philip Watt for introducing and expanding the Rural Health Program; Alex Haynes for expert flying and for building offices, bridges, and schools; Jay Cooper for bringing his amazing computer programs to the bush; Steve Hall for risking his life repeatedly to airlift everything from solar panels to boots for game scouts into muddy bush strips, often in the dark of night; Ronnie Hadley for extending our health care programs; Edward North for his unselfish work in Fulaza village;

and Ian Spincer for improving agriculture in remote villages. Marie and Harvey Hill and Tom and Wanda Canon gave much of themselves in the very beginning. From our Kalahari days to the years in the Luangwa Valley, Kevin Gill helped us identify plants and opened his home to us whenever we were in Johannesburg. Warren Powell, Mike Owens, and Chris Owens helped us in the field.

Some very special people sacrificed much to work with us in North Luangwa: Malcolm and Trish Boulton expertly handled communications, vehicle maintenance, accounting, and complex logistics; secured permits; and supervised the Conservation Education Program. Rex and Anne Haylock managed the field camps, entered data on the computer, supplied game scouts, and met with officials in Lusaka. The Haylocks and the Boultons risked everything to salvage the project during the illegal takeover by corrupt officials, and we will always admire and thank them for their bravery and loyalty to our ideals and us.

Dr. Paul Smith produced the first vegetation survey and map of North Luangwa. His wife, Dr. Debra Shah-Smith, conducted original mycological investigations of the park's mopane woodlands. Judith Hawke and Charlie Ross managed the project's complicated logistics in Lusaka. Our special thanks to David and Carol Harvey for helping us through the project's transition. Dr. Mike Kock is surely one of the most expert large-animal capture specialists of our time — and one of the bravest. He flew, hanging out of the chopper's doorway, into the mountains with Mark — and because he did, we learned a lot about a beleaguered elephant population.

We are grateful to the Frankfurt Zoological Society for financing our field work for more than nineteen years, and we applaud Elsabe Aucamp and Hugo van der Westhuizen for their hard work in continuing the elephant research, with funding from Frankfurt, and for supporting the game scouts of Mano.

The project was also financed by the Owens Foundation for Wildlife Conservation, and we owe so very much to the members for their generous contributions and letters of encouragement and for shipping thousands of pounds of materials to Zambia. A very special thanks to Hank and Margaret McCamish for their remarkably generous donation of a helicopter, pilot training, and operating funds, which literally transformed NLCP by allowing us to reach many more villagers with our programs, even in the rainy season. This aircraft was our single most effective conservation tool. The late Prince Bernhard of the Netherlands provided the park's first radio communication network, perhaps our second most useful conservation tool because it relieved Mark of the need to drop messages in tin cans from the Cessna and because it was essential for coordinating antipoaching patrols and arranging logistics and supply. HRH "PB" supported our work for years and offered his unqualified friendship and encouragement when times were tough. Thanks also to the Turner Foundation, the Williams Family Foundation, the Norcross Wildlife Foundation, the Golden Ark Foundation, the Emily Parker Baker Foundation, and the Frederick E. Cooper and Helen Dykes Cooper Charitable Foundation for generous donations. Special thanks to Diane Parker, H. Turney McKnight, Dick Burgheim, Andrew Filipowski, Mike and Liz Pura, Shana and Andrew Laursen, Elizabeth Holland, Dennis and Sue Umshler, Danny and Barbara Morris, Carol Wong, Jeff Short and the late Barbara Short, Avery and Gerry Doubleday, John and Jane Emrick, John and Theresa Cederholm, Robert and Emmy Cleaves, Phil Osborne, Lois and James Garner, and Alex Carson and the late Johnny Carson for their generous support. Harvest Help has been very supportive of the agricultural assistance programs for years.

Thanks to Paul and Sonja Tudor Jones for their generous contributions and for their vision and funding of the North Luangwa rhino reintroduction programs. Through their conservation fund, they are accomplishing profoundly important conservation work in many parts of Africa, much of it artfully choreographed by our friend Jeremy Pope. Thanks to Jeremy and to Athol Freylink and Adrian Carr of Tudor Safaris for their friendship, support, and dedication to the conservation of wildlife in Zambia, for hospitality in their safari camp, and for Athol's initial help in immobilizing elephants. They were great neighbors in the bush.

Dr. Philip Watt coordinated with AmeriCares to send more than one million dollars' worth of medical supplies to the Zambian people. Dr. Bob and Dana Davis sent thousands of dollars' worth of medical supplies for the Rural Health Care Program. Elefriends of Australia, a generous sponsor, personally delivered educational supplies to us in Luangwa. More than thirty American schools sent art supplies and educational materials to the schools of Mpika District. Delia and Hawk Dykes volunteered their time on numerous occasions to load airplanes or move medical supplies. Our thanks to the "Dear Everybody" volunteers, who stuffed thousands of envelopes over the years, and especially to Vicki Anderten and Ginger Salisbury (deceased) for all the hundreds of ways they helped.

We are forever indebted to the American ambassadors to Zambia

Roland Kuchel and Gordon Streeb, for their astute assistance, encouragement, friendship, and support for many years. They and their wives, Marianne and Junie, were gracious hosts whenever we visited Lusaka. Thanks to President Jimmy Carter for meeting with us to discuss our project and to Delia's mother, Mary Helen Hartley, who helped arrange that meeting. We are grateful to President George H. W. Bush, President Bill Clinton, and President George W. Bush for supporting the United Nations ivory ban.

Our special thanks to John and Carol Coppinger of Remote Africa Safaris for their longtime friendship, for hosting us and our staff at their camps, and for their support in many other ways. Andy Anderson and his family opened their home in Lusaka to us, lifted our spirits, and allowed us to safely park our trucks and trailers loaded with tons of supplies in his yard. Always smiling, Dick Houston offered us cold drinks, warm friendship, old movies, and great accommodations in Lusaka, as did Hal and M. K. Cope, who added more than a dash of moral support and good counsel. Thanks also to Richard Jeffrey for his friendship and support.

Jenny and Derrick Gordon always welcomed dusty travel-worn NLCP staff in from the bush and gave them the run of their home. Thanks so much to Mark Falstad for his professional videotaping of the project — and for his good humor when Mark flew the plane into the lens of his new camera. Oops!

Slim Suleman traveled long distances to help maintain and repair our helicopter in the bush and cooked curry for us in Nairobi. Thanks to Father Thomas for helping us in numerous ways in Mpika, Rick Richey for editing miles of video, and Tom Steeb for designing a great Web site. Thanks to Mwana Bermudes and Nelda Villiness at the American embassy for facilitating grants, shipments, and for offering advice. We are so very appreciative of Trish Parsons and Rob, her late husband, who assisted with our aircraft on special occasions.

The Dallas Zoo designed and shipped NLCP teacher packets for the Conservation Education Program, and Rich Lobello wrote the curriculum. Thanks to Cathy Chiesa and Dr. John King for library research. Thanks also to Bell Helicopter, Inc., for their support, and especially to Bruce Lane, who, though very ill, flew with Mark in our new helicopter during its maiden flight to Marula-Puku.

Delia's brother Lee Dykes drove her all around the state of Georgia whenever she returned home. Leslie Ann Keller designed the Owens Foundation logo, and Bonnie Barney donated her beautiful artwork.

For more than twenty years Dr. Joel Berger has always taken time from his international field work to advise us on scientific matters and has remained steadfast in friendship. We are very grateful to Bernie Lanigan, Brad Jackson, Dana Raybon, and Mary Lou Marocha of Lanigan & Associates for advising us on financial matters for decades. Tammy Johnson has helped with foundation matters in countless ways.

Besides the dedicated officers of the former NPWS and of ZAWA, many people who have worked for years to conserve the Luangwa Valley deserve special appreciation: Phil Berry, Dr. Dale Lewis, the late Norman Carr, Adrian Carr, John and Carol Coppinger, Robin and Jo Pope, Dr. Richard Bell, Dr. Hugh Jackmann, Paul Russell, Adam Pope, Jeremy Pope, Athol Freylink, Mark Harvey, David Shepard, Mike Faddy, and Rachel McRobb.

For comments on the manuscript we are very grateful to Bob Ivey, Jill Bowman, Doug Kim-Brown, Mary Dykes, and Helen Cooper. We are deeply indebted to Alexandra Fuller, one of the most remarkable literary talents of our time, for being a friend to us, to truth, and to Zambia. Thanks, Bo, for writing the foreword to our book.

We thank Harry Foster, our longtime editor and friend at Houghton Mifflin, once again for his talent, patience, and forbearance in helping us mold a ragged, thorny bush manuscript into a book. Peg Anderson did an incredible job of chasing down every redundancy and inserting lost commas. Thanks also to Richard Abate, our literary agent, for his advice and encouragement.

To our old friends and families who make up our roots and troops, our thanks for always being there for us. Our love and thanks always to Margaret, Amanda, and Barbara. And to our "new" friends in Idaho — Doug and Mona, Janet and David, Tim and Joanne, Mike and Jane, Dawn and Rob, David and Mechee, Pat, Wilma and Larry, John and Jen, Sam and Carolyne, Greg and Alicia, and the Pederson clan — thanks for including us in your troop.

INDEX

and closing of NLCP, 174, 178, 185–86
contributions of generally, x
and day-to-day running of NLCP, 153, 154
family of, 129, 185
hiring of, as NLCP staff member, 129
letters from, to Owenses, 185–86
motorbike for, 129, 186
and North Luangwa Community Conservation Development Project (NLCCDP), 187, 191, 211
Owenses' loss of contact with, 179, 184
personality of, 129
in United States, 191–92
village work by, 129, 154, 178, 179, 186–87, 191, 193
and Zambian Wildlife Authority, 212
Smugglers. *See* Ivory smuggling
South Africa, 10, 128, 160
Storms
  in Ohio, 69–70, 72–74, 75
  in Zambia, 33–34, 35, 36, 120–21
Sugar. *See* Chatukwa, Musakanya (Sugar, staff member)
Sunflowers, as crop, 39, 41, 43, 109, 129, 187, 202
Survivor (elephant), 2, 4, 114, 118–19, 158–59, 192

Talky (informant), 14, 161, 162–63
Tanzania, xvi, 10, 160, 193
Tazara, 11–12, 128

Tourism, 207–8
Traditional birth attendants. *See* Midwives
Trichilia trees, 21–22, 91, 112, 169
Tsetse flies, 62, 134, 152

Uapaca kirkiana trees, 152
United Nations, xxiii–xxiv, 9, 11, 14, 159–61, 194

Van der Westhuizen, Hugo, 192

Walker, Amanda and Margaret, 92–95, 188
Wart hogs, 44, 114, 149
Wasps, 22
Waterbucks, 16, 23, 112, 149
Waterfalls, 151–53
Watt, Alston, 82, 129, 130
Watt, Philip, 81, 82–86, 193
Wildebeests, 37–38, 56, 119, 121
Wildlife clubs, 199–200
Wildlife research and ecological monitoring, 210–11
"Wildlife" shops, 202
Windmill, 67–68, 77
Wine, Libby, 48
Winterthorn, 34, 39, 43, 190

Zambia
  Anti-Corruption Commission in, 10, 160, 163
  corruption in, xxv, 9–12, 14, 56, 128, 161, 174–79
  democracy in, xxii, xxv, 128
  history of, 124–28
  independence for, 127
  maps of, xxvi, xxvii